developing new business ideas

A step-by-step guide to creating new business ideas worth backing

Andrew Bragg and Mary Bragg

 Prentice Hall
FINANCIAL TIMES

An imprint of **Pearson Education**

Harlow, England • London • New York • Boston • San Francisco • Toronto • Sydney • Singapore • Hong Kong
Tokyo • Seoul • Taipei • New Delhi • Cape Town • Madrid • Mexico City • Amsterdam • Munich • Paris • Milan

Pearson Education Limited

Edinburgh Gate
Harlow CM20 2JE
tel: +44 (0)1279 623623
fax: +44 (0)1279 431059
website: www.pearsoned.co.uk

First published in Great Britain in 2005

© Pearson Education Limited 2005

The rights of Andrew Bragg and Mary Bragg to be identified as authors of this work have been asserted by them in accordance with the Copyright, Designs and Patents Act 1988.

ISBN 0 273 66325 9

British Library Cataloguing-in-Publication Data
A catalogue record for this book is available from the British Library

Library of Congress Cataloging-in-Publication Data
Bragg, Andrew.
   Developing new business ideas: the fast-track to creating viable new businesses for executives and entrepreneurs/Andrew Bragg and Mary Bragg.
      p. cm.
   Includes bibliographical references and index.
   ISBN 0–273–66325—9 (alk. paper.)
      1. Creative ability in business. 2. New business enterprises. I. Bragg Mary. II. Title.

   HD53.B714 2005
   658.1'1—dc22

                                                          2004066263

10 9 8 7 6 5 4 3 2 1
09 08 07 06 05

Designed by Sue Lamble
Typeset in Melior and Din by 70
Printed and bound in Great Britain by Bell & Bain Ltd, Glasgow

The publishers' policy is to use paper manufactured from sustainable forests.

dedication

to my mother, Peggy Mroczek (née Hurley), whose selfless devotion and love made me all I am, and all I ever will be

about the authors

Andrew Bragg's wide-ranging business career includes general management and marketing roles across the UK and mainland Europe. His chief executive roles have covered the multimedia, print and packaging sectors and have involved a number of entrepreneurial start-ups. He has also worked for book and newspaper publishers and launched a European lighting brand for a major American corporation. He was European General Manager of a leading stationery brand and has also held senior roles in the not-for-profit sector. A graduate of Trinity College, Cambridge, Andrew also gained an MBA from Cranfield University.

Mary Bragg undertook marketing roles within the multinational GlaxoSmithKline before executing a range of consultancy projects in human resource management when seconded to PricewaterhouseCoopers, both in the UK and internationally. Her professional qualifications include a Masters Degree in Organisational Behaviour from Birkbeck College, London University. She combines independent management consultancy with a University career. As Principal Lecturer on entrepreneurship and creativity at London Metropolitan University, she recently designed a portfolio of degree courses on entrepreneurship. She is a Fellow of the Royal Society of Arts and was a founding trustee of the Academy of Enterprise. Her earlier book, *Re-inventing Influence – how to get things done in a world without authority*, won the Management Consultancies' Association award for best management book of the year in 1996. Mary was the first woman in the Association's history to receive this award.

contents

publisher's acknowledgements

We are grateful to the following for permission to reproduce copyright material:

Figure 3.1 reprinted with the permission of Simon & Schuster Adult Publishing Group, from BRAIN POWER by Karl Albrecht. Copyright © 1980 by Prentice-Hall, Inc.; Figure 3.2 from *Patterns of Entrepreneurship*, Kaplan J. © 2003 John Wiley & Sons. Reprinted with permission of John Wiley & Sons, Inc.; Figure 5.6 from T. Monroy and R. Folger, A Typology of Entrepreneurial Styles Beyond Economic Rationality, *Journal of Private Enterprise*, IX, no 2 (1993) 64–79; Table 5.6 from *Entrepreneurship*, J. G. Burch, John Wiley (New York) 1986; Table 5.7 from *Strategic Enterpreneurship: a decision-making approach to new venture creation and management*, P. Wickham, Pearson Education (Harlow), 2001; Min Basadur for text reprinted from Basadur, Min, *The Power of Innovation*, Pearson Education (London: 1995); text reprinted from FIVE STAR MIND by Tom Wujec, copyright © 1995 by Tom Wujec. Used by permission of Broadway Books, a division of Random House, Inc., 134 words from OUR WILDEST DREAMS by JOLINE GODFREY. Copyright © 1992 by Joline Godfrey. Reprinted by permission of HarperCollins Publishers Inc.

In some instances we have been unable to trace the owners of copyright material, and we would appreciate any information that would enable us to do so.

authors' acknowledgements

A great number of creative and enterprising people have helped us to develop this book in accordance with the four-step idea development process which it describes. To all those actual or aspiring entrepreneurs who have contributed generously, albeit anonymously, to our efforts through participation in workshops, on consultancy assignments or through individual feedback, we offer our grateful thanks.

Particular thanks are also due to a number of leading figures who have contributed significantly to our thinking: Robert Heller, Professor Tudor Rickards, Trevor Baylis, Professor John Child, Sue Stedman, Professor John Mullins, Jim Bodoh, Professor David Kirby, Professor Gerard Puccio and Professor Eugene McKenna.

We acknowledge the skills and vision of all those at Pearson who have helped us to develop the book from the initial germ of an idea into a finished product which we hope will help businesses and individuals alike to generate new ideas and thinking: Richard Stagg, Laura Brundell, Kate Salkilld, Catherine Timothy, Elie Ball, Vivienne Church and Stephen Partridge.

Especial thanks are due to all those who have supported, guided and inspired us at various stages of our careers, especially Jean McGinty, Ken Pardey, Gwyneth Lawson, Tom Taylor and John Mroczek.

Our final debt of gratitude is to Tara, whose constant good humour and consistently positive feedback has sustained us throughout.

introduction

At some time in their life, almost everybody has had an idea for starting their own business or for launching an innovative project.

You are probably no different.

The idea might have been sparked by something you saw on a foreign holiday or in a different market sector. You might have been dissatisfied with a product or service which did not work properly. It might have been an article which you read in the paper. Your own experience might have highlighted a particular gap in the market. You might think that your current organisation lets customers down and that you could do better on your own. You might have been made redundant. You might just be fed up with working for others. You might even be one of the favoured few who has had a 'Eureka' moment.

But did you actually do something with your initial idea?

Perhaps you told yourself that your idea was not creative enough.

Perhaps some experts told you why your idea would never work.

Perhaps it was pointed out to you that if your idea was really that good, surely somebody else would already be doing it.

Perhaps you recognised that your idea needed some further refinement, but the business start-up books to which you turned for help rushed straight into the details of implementation without answering your nagging doubts about the strength of your underlying idea.

And if all these issues were not enough, perhaps you read the government statistics which demonstrated that over 30 per cent of new businesses do not survive beyond three years.

And so perhaps you put your idea to one side, remaining within the organisational comfort zone and keeping the security of a monthly pay cheque. Whatever its intrinsic worth, your idea remains useless, however, unless and until it has been implemented into a fully formed product or service which generates new value.

But it doesn't need to be like that.

It is within everybody's power to take that first idea and to follow systematically a structured and creative process to challenge and develop the idea and thereby transform it into a viable business opportunity.

Having the initial idea is a vital first step, but it is only the first step in converting your creativity into a business. It is important not to rush into action with the first apparently feasible business idea you have. Instead, you should follow a process of developing, enhancing and reshaping your initial idea into a real-life business opportunity which will work.

Your original business idea represents only a very first piece of the entrepreneurial jigsaw puzzle. It may turn out to be the piece at the centre which defines the entire puzzle. It is much more likely to be a useful starting point which ends up off-centre or it may turn out to be a bland background piece which is impossible to use until later. It is also possible that you eventually discover that the first jigsaw piece belongs to a quite different puzzle to the one you thought you were working on.

This book shows you how to develop the germ of an initial idea into a viable business opportunity by following a systematic idea development process. This process moves from seeking and shaping opportunities, generating ideas, evaluating and selecting ideas through to planning for implementation.

We show how creativity is an important element of all steps of the process. Creativity is not restricted to the supposed 'Eureka' moment of creating the idea but informs every single step within the process.

We also demonstrate how you can develop your innate creativity, combining analytical thinking with imagination and insight to produce alternative views on situations, together with multiple solutions for capitalising on them, in order to transform your initial idea into a viable business opportunity.

The relentless pressure for the rapidly supplied 'single correct answer' imposed by society in general and by work in particular crushes individual creativity. Conscious that the best way to get a good idea is to generate a lot of alternative ideas, we show you a range of techniques which will allow you to reconnect with the 90 per cent of your creativity which has been drummed out of you.

Each of these straightforward and extremely powerful techniques has a specific role to play at particular steps within the idea development process. Each technique is illustrated by a range of real-life business examples, in both product and service sectors, in both large and small operations, across a range of countries, including Europe, the United States, Australia, Sweden, Japan and the Philippines. Ranging from boundary-hopping to force-fitting, from analogical thinking to reverse brainstorming, from cube-crawling to upside-down thinking, we show how these techniques work and have delivered in practice.

Take a preview at just a few of the enterprising individuals and organisations you will meet in the following pages who illustrate how to – and sometimes how not to – combine logic and intuition, analysis and imagination, in developing the germ of an idea into viable business opportunities:

- **Dame Stephanie Shirley**, founder of the original software company behind Xansa plc, who overcame massive blocks to implementation, including conventional industry thinking which was so male-dominated that she had to sign her early business development letters as 'Steve' in order to be taken seriously.

- **James Dyson**, whose experience of cleaning an old property in the Cotswolds literally brought home to him that existing vacuum cleaners did not work satisfactorily. His subsequent combination of intuitive and technical insight and the business skills to commercialise his ideas, to see the entire idea development process through from start to finish, marks him out as the consummate innovator.

- **Howard Head**, whose innovations revolutionised the worlds of skiing and tennis. He demonstrates the power of challenging convention and the elegant effectiveness of analogical thinking.

- **Sahar Hashemi**, co-founder of Coffee Republic, who realised when visiting her brother in New York that the thing they would both miss most on their return to London was New York's coffee houses.

- **Thomas Edison**, innovator *par excellence* who effectively created the industries of electricity supply, sound recording and motion pictures and consistently delivered on his promise of a 'minor invention every ten days and a big thing every six months or so'.

- **Gary Mueller**, founder of Internet Securities, Inc., one of the few early companies to buck the dot.com trend of high-profile failure and build a high-value and sustainable internet business model.

- **Darryl Lenz**, a working mother and a stewardess with American Airlines, who got her initial business idea when she strapped a child's folding beach chair to her suitcase to make air travel with her young son less of an ordeal and found herself mobbed by passengers anxious to buy the unintended prototype.

- **Jollibee Foods Corporation**, whose structured and creative approach to implementation planning allowed a small fast-food operation in the Philippines to develop sufficient market strength to restrict global giant McDonald's to second place in the market.

- **Trevor Baylis**, who found a brilliant new use for old technology with his clockwork radio, enabling communication about Aids to communities without electricity or batteries.

- **Iridium**, the global mobile phone project which crashed to earth when lack of a structured idea development process meant that catastrophic blocks to implementation, including international politics and inadequate technical performance, were overlooked.

- **Anita Roddick**, founder of Body Shop, who had the insight on breaking bulk in the cosmetic sector while out shopping with her young family.

- **The Sinclair C5**, the battery-powered one-seater pedal-assisted tricycle which offered a single technology-pushed solution before the market need had been fully explored.

- **Phil Knight**, the trained accountant who developed his intuitive 'you're-crazy-it-will-never-work-or-someone-would-already-be-doing-it' idea into global giant NIKE.

- **Bill Bowerman**, NIKE's co-founder, who had the insight from watching his wife make waffles for breakfast that a waffle-patterned outer sole would improve traction and produce faster running times.

- **Gordon and Carole Segal**, who were so inspired by the types of unique, functional and affordable designs which they saw during their honeymoon in Europe that they founded the Crate and Barrel retail concept on their return to Chicago.

- **3M**, whose ubiquitous Post-it® notes were born in part from research into very strong glues rather than the weak glue which characterises the product familiar to us all today.

- **Ray Kroc**, a salesman whose disproportionately high sales of milkshake machines to a particular hamburger joint in remote California led him to discover that the two McDonald brothers had perfected a fast-food operation before the term had been invented.

- **Ingvar Kamprad**, creative and iconoclastic founder of IKEA, for whom expensive solutions were often signs of mediocrity. The key was to 'find simple solutions, scrimping and saving in every direction. Except on ideas'.

- **Stephania Alexander**, who differentiated her plumbing business by meeting the specific needs of women customers with a service including crisp, clean uniforms; portable doormats; carpet protectors; a guarantee on workmanship; plus up-front menu pricing to avoid any stressful quibbles over mysterious 'extras'.

- **Jeff Bezos**, founder of Amazon.com, who left his prestigious and well-paid Wall Street job because of something he read in the newspaper, namely that internet usage was growing by 2300 per cent per year

- **Darryl Mattocks**, who founded the Internet Bookshop at the same time as Amazon.com, but whose research, generation of options and appetite for risk were considerably less than those of Bezos.

- **Michael Bloomberg**, whose close analysis of the online financial information market made him realise that traditional products focused on the needs of the purchasers, the IT managers, not the actual end-users, the analysts and traders.

- **Bette Nesmith**, whose analogical thinking was better than her typing – she transferred to her erratic typing the insight that the window artists decorating the bank where she worked corrected their mistakes by painting over their errors. Liquid Paper was the eventual result.

- **Steve Millar**, managing director of Australian wine company BRL Hardy, whose background in finance and consumer products allowed him to turn conventional industry thinking upside down.

- **Craig Johnston**, professional footballer and developer of the Predator, the world's best-selling football boot, worn by the likes of David Beckham and Zinedine Zidane.

- **Swift-Lite Charcoal**, a UK company originally established to sell charcoal to tandoori restaurants, which discovered a burgeoning market in the Middle East with a product for smoking hookah pipes.

- **Charles Dunstone**, founder of Carphone Warehouse, who realised that his company was not just about providing economical mobile phones, it was also about demystifying the massively complex and opaque charging structures operated by the telephone networks.

- **Katharine Hamnett,** fashion designer, who overturned conventional marketing by barring some buyers and distributors from visiting her exhibition stand in order to generate interest and provoke 'scarcity value'.

- **Scott Cook**, developer of Quicken personal finance software, who acted on his insight that the product's greatest competitor was the pencil, not another software package.

- **Best Friends Pet Resorts and Salons**, whose introduction of hospitality-industry-level customer service, including state-of-the-art customer relationship management software to track the pet-guests' every trait, need and preference, transcended the boundaries of the conventional boarding kennel and vindicated the research finding that 90 per cent of pet-owners view their pets as family members.

- **IDEO**, the American ideas factory which has picked up Thomas Edison's baton and has made brainstorming practically a religion.

- **Hewlett-Packard**, which used the analogy of the food service industry to reconfigure its global supply chain for the HP DeskJet Printer.

- **Sarah Tremellen**, founder of mail-order lingerie company Bravissimo, who had to establish a dummy geographical presence to circumvent a supplier boycott engineered by a local competitor.

- **Stelios Haji-Ioannou**, famous for extending the easyFormula to other markets which were similar, but different, to the airline market and whose easyCinema concept was almost strangled at birth by competitive suppliers.

- **Karan Bilimoria**, who developed the Cobra brand of beer to become so powerful that its production could be moved successfully from Bangalore to Bedford.

- **Howard Schultz**, who founded Il Giornale, a string of speciality coffee stores in Seattle modelled on the typical Italian espresso bar.

The stores were so successful that he went on to purchase Starbucks, to which he had offered the original concept when he had worked for the company several years previously.

- **Andrew Palmer**, who defied expert opinion and successfully persisted with the development of the new production process required to underpin the success of his New Covent Garden Soup Company.

- **Boo.com**, whose technically brilliant internet concept for selling fashion goods online was catastrophically undermined by the inability of some 75 per cent of those who tried to access the website actually to do so.

- **Frederick Smith**, founder of Federal Express, who saw how the bank clearing system provided the solution to an overnight delivery business and who used his wartime experience to put the myriad obstacles which he faced into perspective.

We are convinced that the idea development process represents a key tool in contemporary business and hope that you find the techniques and business examples both informative and inspirational.

Initial business ideas come in all shapes and sizes, across all sectors, in relation to both products and services. There are few ideas which cannot be transformed through the idea development process into a viable business opportunity. Entrepreneurs in even the most apparently unglamorous sectors should be encouraged by Ralph Stayer, CEO of Johnsonville Sausage Company. When challenged by *BusinessWeek* that it was funny that Johnsonville Sausage Company should take pride of place in an article on management meccas alongside Motorola, Hewlett-Packard and Intel, Stayer memorably replied: 'I think it strikes my competitors as a lot less funny.'[1]

We wish you every success.
Andrew Bragg
Mary Bragg
London, November 2004

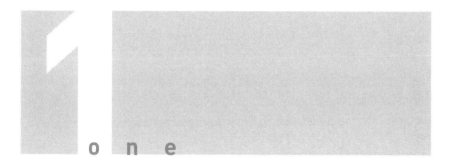

the importance of developing strong ideas

- James Dyson – using the idea development process to clean up
- demystifying the idea development process
- slaying the myth that entrepreneurs are born, not made
- the four steps in the idea development process
- and another thing: benefits of the idea development process
- call in the cavalry or do it yourself?
- Sir Clive Sinclair and the C5 – the perils of a flawed process of idea development

Of course, simply having a good business idea doesn't make you an entrepreneur. Putting one into practice and making it work does. After all, a third of all new businesses fail.

It doesn't matter where your initial idea came from. James Dyson was spurred into action by house-cleaning in the Cotswolds, for example. Very, very few ideas burst from pure Archimedes-like inspiration.

What does matter is what you do with your initial idea.

Rushing to implementation without challenging the problem you are trying to solve is risky. And even when you have correctly defined the business problem, going with the first solution you hit upon is no guarantee of success.

Assessing your emerging solution against other options increases your chances of success. And planning for implementation brings its own opportunities to shape the original idea.

Does all this sound like a process? It should do. The experience of successful entrepreneurs suggests that following a dynamic four-step process, selecting from the wide range of innovative techniques showcased in this book, can transform an initially unshaped idea into an entrepreneurial success.

Put off by the word 'innovative'? Don't be. The idea-generating techniques we demonstrate here allow you to make the best use of your innate creativity alongside more conventional analytical skills. And the techniques are all securely anchored in business reality. Just see how James Dyson follows the four-step process in the following case study.

If you want to transform your own apparently good business idea into an entrepreneurial success, read on.

James Dyson – using the idea development process to clean up[2]

James Dyson's profile demonstrates the entrepreneurial ability to undertake the idea development process from visualising an idea right through to successful commercialisation.

Although Dyson is perhaps most closely associated with the eponymous Dual Cyclone vacuum cleaner, his numerous other market successes include Sea Truck, the award-winning Ballbarrow, the Wheelboat and the Trolleyball.

the idea development process starts with defining or reframing the opportunity. Idea generation is the second step in the idea development process

The idea development process starts with defining or reframing the opportunity. In Dyson's case, the experience of cleaning an old property in the Cotswolds literally brought home to him that existing vacuum cleaners did not work satisfactorily. By the same token, he challenged the conventional product concept of washing machines, undertaking research to reveal that the conventional wash action did not flex the fabric sufficiently to release dirt quickly. In fact, research suggested that washing by hand gave better results than a single-drum machine.

Idea generation is the second step in the idea development process. Dyson had been faced with the problem that air filters in the Ballbarrow spray-finishing room constantly clogged with powder particles. He observed that the air filters clogged just like a vacuum cleaner bag clogs with dust. He solved the air-filter problem by designing and building an industrial cyclone tower which removed the powder particles by exerting centrifugal forces greater than 100,000 times those of gravity. His brilliant insight was that if the air-filter problem was similar to the vacuum-cleaner problem, then perhaps the solution could be similar too. This analogical thinking eventually delivered the first breakthrough in vacuum-cleaner design since the product was invented in 1901, namely the Dual Cyclone.

Dyson's design solution for unsatisfactory washing-machine performance was not to make a yet more powerful version of the conventional product concept but rather to build on the superior effectiveness of washing clothes by hand. From this insight was developed the world's first washing machine with two drums, the Contrarotator, which replicated a hand-washing action to manipulate and flex the fabric to release dirt more quickly.

Idea generation can also be provoked by simple direct questions. Dyson company folklore has it that the casual question 'I like your vacuum cleaners, but when will you make one you don't have to push around?' was the trigger that led to the creation of the Dyson DC06 robot, designed not only to clean properly but also to move around more logically than a human would.

Dyson's belief in the power of challenging conventional thinking and of rule reversal in order to stimulate idea generation was even demonstrated by his design of 'The Wrong Garden' for the Chelsea Flower Show in 2003, when he noted that doing the opposite of what should be done often stimulates creative innovation.

Idea evaluation and selection is the third step in the idea development process. Typical ideas are not born ready-made for the market and must undergo a process of significant challenge and development. In the ▶

case of the Dual Cyclone vacuum cleaner, it took precisely 5,127 prototypes before the specification was finalised, each prototype differing in only one characteristic from its predecessor so that the impact of every modification could be isolated and tracked.

The fourth step in the idea development process involves planning for implementation, identifying and overcoming likely blocks to implementation, and so creating extra value for the original business idea. Because it is often the step at which even the most gifted innovator may stumble, it is also the period when the most persistence is required.

In Dyson's case, supreme persistence was required over the full 15 years which separated conception of the Dual Cyclone from its eventual launch. He encountered numerous unanticipated blocks from his various target audiences. These audiences included venture capitalists whose risk aversion to manufacturing made them ambivalent about the opportunity and about Dyson's design capability.

The major established UK-based manufacturers rejected the new technology represented by Dyson, while a large American manufacturer would meet him only if he agreed to sign over the rights to anything he revealed to them in conversation. Early market research suggested that the clear dust collection bin was not attractive to customers because it might reveal to their neighbours just how much dirt had been picked up in their homes.

Most unexpectedly, the Secretary of State for Wales rejected Dyson's development grant application on the grounds that if the product really did represent a superior offering, then one of the big manufacturers would be producing it. Ironically, this last observation almost proved correct, with Dyson being forced to court to protect his invention from an imitation from Hoover – he eventually gained victory for patent infringement.

If the Dual Cyclone took 15 years from conception to launch, then it took a further ten years from launch to achieve commercial success. It is little wonder that James Dyson entitled his autobiography *Against All Odds*. Dyson cemented his reputation as a leading entrepreneur by providing resources to assist up-and-coming inventors in overcoming some of the problems he had encountered himself. His products are exhibited in such diverse venues as London's Science Museum, San Francisco Museum of Modern Art, Zurich Design Museum and Powerhouse Museum in Sydney.

James Dyson's combination of intuitive and technical insight and the business skills to commercialise his ideas, to see the entire idea development process through from start to finish, are what marks him out as the consummate innovator and not just an inventor.

demystifying the idea development process

The James Dyson case study demonstrates that the idea development process is an iterative process within which ideas are crafted, moulded and reinvented into valuable business opportunities.

One of the most significant yet undervalued business skills is the ability to recognise and develop viable new business ideas for products, processes and services.

Thomas Edison claimed that creativity is '1 per cent inspiration and 99 per cent perspiration'

It was Thomas Edison who once memorably claimed that creativity is '1 per cent inspiration and 99 per cent perspiration'. Any accomplished business person or entrepreneur will confirm that creating an idea is not enough on its own to guarantee success in the market. The business burial grounds are full of headstones commemorating superficially good ideas which were never properly developed, were starved of the resources to reach maturity, were ignored or blocked by those who controlled access to the market place, were stolen by others, or which in the cold light of day simply lacked the strength to live.

just a starting point

The original business idea represents only a first piece of the entrepreneurial jigsaw puzzle. It may turn out to be the piece at the centre which defines the entire puzzle; it may be a useful starting point which ends up off-centre; or it may turn out to be a bland background piece which is impossible to use until later. It is also possible that you eventually discover that the first jigsaw piece which you locate belongs to a quite different puzzle to the one you thought you were working on.

It is the actual completion of the jigsaw puzzle, the systematic and persistent development of the idea into a fully functioning growth business, which is the truly challenging part of the process.

Typically, the ideas which entrepreneurs present to potential investors are only partially formed and lack intrinsic value. The survival rate of the typical business idea is very small: for every 100 ideas presented to investors in the form of a business plan or proposal of some kind, only between one and three usually get funded.

Helena Boas and Matthew Wootliff of Bodas, the lingerie retailer, needed more than £1 million to expand their two-month-old business. To win the necessary funding from business angels Pi Capital, Boas focused her efforts on reshaping and moulding their idea into a really attractive business opportunity. 'The business plan was crucial', says Wootliff. 'Helena spent six months researching and writing it. We did everything from market research to stress tests.' Their efforts paid off, satisfying the requirement expressed by David Giampaolo of Pi Capital that members seek to back a business, not an idea, and gaining Bodas £1.1 million of capital.[3]

over valuing Eureka

The new business that simply bursts from a flash of brilliance is rare. Paul Burns reports Anita Roddick's admission: 'I know that everyone wants to think that it is like an act of God – that you sit down and have a brilliant idea. Well, when you start your own business it is not like that.'[4] Peter Drucker goes further, arguing that 'bright ideas are the riskiest and least successful source of innovative opportunities. The casualty rate is enormous.'[5]

The importance of the 'Eureka' idea is often over rated at the expense of an under-emphasis on the need for products or services which can be sold in sufficient quantity to real customers to generate sustainable cash-flows and profit. As James Dyson's prototyping exercises demonstrate, what is usually required is a series of trial and error iterations, or repetitions, before a crude and promising product or service fits with what the customer is really willing to pay for.

rushing headlong into action

It is a frequent mistake to be so fired up with your idea, so convinced that it is the best solution to a correctly defined market opportunity, that your first instinct is to rush to your financial backers or your managing director and ask for immediate funds to realise the idea. After all, you tell yourself, analysis paralysis risks delay and you have nothing to lose because if things go wrong you can try something else.

This rush to action means that your initial idea may not fulfil its full potential.

Additional and alternative ideas which the very process of validating your idea and searching for new solutions would have produced are lost. 3M's ubiquitous Post-it® notes were born in part from research into very strong glues, for example, rather than the weak glue which characterises the product familiar to us all today. You should always remember the dictum attributed to Tudor Rickards, Professor of Creativity and Organisational Change at the Manchester Business School: 'A good idea is the enemy of a better one. You stop looking for alternatives.'

a good idea is the enemy of a better one. You stop looking for alternatives

solving the wrong problem
More damagingly, your initial idea may be solving the wrong problem. Min Basadur reports how this happened at Procter & Gamble in connection with an automatic car-wash product.[6] A leading competitor had recently launched a hot wax product which was both patent-protected and apparently selling extremely strongly. The research group was tasked to develop a competing product without infringing the patent. The patent involved combining wax from the South American carnauba tree with certain stabilisers and water to produce a stable fluid capable of being sprayed on cars and so overcoming the problem that wax does not dissolve in water.

After 18 months of apparently fruitless labour, the Procter & Gamble team had become bogged down in solving the problem of how to develop a carnauba wax formula without violating the existing patent. Basadur showed the power of asking direct simple questions such as 'Why?' and 'How?'. The response to his question 'how well does the competing product perform?' was very limited. Colleagues believed that it was selling well and that it therefore was performing well. No empirical data existed to support this view. Rigorous testing soon established that the competitor's product did not adhere effectively to cars. In other words, the Procter & Gamble team had been trying to duplicate a product which did not work. Basadur rapidly redefined the problem to the development of a hot wax product for a spray-on water system that would adhere to car bodies and provide a worthwhile benefit.

The failure in the market of the Sinclair C5 battery-powered vehicle also highlights the dangers of incorrectly defining the opportunity, as well as ignoring possible alternative solutions, and is explored more fully in the case study at the end of this chapter.

financial reality

Rushing to implement a business idea can also blind you to its financial realities. Budding entrepreneurs who start new businesses, and executives who have a new idea for their company, particularly when it is for the first time, often radically under estimate their capacity to burn cash in the start-up phase and over estimate their ability to bring in customers and profitable sales. Research undertaken by enterprise guru Jeffry Timmons highlights that for the average start-up it takes 30 months to achieve cash break-even and a full seven years for the investment to be paid back.[7]

dot.com casualties

The dot.com boom of the 1990s exemplifies this type of trigger-happy attitude. Literally thousands of wannabe entrepreneurs rushed into creating and developing web-based companies on the basis of ideas which appeared not to have passed through a robust development process. First-mover advantage was portrayed as paramount; the key objective was to maximise the number of website hits in the untested expectation that hits would lead to market share which would lead to profits.

What was often missing was a sound business model and a recognition of fundamental business principles, such as the need to gain paying customers early and to manage cash. Cash-burn caused the rapid death of many of these Icarus-like companies, epitomised by fashion e-tailer Boo.com.

The number of survivors from the dot.com boom is staggeringly small, with achievement of financial break-even making front-page news even today. For example, e-commerce icon Amazon.com, founded in 1995, took until 2004 to report three consecutive quarters delivering profit. We explore more fully how the application of the idea development process contributed directly to the success of Amazon.com and of online financial information provider Internet Securities, Inc. in later chapters.

For all these reasons, successful entrepreneurs never assume that a first idea represents an immediate opportunity; they systematically plan and follow a structured and creative process to challenge and develop the idea, and thereby transform it into a viable business opportunity.

slaying the myth that entrepreneurs are born, not made
It would be easy to be over awed by the public success of high-profile entrepreneurs and think that all entrepreneurs are born, not made, believing that only those with the gift of creativity can set up their own business or commercialise their idea.

There are certainly plenty of myths surrounding enterprise. According to the myth above, the skills of entrepreneurship are connected with the innate characteristics of entrepreneurs, characteristics which you inherit at birth – these mythical skills cannot be taught or learned. According to other myths, all you need to be an entrepreneur is luck in a chaotic and unstructured world. Further myths position entrepreneurs as impulsively action-oriented, as the gun-slingers of the enterprise world who shoot from the hip and ask questions later. Conversely, myths exist that the best entrepreneurs are just inventors of new products or services.

myths exist that the best entrepreneurs are just inventors of new products or services

All these myths are untrue and misleading.

the tyranny of logic and analysis
It sometimes seems as if business schools perpetuate these myths by focusing their training on cognitive, content-based learning in disciplines such as accountancy, marketing, law and economics, rather than on the process of venture creation and its related disciplines of entrepreneurship, creative idea development, innovation and product design.

In business itself, examples abound of executives undervaluing the skills of idea development, expressing scepticism about the relevance of creativity, innovation and entrepreneurship for large organisations.

These myths and apparent deterrents would not matter if the ability to develop viable business ideas was not so vital to business growth within the economy overall. They also matter because almost everybody, at one stage in their life, wants to develop their own idea – set up their own business, launch a cherished project within an organisation or put skills acquired at work to the social good.

You are probably no different.

everybody has got a business idea

In fact, you probably already have an idea of the product or service which you could provide to satisfy an apparent market opportunity or need. Like Anita Roddick seeking good-quality toiletries in packs much smaller than those conventionally offered by high-street retailers, you might have looked for some service or product in your private life and been surprised when you could not find it; you might have seen an advertisement in the paper promoting a particular skill which you consider you possess; you might have heard customers grumbling about an existing product or an existing supplier; like James Dyson, you might have been dissatisfied with the performance of an everyday product or service; or, like the founders of Crate and Barrel and of Coffee Republic, you might have come across a type of successful company on your holiday abroad which you had never seen at home.

You might have looked at numerous business start-up books which lead with the declaration: 'Now that you have your business idea, here's how to put it into practice.'

But as we outlined above, the premature rush to put the idea into practice carries risks of commission – getting things wrong – as well as risks of omission – overlooking ideas which could be even better.

So how do you break the impasse of having an idea, being aware of the dangers of rushing to implementation, while perhaps thinking that start-ups are just for the born entrepreneur?

capitalising on intuition

We firmly believe that whatever the reasons for the skills of developing viable business ideas being so undervalued and misunderstood, almost everybody can develop the appropriate analytical and intuitive skills.

This book explains how everybody has an innate intuitive side which can be developed, nurtured and used at every step of the process to complement the brain's more logical and analytical skills. Polaroid inventor Dr Edwin Land held the view that creative ability was commonplace but generally uncultivated, reportedly claiming that his 'whole life has been spent trying to teach people that intense concentration for hour after hour can bring out resources in people that they didn't know they had'.[8]

everybody has an innate intuitive side which can be developed, nurtured and used at every step of the process

Trevor Baylis of clockwork radio fame shares this view, claiming that the key to success is to risk thinking unconventional thoughts. Convinced that convention is the enemy of progress, Baylis firmly believes that everybody has the potential to invent something.[9] We develop the theme of whole-brain thinking more fully in subsequent chapters.

creativity is not needed just at the beginning

In addition, emerging research supports our experience that the skills of creativity can and should be applied at every step of the development process and not just front-loaded to the generation of the original ideas – in other words, intuition does not give way to rationally driven implementation once an apparently workable idea has been produced: intuition and logic should interplay throughout the process.

Our book draws on the latest academic research, together with real-life examples from business, the public sector and the not-for-profit sector drawn from our own business practice, consultancy and teaching in order to show you how to acquire and practise these skills. It develops the notion that everybody is capable of creativity and describes the power of consciously harnessing both intuitive and logical skills. Techniques are provided to allow effective switching between these two types of thinking.

This means that almost everybody can develop the germ of an initial business idea into a viable business opportunity by following a systematic idea development process in virtually any organisational setting.

entrepreneurs are ordinary people too

The myths and stereotypes of the entrepreneur are ready to be slayed. After all, over 80 per cent of America's millionaires are reported by Jeffry Timmons to be 'ordinary people who have accumulated their wealth in one generation . . . and do not look like most people's stereotypes of millionaires'. Timmons stresses that these entrepreneurs are not necessarily the gleaming power-players of corporate boardrooms. Rather, they are the individuals who have created outstanding businesses in such sectors as diesel engine rebuilding, meat processing, mobile home parks, pest control and sandblasting.[10]

the four steps in the idea development process

The development of viable new business ideas is a systematic business process, whether the ideas are intended to be used within an existing organisation – intrapreneurially – or within a new organisation – entrepreneurially. The business idea may concern a product, process or service – in every case, the intended outcome is the creation of new value for the organisation.

The process takes as its starting point that you have the germ of a business idea, that is, something which you could provide to satisfy an apparent market opportunity or need.

The four steps shown in Figure 1.1 opposite represent a dynamic and iterative overall process of innovation, where each step informs both the succeeding and preceding steps. The process highlights how new and different ideas, and information of a higher degree of detail, are generated at every successive step and will often be fed back into earlier steps to allow development of alternative ideas. No information or idea is ever wasted, even if an idea is abandoned, because in failure lies the seed of further opportunity.

step one: seeking and shaping opportunities

The first step focuses on exploring your initial business idea by seeking and shaping the opportunity which your business idea intends to address. Quite often, our original business idea is framed as the single solution to one unambiguous opportunity – it is frequently the case that in reality we may not have defined the opportunity correctly in the first place. As we shall see later, it is equally likely that our original idea represents only one of many solutions to the opportunity as initially defined and is not necessarily the best. For this first step, we highlight how specific creativity techniques help you to explore and challenge your initial underlying assumptions about the business opportunity.

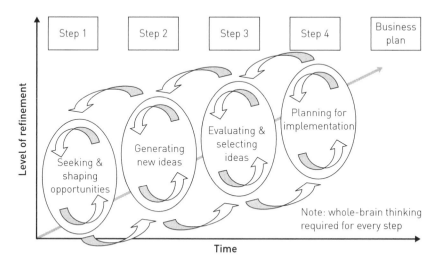

Figure 1.1 The idea development process and whole-brain thinking

As is the recurrent pattern within the total idea development process, these intuitive and divergent techniques are accompanied by more rational and convergent thinking, such as rough-cut estimates of market size and identification of major trends. Analytical and intuitive techniques used for this first step include 'boundary hopping' to escape from the conventional dimensions of a given market, the journalism-inspired '5 Ws plus H' to break opportunities down into their constituent parts, and observing at first hand the core users of products and services to reveal unexpected market opportunities.

The result of this first step is a much greater insight into the market which you are investigating, together with a sharper definition, or quite possibly redefinition, of the opportunity which you wish to seize. Key to this step is an awareness that those who currently serve the market have left gaps which could represent potential opportunities.

The case study on Jeff Bezos, founder of Amazon.com, illustrates best practice in relation to this step, while the case study on Iridium demonstrates the dangers of an elegant solution to an apparent market opportunity based on incorrect assumptions.

step two: generating new ideas
The second step is the generation of new ideas. Building on the insights and information developed in step one, this step uses a further combination of intuitive and rational techniques to develop a range of possible solutions to the business opportunity defined at the previous step.

The six mental workouts and their related routines available in the Mind Gym include the use of stimulus materials, upside-down thinking, analogical thinking and checklists. The techniques will help you generate a significant quantity of ideas which can be clustered into groups and carried forward to the next step. Consistent with the iterative nature of the idea development process, we show how insights from this step may also cause you to go back to step one and redefine the opportunity yet further.

The case study on Howard Head, whose innovations revolutionised the worlds of skiing and tennis, demonstrates the power of challenging convention and the elegant effectiveness of analogical thinking. The case study on Thomas Edison showcases an innovator *par excellence* who effectively created the industries of electricity supply, sound recording and motion pictures.

step three: evaluating and selecting ideas
The third step involves evaluating and selecting the emerging and crystallising business ideas. It typically follows a two-phase process, with a coarse-screen exercise followed by a more detailed, finer-screened evaluation of those ideas which survive the first phase. Frameworks to undertake this process include criteria grids, flowcharts, weighted criteria grids and the idea compatibility matrix.

the third step involves evaluating and selecting the emerging and crystallising business ideas

The criteria to use within the different frameworks can be separated into two broad categories: business-focused, such as the existence of a viable market opportunity, and person-focused, such as your attitude to risk.

As with all the steps within the idea development process, the evaluation and selection step combines left-brain analytical thinking with right-brain insightful thinking, encouraging you to sense the 'bigger picture' rather than become bogged down in spurious detail.

The outcome of this step is the identification of the leading contender to be taken forward to the final step in the idea development process, that of planning for implementation. As was the case with step two, insights arising from ideas 'rejected' at step three may yet provide the stimulus for further ideas and are fed back into earlier steps.

The case study on Karan Bilimoria highlights how his structured approach brought such heady success to his Cobra brand of beer. The case study on Internet Securities, Inc. demonstrates how careful evaluation of opportunities allowed it to buck the dot.com trend of high-profile failure and to build a high-value and sustainable internet business model.

step four: planning for implementation
The fourth step explains how you can increase the likelihood of your idea's success by identifying, and then resolving, potential blocks to implementation. Blocks will adopt many forms, from competitive reaction to lack of technical know-how, from lack of finance to inability to protect your idea.

A range of techniques exists to help you identify the blocks specific to your particular idea, including reverse brainstorming, force-field analysis and commitment charting. The effective application of these techniques continues to require your whole-brain creativity. As we discuss in more detail in the following chapters, planning for implementation is emphatically not just a question of 'non-creative' planners determining the logical steps to commercialise the business idea which their 'creative' colleagues have 'thrown over the wall' to them.

The very process of planning for implementation may lead to modification or refinement of the original business idea. As the 2003 Lambert Review of Business–University Collaboration eloquently phrased it: 'Innovation processes are complex and nonlinear. It is not simply a question of researchers coming up with clever ideas which are passed down a production line to commercial engineers and marketing experts who turn them into winning products. Great ideas emerge out of all kinds of feedback loops, development activities and sheer chance.'[11]

This fourth step of planning for implementation is informed by a number of guiding principles, including asset parsimony, keeping things simple, the need continually to influence and sell, and exercising vigilance and flexibility. The final guiding principle consists of reapplying at a focused level the processes and techniques outlined in the first three steps of the idea development process in order to resolve specific blocks.

Milestone planning will help you identify key events and activities, define their timing and interdependencies, and articulate the assumptions which underlie your business case and which will be tested against reality at each milestone. At the conclusion of this fourth step, you will be ready to codify all the elements of your business idea into a formal and fully fledged business plan.

The case study on Frederick Smith, founder of Federal Express, demonstrates how even the most formidable obstacles to implementation can be overcome. The case study on Jollibee Foods Corporation demonstrates how a structured and creative approach to implementation planning allowed a small fast-food operation in the Philippines to develop sufficient market strength to restrict global giant McDonald's to second place in the market.

making the most of models

We make extensive use of diagrams and models within this book to aid clear understanding, although we fully recognise that models necessarily over-simplify the realities of operational life.

Firstly, the book is laid out in a linear sequence of apparently logical steps, whereas the very nature of innovation is that it is an iterative, interdependent, dynamic and fuzzy process. Insights from later steps continually feed back into earlier ones, as well as feed forward into subsequent steps. The duration of each step will vary according to individual market circumstances. Similarly, the degree of time overlap between individual steps will also vary according to individual market circumstances.

the very nature of innovation is that it is an iterative, interdependent, dynamic and fuzzy process

In addition, real life has a persistent habit of intruding at each and every step of the innovation process. Trevor Baylis had gone as far as yomping across the Namib Desert to test a training shoe which generated electrical power when the arrest of the alleged 'Shoe-Bomber' on board an airline forced him to abandon that particular product idea.[12]

Even products which have gained financiers' hard-earned imprimaturs as commercial winners can fail when presented to the market. Edwin Land, best known as inventor of the Polaroid camera, discovered that the Detroit car industry was just not interested in adopting one of his early and apparently sure-fire inventions, a polarising filter which could eliminate headlight glare and thus reduce the hazards of night driving.

Provided that you acknowledge that real life is chaotic, dynamic and intrusive, however, models fulfil a valuable purpose in providing the clear structures and transparent frameworks with which to make sense of those realities. The model of the idea development process which underpins this book is strongly informed by the outcomes of the Minnesota Innovation Research Program which started in 1983 and ran for 17 years. This major project involved over 30 researchers undertaking longitudinal studies which tracked the development of 14 diverse innovations in real time and in their natural field settings. The researchers observed that the innovation journey is neither sequential and orderly nor a matter of random trial and error. They concluded that 'the innovation journey is a nonlinear cycle of divergent and convergent activities that may repeat over time and at different organisational levels if resources are obtained to renew the cycle'.[13]

This fusion of divergent and convergent activities is echoed by Joline Godfrey, who founded Odysseum, Inc., an international learning company serving the Fortune 500. Godfrey considers that the existence of business plans and the language of business combine to present a misleading impression of business as a rational process. It was her direct experience that starting a business was a series of fits and starts, brainstorms and barriers. As she vividly expressed it: 'Creating a business is a round of chance encounters that lead to new opportunities and ideas, mistakes that turn into miracles.'[14]

and another thing: benefits of the idea development process

The hostility awaiting new business ideas within the economic environment cannot be overemphasised. Any assertion by inexperienced entrepreneurs that all this emphasis on the idea development process is overstated – that once you have got the idea, success is bound to follow – is countered by the facts.

Enterprise guru Jeffry Timmons reports that for every 100 ideas presented to investors in the form of a business plan or proposal of some kind, a maximum of 3 per cent will ever get funded.[15] Rejections are fast and brutal – around 80 per cent of proposals will be rejected in the first few hours, with a further 10–14 per cent being spiked after investors have read the business plan carefully. In other words, a maximum of only 10 per cent of proposals typically generate sufficient interest even to warrant further investigation by the potential backers (see Figure 1.2).

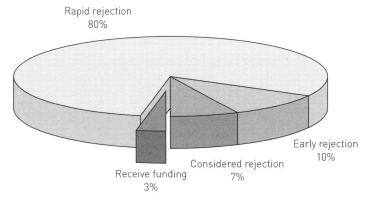

Figure 1.2 Typical life-chances of an initial business plan

For the 90 per cent aspiring but rejected entrepreneurs, such swift and summary dismissal represents a massive investment of time in chasing ideas which are literally going nowhere. The rate of attrition highlights the importance of following a thorough, multi-step process which allows you to proceed to the next step only when the requirements of the previous steps have been satisfied. Only then will you be able to decide effectively whether your business proposal represents a real opportunity or is just another good idea which does not yet merit placing in front of potential backers.

Market hostility once ideas come to fruition is equally harsh, where the record of survival for business start-ups is not good, as demonstrated by

Figure 1.3 below. Data from the Small Business Service at January 2004 shows that across the UK overall, 92 per cent of the new businesses registered in 2001 survived one year.

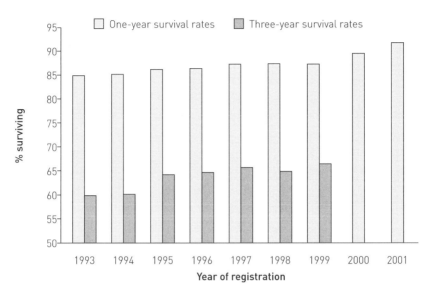

Figure 1.3 Survival rates of UK VAT-registered businesses

Source: Small Business Service, January 2004[16]

The struggle for survival over the next few years does not get any easier. Far from it. The ability to survive three years (as measured from businesses which were VAT-registered in 1999) drops markedly to 67 per cent. While the aggregated figures mask regional and sectoral variations, and while business failures can be attributed to takeover, voluntary winding up as well as business insolvency, the three-year business mortality rate of 33 per cent represents compelling evidence of the need for a thorough idea development process in advance of implementation.

The formality of following a rigorous and structured idea development process offers a number of further benefits.

desperately seeking certainty When starting to develop any business idea, the entrepreneur inevitably experiences initial uncertainty about the dimensions of the particular idea and whether it represents a valid business opportunity. The existence of a business idea might be recognised early on, be it for a product, service or process, but its scale and scope and how the various elements might fit together are totally unknown. By challenging the business problem, generating data and combining rigorous analysis with the creative generation of a range of possible solutions, the idea development process significantly increases the amount of relevant information available to the entrepreneur and thereby decreases uncertainty.

when starting to develop any business idea, the entrepreneur inevitably experiences initial uncertainty

In the case of the ill-fated Iridium project, for example, lack of regular management scrutiny allowed the project to evade the type of challenge offered by the idea development process which would have highlighted in advance the catastrophic blocks to implementation.

quantity creates quality Perhaps one of the most widely recognised benefits of the idea development process is the likely increase in idea quality provided by the generation of a large number of alternatives.

Based on simple probability, the greater the number of alternatives and options generated, the greater the likelihood of generating at least one or two superior solutions. If you jump straight into implementation and the business plan with your first idea, the best possible solution might be overlooked.

15 per cent rule On the corporate stage, the approach to innovation adopted by 3M is widely applauded. The 3M culture includes the 30 per cent rule, requiring a division to generate 30 per cent of its sales from products introduced during the past five years. The culture also includes the 15 per cent 'bootlegging' rule which allows staff to spend up to 15 per cent of their working week on a topic of their choice, provided that it is product-related.

3M's encouragement for new ideas is underpinned by the belief that unfettered creative thinking will pay off in the end and is exemplified by the 3M 'war story' of Francis G. Okie. Retaining his job despite, or perhaps even because of, his suggestion of sandpaper as a viable alternative to razor blades in 1922, Okie went on to develop one of 3M's first blockbusters, a waterproof sandpaper whose superior performance characteristics made it a market-leading product in the auto industry.

20 per cent time It is interesting to note that leading internet search firm Google has emulated 3M's bootlegging rule. The company's proposal to extend into e-mail with its Gmail service stemmed from a Google engineer whose attention was caught by a customer complaint about existing e-mail services. The engineer considered that it might be a good '20 per cent time' project, matching Google's requirement that a day a week is spent on projects which interest staff, unrelated to their day job.[17]

challenging convention for competitive advantage The increased quality of ideas produced by the increased alternatives described above is likely to include challenges to existing concepts of products and services. These challenges may suggest previously unthought-of market opportunities.

It is easy for products and services to become prisoners of their underlying concept. The core competencies which define an organisation can quickly become the 'core rigidities' which make it vulnerable to new competition launching developments outside its defining frame of reference. IBM is always considered to have missed the minicomputer market because the company was convinced that the computing market was defined by the mainframe computers at which IBM excelled.

it is easy for products and services to become prisoners of their underlying concept

We also saw earlier how James Dyson's redefinition of the washing machine concept was rejected by conventional manufacturers.

The watch industry was transformed in the 1970s by reframing the boundaries of the market, a technique which we explore in detail in a later chapter. The reframing exercise switched the focus of attention from time-piece to fashion accessory. As a result, many traditional products were leapfrogged by new products which had more in common with disposable fashion goods than the solid time-pieces of old.

The coffee bar market offers a similar example, in that the conventional market provided a product which was fast and cheap, where the key customer benefit was speed. Operations such as Coffee Republic and Starbucks redefined the market by presenting a chic environment together with a more sophisticated range of drinks, thereby creating a quite different customer proposition.

By the same token, bookseller Tim Waterstone redefined book retailing by moving the focus away from the depth of the range carried towards the quality of the book-buying experience itself. He promoted the expertise of the booksellers themselves and with huge counter-intuitive conviction introduced non-book-selling space in the form of seating areas and coffee shops to encourage book browsing and to enhance the overall experience.

getting stakeholders onside

Following a systematic process for developing new business ideas will also help you more clearly and accurately to meet the needs of the many different constituencies whose backing and support you will need to operationalise your business idea, whether financiers, customers, suppliers or prospective team members.

Every business proposal will be considered by many different people, each one of whom will be influenced by different backgrounds, experiences and expectations. This means that what may seem a good idea to you may be perceived quite differently by them from their particular perspective. As Clive Sinclair succinctly put it: 'What inventors need to recognise is that what is great to them is not necessarily great to other people.'[18]

what inventors need to recognise is that what is great to them is not necessarily great to other people

The various reactions of these expert audiences usually represent major stumbling blocks along the way. The predictability of this behaviour is neatly summed up by Clark's Law of Revolutionary Ideas: 'Every new idea, be it in science, politics, art or any other field, evokes three stages of reaction: "It's impossible. Don't waste my time"; "It's possible, but it's not worth doing"; and "I said it was a good idea all along."'[19]

retuning the opportunity In his heartening and witty autobiography *Clock This, My Life as an Inventor*,[20] Trevor Baylis tells candidly of how two years of 'scorn and rejection' from major manufacturers and financial bodies brought him close to abandoning his quest to turn his clockwork radio into reality. In desperation, he followed the advice of a supportive contact within the BBC World Service and allowed the clockwork radio concept to be televised on *Tomorrow's World*. Luck had it that businessman Christopher Staines saw the programme, immediately contacted Baylis and, together with his South African business partner Rory Stear, quickly joined forces with him.

Staines and Stear possessed the business know-how to turn the basic underlying idea into a viable business proposition, including the ability to address the financial audience in a fashion which Baylis by his own admission could not. Crucially, they had an entrée to influential investors whose faith and money set the project on its way.

In a sense, Staines and Stear took Baylis's idea right back to the opportunity-shaping step in order to initiate a new idea development process. This fresh development process included market research which overturned the initial assumption that the radio had to be miniature; securing funds from the philanthropic arm of the Liberty Life Group; re-engineering the entire radio mechanism to upgrade almost every component and to improve the radio's performance, so that the sound was not distorted 'into a mushy squall' when the volume was turned up; redesigning the radio's exterior to give it customer appeal; and establishing a factory in South Africa using disabled people as a major part of the workforce.

anticipating objections The idea development process therefore provides an excellent opportunity to identify upfront the various target audiences and the different perspectives of their professional expertise and to add the satisfaction of their likely objections to the various screening criteria which you apply to your business ideas.

This anticipation of objections raised by the various gatekeepers is likely to foster the creation of a much more viable, creative and innovative idea. In addition, you will have the knowledge base from which you can accurately assess and evaluate the advice they offer you. It may be the case that the idea development process highlights that you lack the ability to identify what different target audiences may object to. This represents a positive outcome, however, because it identifies early on in the process the gaps in your knowledge which you need to fill.

fast forward to 'yes'

One of the needs of the different target audiences discussed above is to receive sufficient information so that they can be persuaded to grant approval. There is no escape from gaining approvals – to see the eventual light of day, every business idea will need to win approval of some sort from key decision-makers, whether in the form of a board of directors, management committee, venture capitalist or bank manager.

Not only will the idea development process increase the quality of the ideas to be presented, the process also provides an excellent framework for gathering information at an increasingly higher level of detail for inclusion in the approval submission, be it internal project plan or external business plan. The better the idea development process, the greater the chance of success and the less risk of having to commit further time and resources to revisions.

As we saw earlier with the Bodas lingerie company's search for business angel funding, it had to satisfy the investors' need to back a business, not an idea. To achieve this, the founders had to provide evidence that their idea would work, such as a prototype together with proof of market demand.[21]

making it happen

By the same token, a rigorously followed idea development process provides a detailed framework for subsequently managing the business. The wide range of elements addressed – from manufacturing, design, resourcing, benchmarking and quality right through to milestone planning – translates easily into an effective management tool.

individual or corporate: the process works for both

The issues surrounding the contemporary global marketplace are well rehearsed in the modern business literature. These issues include reduced life cycles for both companies and products; the creation of new industries, including those based predominantly on knowledge; the enabling possibilities of information technology; and downsizing into lean organisations. Without wishing to repeat the discussion at length here, it is certainly the case that these issues combine to make innovation a key potential source of competitive advantage for established organisations. The need for this innovation applies equally to products, services and processes.

the need for this innovation applies equally to products, services and processes

This means that all the techniques described in this book are as applicable to organisations as they are to individual budding entrepreneurs. For this reason, we make extensive use throughout the book of examples drawn from the corporate world which are in the public domain. Based on our consultancy and workshop experience, these examples bring the added benefit of representing a common vocabulary for business practitioners from small and large organisations alike. Experience suggests that these types of examples illustrate the innovation techniques more effectively than the anonymous case studies otherwise required by commercial confidentiality.

call in the cavalry or do it yourself?

A whole multitude of business start-up specialists and management consultants exists to advise on all aspects of the idea development process and to charge you for the privilege.

There are undoubtedly some people who would prefer to restrict themselves to the invention end of the process – Trevor Baylis is perhaps a case in point – accepting the inevitable trade-off in terms of financial reward. There is real power, however, in following the whole process yourself from start to finish. It may well be a long haul – following the process through from start to final product is the 99 per cent perspiration evoked by Thomas Edison.

The idea development process represents an invaluable opportunity to test out the robustness and innovation potential of your business ideas, as well as the level of your personal commitment to following them through. Sustained follow-through requires hard graft, self-discipline, dedication and perseverance in the face of what sometimes appear to be insurmountable obstacles. Jane Henry christened these characteristics as the four 'Ps' of creativity – positivity, playfulness, passion and persistence – and these are perhaps best typified by James Dyson.[22]

Positivity represents the consistent habit of seeing problems as opportunities. It embraces the ability to recover rapidly from setbacks and to tolerate criticism. It includes an unwillingness to allow the unanticipated blockages referred to above impede progress.

Playfulness allows an entrepreneur to feel comfortable outside mainstream thinking and action. Drawing on the resources of childhood, it encourages risk-taking and the use of fun and humour in thinking to stimulate flexibility of thought and deed.

Passion evokes the drive of an all-consuming purpose and an obsessive will to achieve goals.

Persistence provides the difference between 'if at first you don't succeed, try and try again' and 'if at first you don't succeed, try something different until you do succeed'.

self-awareness beats the imposition of others

A final point to make in support of undertaking the idea development process yourself is that it is much easier to accept changes and refinements to which you have been inexorably drawn by data which you have generated yourself than to have to stomach changes which have been imposed upon you by outsiders.

Sir Clive Sinclair and the C5 – the perils of a flawed process of idea development[23]

the C5 story offers an
object lesson in the risks of developing a solution before the underlying problem has been fully explored.

Sir Clive Sinclair is an electronics expert whose world-beating products include the executive pocket calculator (1972) and the microvision pocket TV (1977).

His plans to develop an electronic vehicle go back as far as 1973. In 1983 a change in the law for the benefit of disabled drivers and milk float manufacturers allowed for a new type of vehicle, the electrically assisted pedal cycle. The Sinclair C5 was a battery-powered one-seater pedal-assisted tricycle intended to herald a new era of ecological personal transport. It was designed so that anybody over 14 years old could drive it without insurance, driving licence, road tax or crash helmet. The C5's core-benefit proposition was that it was silent, pollution-free, economic and safer than a moped. A number of alternative models of the C5 were created.

The first consumer exposure to the C5 occurred when an early prototype vehicle was presented to 63 families in suburban and town environments in order to research where the controls should be positioned.

The C5's designers were unable to produce radically new battery technology to optimise the trade-off between battery power and weight. This compromised the C5's performance, forcing the driver (when not pedalling) to 'push and coast' – giving a burst of power and then coasting to conserve battery power. The pedals were required when driving up steep hills. The C5 had a published range of 20 miles and a top speed of 15 mph. The battery suffered a significant loss of battery power in freezing weather. It took about eight hours to recharge on the domestic mains.

The C5's boot had a capacity of one cubic foot. The C5 safety booklet commissioned from the Royal Society for the Prevention of Accidents warned of the danger caused by the low height of the machine, which made it difficult for lorry drivers and less alert car drivers to spot the C5. The basic C5 model excluded wing mirrors, horn or indicators, which could be purchased as additional items, as could a high-visibility mast to attach to the car. The fully 'rebundled' cost of the C5, including safety extras, spare battery and delivery, was around £600 rather than the advertised headline price of £399.

The secrecy surrounding the launch limited the tests conducted on public roads to night-time when traffic was light. Private tests included a test-track and accident simulation at the Motor Industry Research Association.

The product launched nationally in 1985 rather than via a rolling launch. A number of the test models failed on hills during the product launch, which was held in January. Distribution in the early stages of the product's life was intended to be by mail order, with delivery from one of the distribution centres direct to the customer's door.

The visuals used in the advertising campaign stressed the leisure component of the C5, featuring women in C5s on a deserted road and ▶

young boys in C5s in a football park rather than images which emphasised the C5's positioning as a serious road transport alternative. Much of the actual advertising copy, however, invited comparison of the C5 with motor cars.

Annual sales were envisaged to grow from 100,000 in the first year to 500,000. From a buoyant start of around 1,000 sales in the first week, sales dwindled and production was discontinued in September 1985 – 14,000 units were produced during the product's lifetime and not all were sold at full price. When the receivers were called in, debts were reported to stand at around £8 million.

key points

- Avoid the temptation to implement your first idea immediately without fully challenging it – you will miss the opportunity to develop a potentially much stronger alternative

- Following the iterative four-step idea development process – seeking and shaping opportunities; generating new ideas; evaluating and selecting the emerging business ideas; and planning for implementation – significantly increases your chances of entrepreneurial success

- Maintain sufficient emotional distance from your initial idea so that you can accept constructive feedback from others or let the idea go if it simply will not work

- Even if you abandon an idea, no information or idea is ever wasted because in failure lies the seed of further opportunity

- Always remember that the acid test of a business opportunity is your ability to sell products or services in sufficient quantity to real customers to generate sustainable cash flows and profit

- Combining rational and intuitive thinking at appropriate steps throughout the idea development process creates new perspectives and competitive advantage for your initial business idea

- Getting started with the idea development process is the best way to evaluate whether your initial idea represents a potentially valid business opportunity and to gauge the strength of your personal commitment

two

applying creativity to the idea development process

- Phil Knight and NIKE – combining logic and intuition into record-breaking success
- why is creativity a must?
- reconnect with your creativity
- creativity and the idea development process
- mastering whole-brain thinking
- Ingvar Kamprad – using logic and intuition to break the mould with IKEA

Since when was an accountant ever compared to Christopher Columbus, using intuition to bravely seek out new and unimagined worlds?

Since Phil Knight, in fact.

Co-founder of the legendary NIKE empire, Knight combined logical analysis and intuition to gain dominance for NIKE in record time across global boardrooms and sports stadia alike.

It was once considered that creativity was the preserve of the favoured few whom the artistic muse would regularly deign to visit. Worse still, it was held that creativity was required only at the start of the idea development process – once a bright idea had been born, it was thrown over the wall to planners and developers to bring to market.

Wrong on both counts. Creativity is needed at every step of the idea development process. Everybody can be creative by combining their innate intuitive ability with the logical and analytical skills which education and the workplace tend to favour. And everybody includes you.

Phil Knight and NIKE – combining logic and intuition into record-breaking success[24]

Phil Knight, the co-founder of the NIKE sportswear empire, exemplifies the benefits of applying a creative approach to every step of the idea development process by combining logic with intuition.

Hailed by many as the success story of the 1970s, NIKE had achieved sales close to $700 million by 1982, with NIKE-wearing athletes having achieved every world record in men's track events.

A gifted athlete who could run a mile in just 13 seconds over the magic four minutes, Phil Knight developed his passion and skill for athletics by running at Oregon State University under the inspired coaching of the legendary Bill Bowerman. Credited with introducing America to the jogging craze in the 1960s, Bowerman went on to become coach to the USA Olympic team in Munich in 1972.

By virtue of studying accountancy at Oregon State University, Knight might appear to fit the stereotype of the left-brain logical thinker. Knight had a strong intuitive side, however. Based on his own running experience, and in the absence of reliable market data, he sensed the opportunity to import Far Eastern products into the American athletics market and thereby emulate what had happened in the markets for cameras and other optical equipment.

The initial business model for what was to become NIKE found expression in an MBA paper on small business management authored by Knight, in which he identified the opportunity to source low-cost but high-quality running shoes from the Far East to compete with the German-based leader of the American market, Adidas.

It is clear that Knight felt that the original concept was right and was enormously excited about marketing his own product line, even though its acceptance in the market was unknown. The NIKE website's depiction of this intuitive insight as 'this you're-crazy-it-will-never-work-or-someone-would-already-be-doing-it idea' is strikingly reminiscent of the refusal of the Secretary of State for Wales to provide a development grant to James Dyson which was highlighted in the previous chapter.

Knight's vision began to become reality during a post-graduation world trip when he used the Japanese leg of the tour to establish a distributor arrangement for the Japanese Tiger brand. Legend has it that in 1964 Knight and Bowerman each contributed $500 to form Blue Ribbon Sports (BRS, Inc.) to distribute the Japanese product. Their promotion to the running community through what Knight memorably termed 'word of foot' was so effective that it could have caused their downfall. The burgeoning sales figures alerted their Japanese supplier to the USA market's possibilities, leading the Japanese to plan direct entry into the market in 1972, either through purchase of a majority stake in BRS, Inc. or by establishing their own network.

The reaction of Knight and Bowerman to this 'whack on the side of the head', as Roger von Oech describes such critical trigger events, showed the mark of the innovative persistent entrepreneur.[25] Instead of selling out to the Japanese distributor, they sensed the opportunity which was not previously apparent to create their own product. From the termination of BRS, Inc.'s import and sales promotion activities, they created the vision of NIKE.

To achieve the vision, they established a deal with one of Japan's largest trading companies to identify manufacturing sources for the new design, as well as to provide financing and export–import services. Finances were under such pressure that Knight was supplementing his modest income from the fledgling company by teaching accounting at Portland State University. Without the funding to retain image and advertising specialists, Knight trusted his right-brain judgement in backing the brand name suggested by Jeff Johnson, the company's first employee. Fittingly enough, the image of NIKE – the Greek goddess of victory – had come to Johnson in a dream.

Knight also trusted his judgement by using the logo created by Carolyn Davidson, a graduate design student whom he happened to meet while he was teaching at Portland State University and to whom he paid the princely commission of $35. Considering that NIKE's 'Swoosh' logo is now known throughout the world, this represents one of brand advertising's more successful investments. ▶

The combination of logic and intuition into whole-brain thinking typified by Knight permeated the whole company.

the combination of logic and intuition into whole-brain thinking typified by Knight permeated the whole company

It was NIKE's co-founder, Bill Bowerman, for example, who while watching his wife make waffles for breakfast realised that a waffle-patterned outer sole would improve traction and produce faster running times. In a classic example of rapid prototyping, Bowerman poured rubber into his wife's waffle iron. Folklore maintains that Bowerman's attention to left-brain detailed thinking apparently extended to removing the branding strips from an athlete's running shoes in order to save even a microscopic amount of weight, and to weighing the ink on the university running singlets. In later chapters, we will see how Clive Woodward, businessman and English rugby manager extraordinaire, used comparable whole-brain thinking to bring his team to World Cup victory in 2003.

Whole-brain thinking was also facilitated in NIKE's early, smaller days by the management culture of perceiving problems as company issues, in whose solution everybody had an interest, rather than seeing problems along departmental lines. In part, this culture was the creative response to the company's financial inability to recruit specialists in every area; instead, NIKE recruited can-do multi-skilled individuals who became 'specialists in the company, not the job'. Significantly, management difficulties arose as NIKE grew and the intuitive sense of senior managers – more street-savvy than Wall Street – was not necessarily shared by incoming managers.

Knight's personal management style combined divergent innovative thinking with convergent evaluation, leading NIKE management to compare the visionary Knight to Christopher Columbus, continually seeking out new worlds. His preferred working style was to spend time alone identifying opportunities and obstacles, conceiving where the company should be and how it was going to get there, before meeting with close colleagues to probe, evaluate and refine the ideas which he had generated. From such unconstrained forward thinking came the realisation that the American market would eventually 'run out of feet' and that other product areas such as clothing and the international market should be explored.

This divergent–convergent pattern of working also led to the insight that the company should convert its vulnerability to import quotas from the Far East into a strategic advantage through innovative improvements to its long-term contractual arrangements with the supplier base.

By the same token, Knight's intuitive grasp of NIKE's business performance was supplemented by a strong left-brain focus born of his training as an accountant, which allowed him to focus on a few key quantitative performance indicators. Whole-brain thinking has allowed NIKE to race across the business and athletic worlds. From its humble beginnings, NIKE now turns over more than $12 billion per year.

why is creativity a must?

Phil Knight's success with NIKE vividly illustrates how creativity must be applied at every step of the idea development process. Certainly Knight had the initial creative vision of the market potential for high-quality, economically sourced running shoes which led to the creation of Blue Ribbon Sports (BRS, Inc.), but it could all have come to nothing when the Japanese exporters threatened BRS, Inc.'s very survival. This threat to Knight's initial vision led him to renew his vision and to break the conventional rules by designing and sourcing his own NIKE-branded product.

creativity must be applied at every step of the idea development process

He continued to apply creativity throughout the idea development process, whether structuring innovative deals with Far Eastern manufacturers to secure capacity at economical prices or using heavy brand advertising to reinforce the expert endorsement of Olympic-winning athletes.

don't front-load creativity

As we saw earlier, it is a mistake to assume that a superficially attractive business idea can automatically be developed into a profitable business. This mistaken assumption is perpetuated by the conventional model of the innovation process, which 'front-loads' creativity into the idea generation phase. Drawing in part from NASA's early project management techniques, the conventional stage-gate model of innovation is shown in Figure 2.1.

Figure 2.1 The conventional stage-gate model of innovation

Under this model, each stage of activity has to report to a 'review gate' before it may proceed to the next stage with military precision. Each review gate has the power of issuing a go/no-go decision. According to this conventional model, creativity is restricted to the creative specialists and once the creative moment has occurred, responsibility for commercialising the idea is 'thrown over the gate' to the logical and analytical implementers.

Not only does 'front-loading' creativity in this way downplay the importance of logic and analysis in the idea generation step, it also ignores the important role of intuition and imagination in the three subsequent steps.

intuition and logic – equal partners It is increasingly

accepted that both intuition and logic have a part to play at every step in the idea development process, albeit with different levels of emphasis, and these are not just confined to specific steps of the process.

both intuition and logic have a part to play at every step in the idea development process

At the step of seeking and shaping opportunities, for example, both logic and intuition perform supporting roles. It was an inquisitive and analytical salesman of milkshake machines who noticed that one of the food outlets to which he sold the machines bought comparatively more machines than the selling space and location seemed to warrant. Closer investigation of the store revealed to the salesman that the proprietors had set up a highly effective system to standardise the production of their food, generating high turnover at good margins. The salesman had the imaginative insight to realise that this formula could be rolled out on a much bigger scale. From such analysis and imagination was the McDonald's concept created by Ray Kroc.[26]

By the same token, insight and imagination have a key role to play during the planning for implementation step, which is not just the logic-oriented set of conventional textbook approaches you might expect. This is the type of creativity exemplified by the fashion designer with no marketing budget who banned fashion critics from attending her shows in order to generate interest; or the mass-market sandwich producer who realised that the principles of silk-screen printing could be transferred to buttering bread in high volumes. We will investigate all these imaginative examples in more detail in later chapters, including the furniture retailer who broke all the conventional rules – Ingvar Kamprad of IKEA – who features in the case study at the end of this chapter.

the traditional view of creativity

The limitations of the conventional model of the innovation process are compounded by the traditional view of creativity which held that only right-brain thinkers could be creative. Blessed with right-brain dominance, these creative types were deemed capable of exploiting their unconventional, unsystematic, artistic and unstructured approach to generate an endless supply of workable ideas. Those not blessed with the artistic temperament were deemed to be logical, commonsensical and analytical. The two groups were held to be mutually exclusive.

Not only do we disagree with the conventional view of the innovation process, we believe that creativity is wider than just right-brain thinking. In our view, creativity can best be defined as the effective combination of intuition (divergent or right-brain thinking) and logic (convergent or left-brain thinking). Our experience is that everybody can be creative by combining divergent with convergent thinking, although this view of creativity runs counter to tradition and practice.

creativity can best be defined as the effective combination of intuition (divergent or right-brain thinking) and logic (convergent or left-brain thinking)

education kills creativity
Almost from the moment we enter school, we are trained to think convergently, to find the single correct answer by following a logical train of thought. Lewis articulated the powerful role which education systems play in reinforcing the analytical over the imaginative when he wrote:

'In class, students are expected to acquire knowledge one step at a time, adding methodically to their storehouse of facts until they have sufficient to pass an examination. This demands left-brain skills. The problems students are given to solve more often demand an analytical than an intuitive approach. This, too . . . is a task for the left hemisphere. Written work, by which ability is chiefly evaluated, must be organised, well argued and logically structured . . . all left-brain skills. The students considered most intelligent and successful are those who strive after academic goals, can control their emotions in class, follow instructions, do not ask awkward questions, are punctual and hand in class assignments on time. Goal-setting, emotional restraint, time-keeping and matching your behaviour to other people's expectations are all left-brain skills.'[27]

Given the extent to which the contemporary education system is target- and performance-driven, it is little wonder that children are trained to seek single correct answers in all that they study. The skills of imagination and intuition risk being lost from an early age.

What would you expect a group of four-year-olds to think the following small shape on a whiteboard represents?

Typical answers might include a squashed beetle, an upside-down fried egg, an eskimo's fishing hole, a flower, a black cloud, the top of a pole, a cigarette butt, a pen leak, a hole in a tent, a wine spill, an island and so on.

Ask the same question of a group of 14-year-olds and you would be lucky to be told it was a black blob – the unremitting search for a single right answer has closed off any search for other and more imaginative answers.

Even business and management course at universities and business schools contribute to the stifling of creativity, often favouring the logical and analytical disciplines of accountancy, finance, operations and marketing over more intuitive approaches. The mythology of single right and wrong answers is perpetuated by never-ending assessment – indeed, American commentators have estimated that the average student who has completed four years of college has taken more than 2,600 tests.[28]

It is worth noting how many business schools use the globally recognised GMAT test (Graduate Management Admission Test), whose emphasis on logical reasoning and numerical dexterity may eliminate at admissions stage right-brain thinkers with a tendency to think contemplatively and to see problems not just in terms of right and wrong solutions. In other words, the GMAT assumes that all good management thinking is left-brain dominated and then contributes to the perpetuation of that myth.[29]

logic fits the work culture The focus within education and training on the single correct answer tends to continue in the workplace, where it is often the logical thinker who will fit the culture who is preferred over the intuitive and imaginative. Given all these different aspects, it is hardly surprising that the one-correct-logical-answer syndrome has become such an inherent part of our thinking that we are estimated to use only about 2–10 per cent of our creative potential.[30]

But creativity is so important that if you cannot use your whole-brain thinking to be creative, you risk your business idea being literally half-brained. This risk is all the more real during the process of idea development because the team responsible for developing the idea is probably restricted to just you, with one or two other partners at most.

The challenge is to reconnect with the more than 90 per cent of the creativity which has been educated out of you.

the challenge is to reconnect with the more than 90 per cent of the creativity which has been educated out of you

reconnect with your creativity The 1981 Nobel prize-winning work of neurosurgeon Roger Sperry on split-brain theory provides reassurance that everybody can be creative by combining logic and intuition. He demonstrated that the right and left hemispheres of the brain perform fundamentally different functions and process information in quite different ways.

right brain: intuitive

The right side is the domain of visualisation and intuition. Operating in terms of sensory images and non-rational modes of thought, the right side represents the source of dreaming and feeling. Right-brain thinking draws on the power of divergent reasoning, which is the ability to create a multitude of original, diverse ideas and to investigate issues from the widest set of perspectives.

Rosabeth Moss Kanter is Professor of Business Administration at Harvard Business School and author of such classic management texts as *The Change Masters* and *When Grants Learn to Dance*. She coined the term 'kaleidoscopic thinking' to describe this capacity to question, rearrange and see things from a different angle.[31]

The importance of hearing and trusting the inarticulate voice of intuition is highlighted by research by Marton and others, which revealed that 90 per cent of the 83 Nobel science laureates surveyed relied upon intuition in one way or another.[32]

left brain: logical

In contrast, the left side is characterised by thinking in terms of symbols and words. It performs logical thinking, judgement, speaking and mathematical reasoning. The left side is the domain of the so-called rational and logical functions. Based on convergent reasoning, it is the left side which evaluates multiple ideas and selects the best solution to a given problem with a highly detailed focus. The contrast between left- and right-brain thinking is illustrated in Figure 2.2.

Sperry's split-brain theory held that our habit of using one side of the brain more than the other influences our problem-solving skills, physical and mental abilities, as well as our personality traits. In other words, we tend to possess a dominant and preferred thinking style. These preferred thinking styles can be categorised as either left-brain (convergent) or right-brain (divergent). The characteristics of each thinking style are shown in Table 2.1

CONVERGENT THINKING

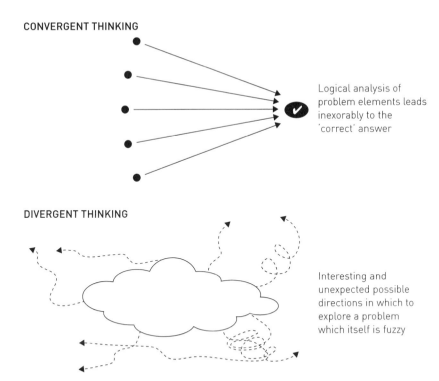

Logical analysis of problem elements leads inexorably to the 'correct' answer

DIVERGENT THINKING

Interesting and unexpected possible directions in which to explore a problem which itself is fuzzy

Figure 2.2 Overview of convergent and divergent thinking

Table 2.1 Comparison of convergent and divergent thinking

Left brain/convergent	Right brain/divergent	
Positive	Intuitive	
Analytical	Spontaneous	Holistic
Logical	Emotional	Playful
Linear	Non-verbal	Diffuse
Explicit	Musical	Shape recognition
Sequential	Visual	Physical
Verbal	Artistic	Sensory
Concrete	Dreaming	Visualisation
Rational	Imaginative	Images
Active		
Goal-oriented		
Judgemental		
Speaking		
Mathematical		

debunking the myth of the 'creatives'

Prior to Sperry, popular thinking had it that only dominant right-brain thinkers, the 'artistic types' and 'creatives', could be creative. Sperry's work demonstrated that everybody can tap into their right-brain and overcome the conventional preference for left-brain thinking which age and the education system conspire to create. Later sections of this book will show you how.

There are strong precedents for Sperry's depiction of creativity as requiring the use and co-ordination of both sides of the brain. This combination facilitates the analysis by the left-brain of the flashes of insight and intuition from the right-brain. It is claimed that Einstein was lying on a hillside one summer's day, contemplating the light rays shining into his half-closed eyes. Dreaming of how it might feel to travel down a light beam, he experienced the sudden right-brain intuition of what it would be like. Only later did the Theory of Relativity find left-brain elaboration and expression in words and mathematical symbols.

The precise chemistry of carbon compounds owes a large part to 19th-century German chemist Friedrich August Kekulé. By a strange set of circumstances, Kekulé was a witness at a murder trial where the victim's distinctive ring formed a crucial part of the evidence. The ring featured the old alchemy seal of two intertwined serpents biting each other's tails. Many years later, while agonising over the structure of benzene which logic alone seemed unable to resolve, Kekulé fell asleep in front of the fire. He dreamt of the twining serpents on the old ring, whirling in the flames. Finally the serpents caught each other's tails and formed a circle. The visual imagery generated by turning his dreams loose on a seemingly intractable problem and by breaking the thread of logic had produced a sudden intuitive insight, namely that benzene was formed of a hexagonal ring. As he wrote in his diary: 'As if by a flash of lightning I awoke; and . . . spent the rest of the night in working out the consequences of the hypothesis.'

'as if by a flash of lightning I awoke; and spent the rest of the night in working out the consequences of the hypothesis'

Bill Gates, founder of Microsoft, provides a further illustration of this powerful combination of left- and right-brain thinking. In 1974, a like-minded friend, Paul Allen, spotted an article in *Popular Electronics* about the world's first home computer, the Altair 8800. Primitive by today's standards, the Altair lacked software which would allow it to achieve something. Gates not only perceived the opportunity, he sensed that he and Allen were capable of writing a software program for the Altair. On the strength of this right-brain intuition and before writing a single word of code, Gates called the president of Altair's manufacturer with the claim that they had created a version of the popular computer language BASIC for the Altair. Gaining a positive response from the president, Gates and Allen proceeded to create a program which worked perfectly and swiftly led to the foundation of Microsoft.[33]

artist as businessman – a contradiction in terms?
To demonstrate that whole-brain thinking was a long-standing phenomenon just waiting to be discovered, consider the example of leading 18th-century English portrait painter Thomas Gainsborough.

Gainsborough combined exquisite artistic right-brain skill with a finely developed left-brain financial instinct. Having prudently married into money, he moved from the relative wilds of Ipswich to the splendour of Bath, which was rapidly becoming a fashionable winter resort for wealthy Londoners, in order to pursue what he described in his private letters as 'the curs'd Face Business'. He would often paint only the face and sometimes the hands of his subjects, leaving his lesser qualified staff to paint the backgrounds, while charging a price as if the entire creation was his alone.

creativity and the idea development process

Creativity lies at the heart of the idea development process because each of the four steps of the process represents a cycle of divergent–convergent thinking, as shown in Figure 2.3.

Each divergent thinking phase generates ideas imaginatively, seeking quantity of ideas, the more intuitive and innovative the better. Judgement and evaluation are suspended. Each convergent thinking phase seeks to refine and improve the options and to select the elements to pass on to the next step.

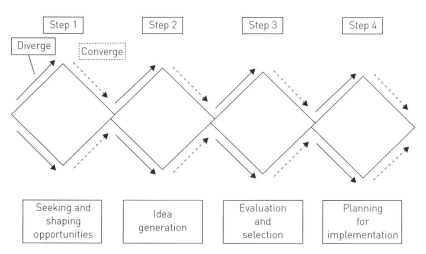

Figure 2.3 Divergent–convergent thinking throughout the idea development process

the innovation journey

As we saw in Chapter 1, the Minnesota Innovation Research Program, a major longitudinal study led by Andrew van de Ven and others which involved 30 researchers tracking 14 diverse innovations in real time and in their natural field settings, concluded that the innovation journey is a 'cycle of divergent and convergent activities that may repeat over time and at different organisational levels if resources are obtained to renew the cycle'.[34]

Later chapters of this book illustrate convergent and divergent techniques which are particularly well suited to specific steps of the process. It may appear paradoxical that some of these divergent techniques may at first almost 'force' an imaginative approach. Our intention is to offer you a structured approach which over time will become natural and intuitive to you. It is no different to learning how to drive a car: after all, how many times did you almost crash as a learner because you were so busy looking down at the gearstick? How many years ago did you last need to do that?

finding the correct balance

While both intuition and logic are required at each of the four steps, the relative weight of each style of thinking varies at each step. The shift of emphasis is shown in Table 2.2.

Table 2.2 How the emphasis on thinking style changes for each step of the process

Step	Description	Thinking style
1 Seeking and shaping opportunities	Identifying and exploring different opportunities, followed by analytical judgement	Divergent and convergent whole-brain thinking equally dominant
2 Generating new ideas	Creating significant volumes of innovative, imaginative and associative ideas	Divergent thinking is dominant
3 Evaluating and selecting ideas	Screening the best from the rest and then evaluating those few in detail	Convergent thinking is dominant
4 Planning for implementation	Identifying and overcoming blocks to implementation	Divergent and convergent whole-brain thinking equally dominant

You are now aware that you must combine intuition and logic at every step in order to be creative; the insights on whole-brain thinking should have also made you confident that you can. So why not start improving your skills of convergent and divergent thinking?

mastering whole-brain thinking

There are three key steps to mastering whole-brain thinking as it applies to the idea development process:

- Identify your preferred thinking style
- Strengthen your non-preferred thinking style
- Make the most of divergent and convergent thinking phases.

We will deal with each of these in turn.

step one: identify your preferred thinking style

Complete the following exercise to test your left-brain/right-brain dominance.[35] The exercise can also be found at www.angelfire.com/wi/2 brains.

Take a blank sheet of lined paper. Read through the list below and each time you find a description or characteristic which applies to you, write down its number on the sheet of paper. There is no particular number of characteristics you must choose.

After you have completed this, refer to the key printed at the end of the exercise in order to write next to every number on your paper whether it was an L or an R. Count up the number of Ls and Rs. Whichever number is higher represents your dominance.

If the numbers are close, that means you use both sides of your brain equally. Having talents in both left- and right-brain thinking, together with the ability to shift appropriately and effortlessly between the two styles, puts you in the position of the master whole-brain thinker, exemplified by Ingvar Kamprad of IKEA whom we will meet later on in this chapter.

Questionnaire on left-brain/right-brain dominance

1 I always wear a watch
2 I keep a journal
3 I believe there is a right and wrong way to do everything
4 I hate following directions
5 The expression 'Life is just a bowl of cherries' makes no sense to me
6 I find that sticking to a schedule is boring
7 I'd rather draw someone a map than tell them how to get somewhere
8 If I lost something, I'd try to remember where I saw it last
9 If I don't know which way to turn, I let my emotions guide me
10 I'm pretty good at maths
11 If I had to assemble something, I'd read the directions first
12 I'm always late getting places
13 Some people think I'm psychic
14 Setting goals for myself helps keep me from slacking off
15 When somebody asks me a question, I turn my head to the left
16 If I have a tough decision to make, I write down the pros and the cons
17 I'd make a good detective
18 I am musically inclined

19 If I have a problem, I try to work it out by relating it to one I've had in the past

20 When I talk, I gesture a lot

21 If someone asks me a question, I turn my head to the right

22 I believe there are two sides to every story

23 I can tell whether someone is guilty just by looking at them

24 I keep a 'to-do' list

25 I feel comfortable expressing myself with words

26 Before I take a stand on an issue, I get all the facts

27 I've considered becoming a poet, a politician, an architect or a dancer

28 I lose track of time easily

29 If I forgot someone's name, I'd go through the alphabet until I remembered it

30 I like to draw

31 When I'm confused, I usually go with my gut instinct

32 I have considered becoming a lawyer, journalist or doctor

Key to questionnaire on left-brain/right-brain dominance

1–L	9–R	17–L	25–L
2–L	10–L	18–R	26–L
3–L	11–L	19–R	27–R
4–R	12–R	20–R	28–R
5–L	13–R	21–L	29–L
6–R	14–L	22–R	30–R
7–R	15–R	23–R	31–R
8–L	16–L	24–L	32–L

step two: strengthen your non-preferred thinking style

The following sections suggest how you can strengthen your non-preferred style by improving your ability to switch between left-brain and right-brain thinking and by deliberately stretching your non-preferred thinking side.

switching between thinking styles Before moving into the brain-stretching exercises, we will start with a few warm-ups to get you used to the movement between convergent and divergent thinking, generating new perspectives on things which your left-brain told you were unambiguously true.

Look at the picture below and describe the woman you see.[36]

Conventional left-brain thinking would say that a picture can communicate only one image. But what do you see? An old woman? Or a young woman with a boa? Consider which detail it was that drew you to your initial interpretation – it shows the power of the first impression to colour your judgement. Once you have spotted both, reflect on what it feels like to shift perception from one perspective to another: it will make it easier for you actively to manage the conscious transition from convergent to divergent thinking which is such an important part of creativity.

Look at the second ambiguous picture below. Do you see a vase or a pair of twins?

Again, reflect on what it feels like to move between the differing perceptions – focus on the vase and then on the twins, and then back again. And as with the previous picture, why stop at two images? Can you shift your perception to identify the whale fin, the key hole, and what else? Use all the tricks at your disposal – focus on particular sections of the picture, turn it upside down, transpose black with white – before comparing your solutions against ours, which are shown in Appendix 1 on page 249.[37]

As a final warm-up, make a list in two minutes of the uses to which you can put a leather belt with a buckle, other than to hold up your trousers. Ideas from our workshop participants have included matching accessory for shoes; rescue a drowning person; sharpen razor; start a leather belt collection; straight edge; flash a signal in the sunlight; bookmark; secure a suitcase with a broken lock; dog lead; bracelet; hole-punch; fire-lighter; bottle opener; measuring tool; hold a door shut; tapping out Morse code; whip; template for other leather belts; door hinge.

Clearly there is no correct number of correct answers – the important aspect to consider is how comfortable you felt generating ideas: did you struggle to write down the ideas as they poured out or did you stop at just four or five? Did you decide against some ideas because they felt frivolous? Did you think that cutting the belt into smaller pieces was breaking the rules? Did you focus just on the belt's original uses? Did you ignore the uses to which the buckle could be put? How you fared will tell you a lot about your ability to be actively imaginative and to defer your critical judgement.

how you fared will tell you a lot about your ability to be actively imaginative

stretching your right-brain Whether the earlier questionnaire identified your preferred thinking style as left-brain or whether you are a natural right-brainer who wants to see whether you can be even better, the following exercises will help you stretch your right-brain. Many of the activities are also effective for when you want to make a conscious transition from left-brain to right-brain thinking.

- Use metaphors and analogies to describe things and people in your conversations and writing
- Make eye contact with people you meet in order to help feel their point of view
- Take off your watch when you are not working
- Suspend your initial judgement of ideas, new acquaintances, movies, TV programmes
- Record your hunches, feelings and intuitions and calculate their accuracy
- Take a stroll to no place in particular
- Surf the net just to see where it takes you
- Indulge in detailed day-dreaming and visualising things and situations in the future
- Do some doodling and draw faces, caricatures and landscapes
- Perceive the bigger picture and float above the details
- Collect junk mail and peruse it for unusual ideas
- Place a deliberate spelling mistake in your next letter or business paper and check whether the world falls in.

stretching your left-brain The following exercises are useful for stretching your left-brain and for making a conscious transition from right-brain to left-brain thinking.

- Establish a timetable for all your work activities during the coming week and check your progress every hour
- Make a step-by-step plan of your life activities for the next ten years
- Read a book on logic
- When you next buy a piece of electrical apparatus, read the instruction manual from start to finish (before using the apparatus)
- Learn how to use a new computer program
- Complete a crossword puzzle
- Compile a detailed broken-down analysis of the three major issues facing you at work
- Volunteer to make public presentations at every opportunity
- Write out the detailed search strategy which you intend to follow when you next go on to the internet looking for specific information.

step three: make the most of divergent and convergent thinking phases

Awareness of the ground rules for convergent and divergent thinking will help you make the most of whole-brain thinking. It is highly important to keep the phases separate from each other in order to preserve their distinct identities. We will look at ground rules first.

keep the phases separate from each other in order to preserve their distinct identities

ground rules for divergent thinking The ground rules are intended to allow divergent thinking to generate freely ideas in quantity:

- Remember that you personally are capable of effective divergent thinking
- Suspend and defer judgement – this means no criticism, no praise, no logic, no evaluation
- Aim for a high volume of ideas – the more ideas you generate, the higher the probability of hitting upon a truly unique or novel solution

- Avoid searching for the one 'right' answer
- Allow yourself to express wild, crazy, radical and impossible ideas – it is easier subsequently to tame a wild idea than to breathe life into a weak idea, and radical ideas offer completely new insights
- Avoid worrying about being logical or correct – relax, indulge your brain and embrace non-logical thinking
- Ignore the wish to be practical – imagining impractical answers to 'what if' questions can create powerful ideas
- Think in pictures – visualise the idea to make it real and don't be afraid to use your other senses literally to feel your way towards further ideas
- Maintain an uninterrupted flow of ideas – treat each idea as a stepping-stone to the next
- Build, combine and develop ideas or fragments of ideas as they arise, creating novel associations wherever you can
- Celebrate the playfulness associated with imaginative thinking – avoid falling into the (left-brain) trap of secretly thinking that imaginative exercises are somehow frivolous
- Avoid too much detail – ambiguity can be a powerful imaginative stimulus
- Have the confidence to challenge convention – social norms are such that you are bound to fear that you will look foolish in suggesting outlandish ideas which challenge conformity.

ground rules for convergent thinking

- Emphasise the quality of ideas, not their quantity – one workable idea beats five ideas which cannot deliver
- Avoid waiting for absolute perfection – move good ideas forward
- Apply robust judgement and logic
- Be affirmative – this means thinking about what you like most about the idea first rather than rushing to identify concerns
- Ignore preconceptions – always go back to first principles to evaluate ideas
- Avoid the 'safe' option as the easy way out of elaborating more novel and potentially superior solutions

- Check your objectives – you should always establish whether the idea really applies to the problem you are trying to solve

- Improve ideas – where ideas look close to what you need, improve and strengthen them

- Avoid discarding potentially good ideas prematurely

- Be open to novelty – this involves keeping an open mind because radical ideas by their very nature sound absurd and may otherwise invite instant rejection.

actively managing the different phases It is vital to separate the two different thinking phases so that the particular objectives of each phase can be achieved.

You must allow each phase to run its due course.

allowing divergence to deliver The generation of imaginative ideas during a divergent thinking phase can be stopped dead in its tracks by criticism, evaluation or judgement.

You might just have thought up an innovative idea based on a particular statistic or piece of market data and then you start to worry whether this piece of data was correct. Or you might have rushed ahead in your mind's eye to checking that the idea could be implemented and are now starting to grapple with objections and obstacles. Or you might have realised a flaw in the idea which you have just put forward. Or you might have discovered a solution which intuitively works – indeed, your solution may work in practice, but that is not to say that there is not a better solution just waiting to be found.

With each of the above examples, you have allowed judgement to interfere and thus break the stream of idea generation. The successful business leader identified by Alex Osborn had it right when he claimed that chief executives have just one purpose, namely to 'keep closed minds open'.[38] Judgmental thinking stifles imagination.

chief executives have just one purpose, namely to 'keep closed minds open'

using convergence to complete It is equally important that you respect the integrity of the convergent phase and avoid slipping back into divergent thinking. You must not get carried away with developing alternatives to the idea under review, reverting to right-brain thinking in order to open up further ideas. All you will do is muddy the waters and so make it impossible to complete the crystal-clear evaluation process for the original idea.

Actively managing the divergent and convergent phases is no different to using the brake and accelerator pedals in your car – you never apply both pedals together, and if you alternate rapidly between brake and accelerator, your progress tends to be erratic and dangerous. The driving analogy holds for the entire idea development process – use only the accelerator (divergent thinking) and you will run out of road; use only the brake (convergent thinking) and you will come to a stop. As the following IKEA case study shows, judicious and considered use of both convergent and divergent thinking at the appropriate time is the key to a successful idea development journey.

Ingvar Kamprad – using logic and intuition to break the mould with IKEA[39]

the story of Ingvar Kamprad and IKEA demonstrates the power of whole-brain thinking.

Born in 1926 in Småland, a rugged region in southern Sweden, Ingvar Kamprad started to make money even as a boy by selling to his neighbours individual matches which he had bought in bulk from Stockholm.

When Kamprad founded IKEA in 1943, the company initially distributed a wide range of consumer products, from pens to picture frames. The portfolio was united through its low-price proposition. Advertising in local papers was supplemented by a makeshift mail-order catalogue, with deliveries achieved through the local milk van and rail network. The positive market response to the introduction of furniture into the range led Kamprad to discontinue all other products in order to focus on low-priced furniture. The first IKEA furniture catalogue was published in 1951.

At that time, the Swedish furniture market was typical of the worldwide furniture market: fragmented along country lines, national markets comprised small manufacturers and distributors catering to local demands. Close associations between suppliers and retailers meant that the Swedish furniture market operated as a cartel.

Kamprad was quick to identify the potential of the market, driven by the increasing post-war prosperity; the erosion of the Swedish tradition of handing down custom-made furniture from generation to generation; the emergence of young house-owners seeking new but economical furniture to furnish their first homes; the impact on shopping habits of the wider availability of the car; and the post-war baby boom.

Kamprad's awareness of the post-war social issues, together with the cartel operating in his chosen market, led to his vision for IKEA extending beyond mere furniture – it was more of a quasi-philosophical mission to improve the lot of the masses by 'siding with the many'. The published company vision is explicit in asking 'the customer to work as a partner . . . so together we can create a better everyday life for everyone'.

The Swedish retail cartel was united in escalating its efforts to prevent IKEA penetrating the market. From stopping IKEA selling direct to customers at the annual trade fair, the retail cartel moved to exerting pressure on the manufacturers not to sell to IKEA. The boycott by suppliers forced IKEA to develop its own furniture and to establish its own manufacturing and distribution networks. IKEA's first furniture showroom was opened in 1953, with the first IKEA store opening in 1958.

Folklore has it that the flat-pack concept arose in 1955 through chance, when an employee removed the legs from a table to allow it to fit into his car.

The flagship IKEA store which opened in Stockholm in 1965 incorporated a number of defining product/service IKEA elements, including out-of-city location with ample parking space. The Stockholm store did not initially include a self-service warehouse – it was the manager's attempts to cope with over-crowding at the opening which led him to allow the customers to collect their products from the warehouse. This creative and simple reaction became a core element of the design of subsequent IKEA stores.

The core IKEA offering comprised a wide range of well-designed products offered at an economical price. Low-cost sourcing was therefore a particularly important requirement. Good relations were forged with low-cost Polish manufacturers in the 1950s and 1960s. ▶

Non-traditional production sources included ski manufacturers, from whom spare capacity was bought on extremely economical terms to make tables, and a shirt manufacturer whose spare capacity was bought to make cushion covers. IKEA made use of a supermarket trolley manufacturer's knowledge of strength and stability when designing its 'Moment' sofa in 1985.

IKEA challenged convention in its choice of raw materials: in the 1960s, the company led the trend to replace teak with less costly oak materials, and in the 1970s it championed acceptance of inexpensive pinewood furniture.

Cost control was paramount – company mythology relates the stories of Kamprad driving around a city at night in order to find an appropriately economical hotel and preventing a senior executive from flying first-class to an important meeting. IKEA's value statement, *Testament of a Furniture Dealer*, which Kamprad wrote in 1976 to communicate the IKEA vision within an increasingly dispersed organisation, stressed that 'expensive solutions . . . are often signs of mediocrity. We have no interest in a solution until we know what it costs'. The company website promotes the IKEA value of 'finding simple solutions, scrimping and saving in every direction. Except on ideas'.

The IKEA retail experience was standardised with a strict conformance to a tight specification, whether it applied to in-store displays, the traffic flow, which maximised customers' exposure to products by taking them through a four-leafed clover pattern, or in-store facilities.

Unlike traditional furniture retailers who relied heavily on in-store sales as a key promotion tool, Kamprad followed an aggressive and unconventional marketing strategy to pull customers into the stores, where displays, catalogues and good layout combined into highly cost-effective 'silent salesmen'. Advertisements consistently positioned IKEA as a non-conformist within the industry.

New store openings were rolled out with military-style precision, with three distinct waves of activity: a 'construction' phase to establish the new store, a 'build-up' team to ready the staff and operations for opening, and an 'operations' phase which would kick in around one year after store opening. Where innovations in individual stores such as in-store cafés and supervised play areas for children were successful, they were progressively implemented across the retail network.

Managers were routinely rotated across functions in order to gain an holistic view of the business, although purchasing, distribution and design experts tended to remain in their specialist function. The company ran 'anti-bureaucrat weeks' which required all managers to work for a given period every year in the warehouses and showrooms, so that they knew the business from 'the sharp end'. The company tended to recruit on potential rather than on past performance, favouring the freshness, adaptability and absence of prior 'corporate brain-washing' over the fixed mindset associated with conventional business training.

Through personal visits, a tight cadre of like-minded managers, the creation of internal IKEA ambassadors and such formal communication tools as the IKEA value statement, Kamprad's philosophy and values dominated the company.

Kamprad promoted the transformation of problems into opportunities and continually sought to demonstrate that it was not dangerous to be different. Revered as a visionary within IKEA, he is alleged to have mapped out IKEA's entry strategy into Russia and East Europe during the 1980s on a table napkin, dubbed by company insiders as Kamprad's 'Picasso'. This eastern expansion did not take place until the late 1990s and even then only because Kamprad's persistent awareness of the market opportunity overcame internal concerns about the economic and political obstacles which the venture faced.

Kamprad continually favoured simplicity over complexity, informality over hierarchy. His statement of values contends that 'bureaucracy complicates and paralyses. Exaggerated planning can be fatal'. As he went on to write: 'Only while sleeping one makes no mistakes. The fear of making mistakes is the root of bureaucracy and the enemy of all evolution.'

Kamprad's visionary skills were matched by a legendary attention to detail, including detailed manufacturing and sales knowledge for each of the company's major product lines. He was renowned for discussing purchasing and design intricacies with managers five or more levels below him. One company catch-phrase held that 'retail is detail'.

Employing over 65,000 workers across a global retail network of over 200 stores in more than 30 countries, IKEA is now recognised as the world's largest home furnishings retailer.

key points

- Add value by applying creativity to every step of the idea development process, not just to the initial generation of the business idea

- Creative whole-brain thinking is not some mysterious and rare talent reserved for a select few – it represents a set of skills which can be developed by actively combining convergent (logical) and divergent (intuitive) thinking

- Apply the two types of thinking – logical and intuitive – with different emphasis at each step of the idea development process

- When you're thinking in a particular style, keep in that style until that specific phase is finished

step one – seeking and shaping opportunities

- Amazon.com – shaping the internet opportunity
- don't rush to headlong action
- give yourself time to develop alternatives
- treat your first business idea as purely tentative
- total immersion in the market
- fact-finding
- tools for seeking and shaping opportunities
- moving to step two – acknowledging Catch-22
- Iridium – the imperfect solution to an opportunity which never existed?

To go headlong after a market which does not exist may be regarded as unfortunate. To stick slavishly with an unworkable business solution for that market mirage looks like carelessness.

But Iridium, the would-be global telephone service provider, did precisely both. As a result, Iridium serves as a warning beacon for all those who want to rush in with a preferred solution without adequately seeking and shaping the business opportunity which they think they have seen.

In contrast, Jeff Bezos took his time. Not so much time that he sacrificed first-mover advantage in the emerging internet-based retailing sector. Nor so little time that he could not immerse himself fully in the sector and short-list 20 possible product areas before selecting books.

That's why the story of Amazon.com makes essential reading.

Amazon.com – shaping the internet opportunity[40]

the success of this iconic internet-based retailer highlights the benefits of investing time in assessing and shaping the opportunity, and thereby translating fuzzy possibility into big vision reality.

This fuzzy opportunity brought about by technology was recognised in early 1994 independently by two men, a Briton and an American, who were both in their early thirties. The Briton, Darryl Mattocks, was a computer games specialist whose wife worked in publishing. Jeff Bezos was a Wall Street whizzkid who had graduated *summa cum laude* from Princeton University in computer science and electrical engineering. He had risen swiftly to become the youngest ever senior vice-president in the history of D. E. Shaw investment bank.

Chance reading led Bezos in 1994 to the statistic that internet usage was growing by 2,300 per cent per year. 'Anything that is growing that fast is going to be ubiquitous very quickly. It was my wake-up call,' recalled Bezos.

Cushioned by the financial rewards of his brief yet successful Wall Street career, Bezos left his job in order to immerse himself fully in seizing and shaping the opportunity which intuition told him that the internet represented. At this stage, the opportunity was just 'fuzzy'. Bezos' first step was to deepen his understanding of the opportunity by systematically researching the key factors required to build a successful internet business, a research exercise which *The Economist* later applauded as a 'model of financial rigour'.

Bezos also invested time in thoroughly investigating the full range of product categories which might meet those critical success factors. He generated a list of around 20 potential markets, including videos, computer hardware, computer software, clothing, books and music. By interrogating the options, he narrowed down the alternatives to two – music and books – on the grounds that these two markets presented a characteristic which offered a significant competitive advantage for internet-based selling as opposed to physical retail sales – far too many product titles for a single store to stock.

His research in these two markets led him to prefer books over music because there were 1.5 million English language books in print and because consumers kept demonstrating that they valued authoritative selection. As he noted, the biggest phenomenon in retailing was the big-format store – the 'category killer' – whether in books, toys or music, yet the largest physical bookstore in the world had only 175,000 titles. With the two biggest booksellers, Barnes and Noble and Borders Group Inc., accounting for less than 12 per cent of sales, and a fragmented supplier base of over 4,200 US publishers, Bezos was confident that there 'weren't any 800-pound gorillas in book-selling'.[41]

A 'total' product range was not the only element in the proposed offer with which Bezos planned to attack traditional book retailing. Bezos had a keen sense of what the traditional book-buying experience represented in its total (and worst) form: going out shopping on a rainy day, searching for books you cannot find, queuing for help, queuing to pay, waiting for out-of-stock books which no one tells you have been delivered and then starting the whole process all over again.

He also realised that a large part of the pleasure of book buying is browsing, being guided to recently published books which may be of interest and comparing notes with others. He realised that an opportunity existed for an internet service which did not just replicate a 'bricks-and-mortar' operation which sold books, but which actually offered an enhanced service. This service could include information, advice and recommendation customised to individual reading profiles. His insight into buyer behaviour recognised that customers valued not just the ability to purchase books but also the ability to access the information which led to their purchase.

Bezos realised that the internet could personalise every customer interaction and 'own' the customer relationship rather than be restricted to mass production of a standard service to a mythic average customer. This insight allowed him to challenge the traditional retailer–buyer relationship. Rather than act as administrative middle-man for routine transactions between book publisher and book buyer, Amazon.com created a new role of 'go-between service provider', assembling a range of different service elements which provided the customer with a ▶

superior integrated result at a low delivered cost. In addition to the online personalisation offered by Amazon.com, the emotional element of the customer relationship was reinforced with a high level of regular e-mail correspondence.

challenge the traditional retailer–buyer relationship

Bezos did not create artificial boundaries for himself. His business would be global, evoked by the name of the world's longest river (albeit after the first incorporated name of Cadabra had been discarded). By the same token, he did not restrict the subject areas where his company would compete; quite the reverse. As Bezos himself admitted: 'When Amazon.com started, there were smaller online bookstores, but none of them had the goal of having every book in print in stock and that certainly has been our goal from day one.'

Mattocks' Internet Bookshop was dominated by just one niche – science fiction. Mattocks had lived most of his life in the university city of Oxford and had no desire to leave, although it was miles away from the nearest book warehouse or distribution centre. In contrast, Bezos kept an open mind on where the physical operation should be sited. Research finally led Bezos to relocate from the East to the West coast and site operations in Seattle. Microsoft's home town provided easy access to America's largest book wholesaler, a pool of computer experts from which to recruit talent and proximity to Silicon Valley's computer gurus and venture capitalists.

Nor did Bezos define his business within the boundaries of conventional book retailing. He recognised that the critical expertise for his business lay in information technology, systems, retail and logistics. Early executive appointments included functional experts from Wal-Mart and Microsoft. Alongside hiring the best people, he bought the best computers; he scrimped on almost everything else – doors were turned into desktops, a sheet of paper stuck in a plant in the lobby announced Amazon.com's headquarters.

Bezos recognised that the critical expertise for his business lay in information technology, systems, retail and logistics

Within four years, Mattocks had sold his Internet Bookshop to W H Smith for £10 million.

With reported profits of US $111 million for the first quarter of 2004 representing its third quarterly profit in a row, Amazon.com has achieved a market capitalisation of around $14,370 million. Bezos' superior ability to shape the web-based opportunity which the giants of book publishing and retailing had failed to see has made Amazon.com a true icon of the e-commerce era.

don't rush to headlong action

Jeff Bezos represents best practice in taking time to give shape to a business opportunity rather than rushing into headlong action.

When you first hit upon your new business idea, your natural instincts are to forge ahead, get your hands dirty and start the business. You tell yourself that you know the market, you are aware of the gaps, problems and issues which exist, and you have good insight into customer motivation. You also remind yourself that any delay may be dangerous because the apparent window of opportunity may slam shut. So why waste time on testing out your ideas when all your gut instincts are to proceed?

stumbling at the first fence

It is surprising just how many people do start up their businesses with just this set of assumptions. It is perhaps less surprising that the vast majority stumble at the first fence, gaining experience through failure rather than earning the fame and fortune which they initially intended.

Trailfinders is a well-established award-winning specialist travel agency. Mike Gooley, its founder, learned about business start-ups the hard way, however. Gooley's first business venture on leaving the army was to put up £2,000 with five ex-army colleagues and head off for the jungle in Guyana. Their efforts to establish a gold and diamond prospecting business there foundered rapidly, because their venture upset an 'understanding' between the locals and the government. They were strongly encouraged to return to England.[42]

This example illustrates effectively how the level of emotional commitment to the business idea was so high that the underlying assumptions were not challenged, the overall market context was not explored and the business proposition was not defined. In their rush to action, Mike Gooley and his colleagues were unable to identify what specific problem in the market they were trying to address, let alone what their business idea would represent. In addition, their research had not identified the major impact which the political infrastructure often has on businesses in third world countries.

give yourself time to develop alternatives It is

important that you give yourself the time to identify the correct market opportunity to address before you rush to find a means of seizing the opportunity, let alone implementing it.

Although creating alternative perspectives on the opportunity and subsequently on the solution is such a critical part of the process, it is one that is too often ignored.

rising above solutions 'which will do' The research study

on decision-making reported by Paul Nutt highlights just how frequently managers search rapidly for solutions 'which will do' and then move to immediate action. In 85 per cent of the decision-making situations reviewed, there was little or no viable search for alternatives. Instead, decision-makers tended to copy solutions followed by others, accept off-the-shelf solutions from third parties or seize upon ideas of unknown or debatable value and then search for evidence to support them.

Even in the 15 per cent of cases where deliberate efforts were made to develop viable alternatives, there was a tendency to stop the search for alternatives once a few possibilities had been identified.[43]

identify the opportunity before the solution As we will

with Iridium see later on in the chapter, there is no point in an elegant solution to a market opportunity which is based on incorrect assumptions. The more alternative views of the opportunity which you possess, the more you have challenged the assumptions underpinning the opportunity, the greater the likelihood that the definition which you eventually select will be sufficiently robust to allow you to produce viable business ideas.

In many ways, identifying the correct opportunity to seize is as important, if not more important, than creating the means of seizing it.

We saw in Chapter 1 how the hot wax team at Procter & Gamble beavered away in an attempt to emulate a competitor product which in practice did not work effectively. Albert Einstein declared that 'the formulation of a problem is far more often essential than its solution, which may be merely a matter of mathematical or experimental skill'.[44]

identifying the correct opportunity to seize is as important, if not more important, than creating the means of seizing it

This view is shared by Mihaly Csikszentmihalyi of Claremont Graduate University and others, who contend that the ability to identify the key problem or opportunity in a given situation, and then to recognise how existing knowledge might be applied to it, is more important than solving the problem. It could be argued, for example, that Crick and Watson's creative accomplishment in discovering DNA's structure lay not merely in the final model which they produced but also in the recognition that DNA represented the correct problem towards which they should direct their skills and efforts.

'me-too' heralds disaster A study of three decades of enterprise policy in the Tees Valley published in 2004 highlighted the danger of establishing businesses without clear differentiating benefit. The study suggested that government efforts to stimulate new business creation in the 1980s through start-up subsidy had the unintended consequence of encouraging 'me-too' businesses which competed purely on price. Having undercut the competition, but lacking sustainable differentiation, these new businesses would in turn cease trading. This churn phenomenon merely served to drive down prices in the market rather than add to the total stock of value-adding businesses.[45]

the power of the open mind Research supports the effectiveness of an open approach which allows opportunities and ideas to develop. Jacob Getzels and Mihaly Csikszentmihalyi tracked the careers of a cohort of art students whose approach to a particular piece of work they had observed.[46] The students had been asked to select and arrange objects for a still-life drawing. The researchers noted that the most creative students – identified as those who were most successful seven years later – had played with more objects, studied them more carefully and chosen the most unusual objects for their composition, in comparison with their peers. In other words, the most creative students did not start with a fixed idea of their drawing; their visual themes emerged only as they actually handled the still-life objects.

The power of an open mind is not a new discovery. Over two centuries ago, the German poet and playwright Friedrich Schiller wrote to a friend who had asked for advice on generating new ideas as follows:

'The reason for your complaint lies, it seems to me, in the constraint which your intellect imposes upon your imagination . . . Apparently it is not good – and indeed it hinders the creative work of the mind – if the intellect examines too closely the ideas already pouring in, as it were at the gates . . . In the case of the creative mind, it seems to me, the intellect has withdrawn its waiters from the gates, and the ideas rush in pell-mell, and only then does it review and inspect the multitude. Your worthy critics, or whatever you may call yourselves, are ashamed or afraid of the momentary and passing madness which is found in all real creators . . . Hence your complaints of unfruitfulness, for you reject too soon and discriminate too severely.'

deciding when to decide More recently, Karl Albrecht has coined the term the 'creative procrastination zone' to describe an area which you must learn to dominate, but where western action-oriented management culture tends to make us uncomfortable.[47] Albrecht recognises that timing is everything – there is a right time for each specific opportunity, neither too soon nor too late. The trick lies in deciding when to decide. You need to judge how much time you can give yourself to shape the opportunity before you start to risk paying a penalty for delay. Jumping too soon in order to be ahead of the game, but when the opportunity is still very fuzzy, is as dangerous as leaving things too late, when you risk having only 'me-too' products with which to react. The power of a decision deadline is that it allows you to generate options and keep alternatives open rather than close them earlier than you need to. Crucially, it maximises the amount of time for you to suspend judgement.

Albrecht also highlights how the level of analysis undertaken in shaping an opportunity is significant as well – being overly reflective and analytical can waste time and energy in studying unnecessary details and issues, while being under-analytical can lead you to jump the gun, unaware of difficulties or ignorant of different, and possibly better, alternatives.

The scales of timing (reactive–anticipatory) and of analysis (reflective–impulsive) are combined in Albrecht's elegant model, shown in Figure 3.1.

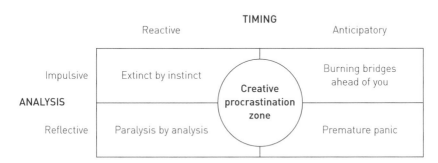

Figure 3.1 Albrecht's creative procrastination zone[48]

The first mining venture of Trailfinders' Mike Gooley would probably exemplify an impulsive anticipatory attack on a market, while many of the early dot.com companies could be described as impulsively reacting to the internet frenzy.

The response of media giant Bertelsmann to the opportunities of the internet reveals the dangers of over-analysis, as its newly appointed chief executive admitted to *The Economist*: '[For two years] we had tremendous discussion about book retailing on the internet. In the meantime Amazon took the market. On the internet, three months is a year. They have two years' start on us. That means eight or ten years.'[49]

While the timing of Darryl Mattocks' Internet Bookshop matched that of Jeff Bezos, the intensity of Mattocks' research and the extent to which he generated options were much more limited. Jeff Bezos firmly occupied the creative procrastination zone – he recognised the time-is-precious urgency of the emerging internet phenomenon and gave up his job so that he could immerse himself in understanding the new market. He gave himself time, however, to generate options for the product areas in which he was going to specialise before settling on books in a way which was to revolutionise e-commerce.

However uncomfortable it may feel in an action-oriented management culture, you should have the confidence to decide when to decide, not in order to avoid committing to action but rather for the purpose of creating alternatives and increasing your understanding of the market. It is no different to being on top of a mountain – only from that vantage point can you see all possible approaches by foot to the top. If you don't look at all the possible approaches, how can you be sure that you have seen the best possible route to the top?

if you don't look at all the possible approaches, how can you be sure that you have seen the best possible route to the top?

treat your first business idea as purely tentative

Even if you think that you may already have an apparent solution to an apparent market opportunity, you must not allow the investigative stage to be constrained by focusing merely on aspects of the market which your current solution seeks to address.

gather the clues

Rather like a detective coming fresh to a crime scene, your task is to gather as many clues as possible before forming a view as to who the main suspect might be. This is not the same as arriving at the scene with a preconceived idea as to the suspect and then collecting only the clues which confirm your preconception, or jumping to the very first conclusion suggested by a cursory examination of the evidence.

As we will see later with Iridium, this open-mindedness is often difficult to achieve and has led authorities such as Bettina von Stamm, Head of the Innovation Exchange at London Business School, to comment that: 'Another issue with market research is that it is often undertaken to confirm results or beliefs rather than to gain new insights.'[50]

blinkered by convention

If you work in a particular business or industry, you might consider that you know from first-hand experience as a supplier or customer where the market opportunity lies. However, there is a risk that you may perceive the problem in conventional industry terms – have you actually asked why systems need to operate in a particular fashion? Are you aware of what innovations are being developed in other lead markets? Do you know from first-hand experience how products are actually used by the end-user or do you just think you know? Are you aggregating the market at such a high level that the different motivations of the different component segments are being lost? Are your real competitors different to those identified by industry custom and practice?

You should never forget that the greater your eventual knowledge of the market and of its many angles, the greater your chances of creating a range of opportunities for you to shape further. Having the luxury of choice increases your chances of creating a truly innovative idea.

emotional detachment All these factors mean that you must not become so wedded to your initial business idea or interpretation of the market that you start to screen out other and possibly better ideas.

You need to develop detachment and remoteness so that, if needs be, you can let go of your first 'business baby' without emotion in order to replace it with another. The views of Tom Kelley of IDEO in connection with prototypes are just as applicable to problem definitions when he describes how his team tries not to get too attached to the first few prototypes. The team knows that the prototypes will change because no idea is so good that it cannot be improved upon. IDEO, one of the world's leading design consultancies, plans right from the start on a *series* of improvements.[51]

In other words, every business idea remains tentative until the launch has proved successful. It is quite likely that at every step of the idea development process new information and insights or external events will emerge which require you to cycle back to an earlier step. This runs counter to the conventional model of innovation, where implementation runs inexorably towards launch once the initial 'creative phase' has spawned the new product or service. As we saw with Albrecht's concept of 'creative procrastination', this continual openness to review also challenges the western management predisposition to action in preference to considered reflection and analysis.

increasing the chances of success

But you must persevere with this opportunity-shaping step because investment in time and resource now increases the chances of successful implementation. Further, if you have to recycle back to this step, you will already have generated considerable background information and insight which you can revisit in order to generate alternative definitions of the opportunity.

Lack of clear definition of the intended business opportunity is one of the biggest reasons for business failure. The techniques outlined later in this chapter will help you improve your opportunity-seeking and shaping skills and improve your ability to develop a degree of remoteness from your initial definition of the business idea.

lack of clear definition of the intended business opportunity is one of the biggest reasons for business failure

The outcome of this first step will be a single high-powered definition of the market opportunity, or at most several, to which the idea generation techniques described in the next chapter can be fruitfully applied.

total immersion in the market

The important factor at this step is to become totally immersed in the market, unearthing aspects which you had not previously considered, challenging all your assumptions and using information to generate further ideas about which you gather more information and insight. This immersion, using creative as well as analytical techniques, will help you develop a variety of perspectives on the market and the opportunities which it presents.

The problem or opportunity as you first perceive it may not resemble the problem as you finally perceive it. You need to open up your mind to as many potentially relevant facts and insights as you can so that you can improve the final perception. Time invested now is time well spent. As the President of Harvard Business School is reported to have once said: 'If you thought that knowledge was expensive, you should try ignorance.'

For Joe Moya and Joe Raia, owners and founders of Joe Designer Inc., a New York City-based product development and graphic communications firm whose client list includes Kodak and Warner Media Services, this initial investigative stage is crucial. Raia claims: 'It's really not so much a sit-down-at-the-library type of thing; it's just about keeping an open mind to different elements, things you can use in your design.'

This openness to sources of inspiration, whether past or present, silly or sublime, is supplemented by analytical activity. As Raia continues: 'We familiarize ourselves with market trends, the past history of the product, the past history of the trends of that product. We research by flipping through magazines. We pin articles, photos, everything up on the walls and familiarize the whole team with what the history is.'[52]

We have already seen how Jeff Bezos left his Wall Street job in order to immerse himself in the dynamics of the emerging internet. There are many other examples of the power of this immersion technique: Arthur Hailey lived in the Roosevelt Hotel in New Orleans to research his best-selling novel *Hotel*; naturalist Jane Goodall lived in the African bush for 28 years observing chimpanzees; and Herman Melville read every account of whaling which he could obtain before he settled down to create *Moby Dick*.

whole-brain thinking
It is important to recognise that as with so many aspects of the idea development process, this step of seeking and shaping the opportunity involves both divergent and convergent thinking. This step is also highly iterative – a piece of data may provoke you to investigate a further avenue and this investigation may provoke further ideas. Your intention should be to create a virtuous circle, where the more extensive your research, the greater will be your exposure to new situations, fresh ideas and new possibilities, which in turn allow you to generate new perspectives on your initial business idea.

The cardinal rule when gathering ideas and information is to pursue quantity. Search for as much information as you can and then track down some more. If you feel that you have exhausted your research, use divergent techniques to generate ideas for other sources of information which you can investigate.

the cardinal rule when gathering ideas and information is to pursue quantity

fact-finding

Fact-finding is a precursor to, and then an iterative companion process to, seeking and shaping the opportunity. Fact-finding is intended to increase your overall understanding of your initial opportunity. It helps you collect relevant data that can suggest different ways of restating your original definitions of the opportunity.

Some of the information will be the relatively straightforward 'sit-down-at-the-library' research described by Joe Raia. This information will cover market size, competitor data, information on customers and suppliers, industry trends and so on. The sources for this type of information are well rehearsed and include brochures and annual reports, competitor and supplier websites, market research reports, analyst reports, trade press and trade shows, seminars, industry associations, quality newspaper special features on specific industries or technologies, business magazines and journals, conference papers and government statistics.

The internet is an increasingly powerful tool for undertaking extensive and detailed desk research and is excellent for making creative jumps to unexpected and unusual information sources. It also provides a rapid and inexpensive window on foreign markets.

All these types of information need to feed into, as well as be informed by, the insights which you are generating through the other techniques described in this chapter.

the stimulus of searching

The very act of searching for information may provoke further insights and avenues to explore. This is not so surprising when you consider that some of the data you may be looking for may not exist, especially if the product or service is new to the market without existing comparable data. This means that you must engage divergent thinking to identify sources of data which might stand as proxy to the market you are researching. As you look for this data, going off the beaten track may offer new opportunities. When your left-brain tries to stop you leaving the beaten track by telling you that you are wasting time and breaking the rules, remind yourself of the importance of 'creative procrastination'.

None of the information which you gather will ever be wasted. Either it will provoke new ideas, or it will be used in subsequent evaluation stages, or it will provide the market evidence within the business plan, or the information can be stored for later review when it may offer insights which you are not yet ready to perceive. This means that you should never discard or screen out information or ideas because they do not immediately appear useful.

If you doubt this, be heartened by the story of penicillin. As Alexander Fleming acknowledged at the time of winning the Nobel prize for medicine in 1945: 'Nature makes penicillin. I just discovered it.' The reality is more complex than that. It is true that Fleming discovered penicillin in 1929 by accident, when a forgotten culture plate developed a large growth of green mould. Observing that a host of dead microbes lay between the mould and the clumps of yellow bacteria, Fleming deduced that something emanating from the mould had killed the bacteria. He named his discovery penicillin but concluded that it offered little opportunity for applied use. He published an academic paper about its laboratory properties and then moved on.

It was a full ten years later, however, before a team of Oxford scientists recognised the opportunities represented by Fleming's discovery and with great difficulty produced sufficient penicillin to conduct the trials which established it as the miracle drug of the 20th century.[53]

reworking the facts
As you collect your various facts and figures, it is important not just to file them away as static representations of a given market but continually to challenge the facts for other avenues to pursue and for other insights to develop. You must keep reviewing the data during the entire idea development process – market data is itself dynamic; new data may emerge which challenges the accuracy of earlier analysis; and data whose potential you initially could not perceive may suddenly offer rich pickings.

The existing management and marketing literature gives wide coverage to the conventional SWOT technique. SWOT analyses a company's internal *strengths* and *weaknesses* relative to the competition and identifies the *opportunities* and *threats* which lie outside an organisation's direct control. SWOT provides an effective tool for starting to structure the data. By the same token, undertaking an audit of the external environment under the headings of *political*, *economic*, *social* and *technological* change – the well-known PEST analysis – provides a useful additional feed for the opportunities and threats sections.

While populating your PEST and SWOT analyses, you must keep asking yourself how you can transform threats into opportunities or translate technological developments in the external world into opportunities. In other words, fact-finding should be as much about seeking and shaping new opportunities as describing the context to existing opportunities. Jeff Bezos represents a particularly spectacular example of being inspired by one statistic – the internet's 2,300 per cent annual growth rate – to create Amazon.com, the iconic online retailer.

tools for seeking and shaping opportunities

In addition to the fact-finding sources identified above, a wide range of predominantly divergent tools can help you seek and shape market opportunities and so avoid the trap of considering your first idea as your best and only idea. These are listed in Table 3.1.

Table 3.1 Tools for seeking and shaping opportunities

- The power of 'Why?'
- The '5 Whys?'
- The '5 Ws plus H'
- Observing core users
- Lead users
- Seek inspiration from the unfamiliar
- Boundary examination
- Boundary-hopping

You will not need to use all of the techniques all of the time. You will also find that some of the techniques overlap with each other. Between them, though, they represent quite a formidable armoury and every technique will be useful to you at some point.

There is no right and wrong way to approach this step of seeking and shaping opportunities. You should have the confidence to use a variety of the techniques to provoke as many different angles and as much fresh and provocative thinking as you possibly can. This chapter discusses each technique in turn, so that you can become familiar with them and develop your skills in selecting techniques appropriate to the task in hand.

Cast your mind back to the rules of convergent and divergent thinking and to the active management of the different phases outlined in Chapter 2. This opportunity-shaping step will involve switching between divergent and convergent thinking. Some divergent thinking may have suggested a previously unconsidered market segment. Some left-brain market research reveals a lack of data. You move back to divergent thinking to consider other ways of getting the data you need and what other data you could collect which would serve as proxy data. And so a series of convergent and divergent episodes ensues.

You must learn to feel comfortable actively managing the transition between left- and right-brain thinking because this dichotomy underpins the entire idea development process. As Albert Rothenberg, a clinical professor of psychiatry at Harvard University and a leading writer on creativity in the arts and sciences, has argued: 'The creative process is a matter of continually separating and bringing together, bringing together and separating, in many dimensions – affective, conceptual, perceptual, volitional and physical.'

the creative capacity of questions
Asking questions is one of the simplest and most effective ways of challenging assumptions and convention, creating additional perspectives on existing opportunities and highlighting new and unexpected gaps in the market.

We saw in the first chapter how the creative trigger which unleashed the Dyson DC06 robot was the casual question, 'I like your vacuum cleaners, but when will you make one you don't have to push around?'.

the creative process is a matter of
continually separating and bringing
together, bringing together and separating

casting fresh light on the familiar
Asking questions intensifies your interest in, and understanding of, ideas and concepts. Tom Wujec reports the unusual but inspired way in which Amsterdam's Rijksmuseum stimulated interest in Rembrandt's famous painting *The Night Watch* when it was returned to the gallery after restoration.[54] The curators asked visitors to submit questions about the painting and prepared answers to the 50 most popular questions. The questions and answers were not restricted to 'conventional' art-related issues – they included issues of forgery, the value of the painting, technical errors in the painting and so on.

The curators published the questions and answers on the walls of an adjoining room through which visitors had to pass before viewing *The*

Night Watch. The experiment revealed that the average length of time people spent viewing the painting increased from six minutes to over half an hour. Visitors reported how the questions stimulated them to create richer ideas about the painting by encouraging them to look longer, to look closer and to remember more.

Your aim should be to establish a virtuous circle of creating greater understanding of the market area, which creates a greater propensity to generate valuable insights which then promote further enquiry. Active questioning should be used at each and every step of the idea development process.

Three variants of questioning technique exist – 'Why?', '5 Whys' and '5Ws plus H'. We describe each in turn.

the power of 'why?'

The surprising capacity of asking 'Why?' to reveal the unexpected is well illustrated by the story of how the Polaroid camera was invented. History relates that it was the innocent challenge of a child which provided the initial stimulus to its invention. On holiday in Santa Fe in December 1943, Edwin Land suggested to his three-year-old daughter that they take the camera film which he had just finished to the shop for processing, adding how much he was looking forward to seeing the pictures in a week's time. Her immediate response was: 'Why do I have to wait a week to see my picture?'

This instinctive challenge by the child to the status quo, the devastatingly simple question 'Why?', identified a worthwhile problem to Land which he had never previously considered, namely: 'How might I make a camera which yields instantaneous pictures?' He is reported to have formulated several possible solutions the very same day, to the extent that he spent several hours with his patent attorney that evening. Land commercialised the product within about four years.

In similar vein, Anita Roddick was out shopping with her children and had been into the grocers and sweetshop before going to the chemists. She asked herself what seems now to be a blindingly simple question: 'Why are cosmetics not sold in smaller sizes with the level of choice – as much or as little as you like – offered by the greengrocer and the sweetshop?'[55] This simple challenge born of everyday experience provided a significant input to the creation of Body Shop.

Asking 'Why?' at every step of the idea development process is sound sense. It can highlight market opportunities, provided that you maintain an open mind, unblinkered by industry or sector convention. It can also provide a constant challenge to your opportunity definition, and avoid you rushing down the type of blind alley highlighted in the earlier hot wax story.

the '5 whys?' technique
This straightforward but effective technique stemmed initially from the world of manufacturing production. Toyota pioneered the technique in the 1970s to attack the root causes of manufacturing problems rather than treat the symptoms or the contributory causes. The technique recognises that very often the ostensible reason for a problem will lead you to another question. Four or five repeated questions tend to be sufficient to peel away the layers of symptoms to reveal the root cause of a problem and show how the total problem is structured.

It is most useful to you during the opportunity-shaping step as a technique to break down market opportunities into their constituent parts and to generate market insights.

Imagine that Ray Kroc had used the '5 Whys' technique when he discovered while selling milkshake machines to hamburger joints in 1954 that one particular outlet in remote California was buying more than its location and floor space seemed to justify:

Why is the outlet buying more milkshake machines than its floor space would suggest?

> *Because the outlet is attracting a greater throughput of customers than its competitors.*

Why?

> *Because customers find its offering more attractive than that of the competitors.*

Why?

> *Because the food served is consistently tasty and does not involve the customer having to wait.*

Why?

> *Because the store staff are very effective at what they do.*

Why?

> *Because the menu is very limited and the staff are directed to specialise in a very small number of highly systematised tasks.*

Owned by two brothers, Dick and Maurice 'Mac' McDonald, the hamburger restaurant offered a very limited menu, concentrating on just a few items: hamburgers, cheeseburgers, French fries, soft drinks and milkshakes, all at the lowest possible prices. Ray Kroc realised the potential of this standardisation process and saw the opportunity for plenty of new milkshake machine orders, if only the brothers would open more restaurants. Kroc volunteered to run them. In 1955, Kroc opened his first restaurant under franchise. He bought out the McDonald brothers for $2.7 million in 1961.[56] [57]

The '5 ws plus h' technique

The '5Ws plus H' technique provides a useful framework to generate new perspectives and gather new information about your initial business opportunity. Borrowed from the world of journalism, the technique asks 'Who?, What?, Where?, When?, Why? and How?' in order systematically to explore what you know, what you don't know and what you had not perhaps considered about your business idea. It effectively deconstructs the initial opportunity into a multiplicity of smaller elements, which can then be reassembled in a variety of different formulations.

You start by phrasing your business idea in the format 'In what ways might (IWWM ... ?)'.

Imagine that you are Michael Bloomberg, considering the online financial information industry in the early 1980s. Reuters and Telerate dominated the market, providing news and prices in real time to the investment and analyst communities. You might frame an initial business opportunity as: 'In what ways might I improve the provision of financial information?'

You should then generate separate lists of questions relevant to the general problem against each of the '5Ws plus H' questions. You then examine your answers to each question, interrogating the answers for stimuli to help you redefine the opportunity.

Against 'Who?', for example, your list might include:

- Who uses the systems?
- Who purchases the systems?
- Who judges whether the systems are effective?
- Who says there's anything wrong with current systems?
- Who might want something different?

Against 'What?', for example, your list might include:

- What are the biggest drawbacks to users of the current system?
- What offline processes could be replaced by online functionality?

- What would make a new system faster?
- What would make a new system more user-friendly?
- What could a new system do to help users achieve their objectives?

breaking free of conventional thinking Just asking these simple but provocative questions in a phase of divergent thinking can open up previously unthought-of avenues and issues. It helps avoid the risk that you become stuck in conventional thinking.

In Michael Bloomberg's case, he discovered that conventional thinking in the IT industry focused on selling to the IT managers, for whom standardisation was a key criterion. The actual needs of the end-users, the analysts and traders, appeared of secondary importance.

Having decided to explore the end-user angle more fully, Bloomberg could then have rephrased the question as: 'IWWM we make the systems better able to help the actual users achieve their objectives?' In reality, Bloomberg did design a system which directly addressed the traders' needs and objectives, with multiple monitors to avoid opening and closing endless windows, easy-to-use terminals and integral analytic capability to render offline calculations unnecessary. Further exploration of users' objectives highlighted that these extended to personal as well as professional issues. Bloomberg included information and purchasing services to allow the cash-rich but time-poor traders to achieve their social goals as well.

Undertaking this deconstruction exercise for each of the '5Ws plus H' down to as many levels as you wish is a powerful tool to generate a range of further perspectives on your initial opportunity.

challenging received wisdom If you work in a particular market or industry, the chances are that you consider you know everything about how the market ticks, why customers buy and how users actually consume the products and services. But do you?

Industries tend to have particular ways of viewing themselves. Have you been brain-washed into conventional thinking?

yours sincerely, steve', she wrote When Dame Stephanie Shirley founded the original software company which was to develop into the massive Xansa plc, industry convention was that software was something given away for nothing. In addition, conventional industry thinking was so male-dominated that she had to sign her early business development letters as 'Steve' in order to be taken seriously.

When Steve Millar joined BRL Hardy, the Australian wine company, as managing director in the early 1990s, his background in finance and consumer products gave him a quite different perspective on the wine market's conventions. He swiftly realised that wine companies tended to belong to wine makers who focused more on their craft than on the market. As we shall see later in this chapter, Millar went on to adopt an innovative, marketing-led approach to transform his company.

conventional industry thinking was so male-dominated that she had to sign her early business development letters as 'Steve'

escaping from marketing myopia Alternatively, your assumptions on product usage may be constrained by your past understanding of the market or by your knowledge of the original intentions behind the product or service. Marketing brand managers are often brought down to earth with a bump when they first listen to focus groups discussing their products, precisely because focus groups 'speak it as it is' about the products, without a manufacturer's frame of reference and respect for the product.

While focus groups can help your understanding of an existing product's usage and can possibly identify problems associated with it, users may lack the language or insight adequately to explain what is wrong and, perhaps even more importantly, what might be missing. Equally, relying on written customer feedback and user questionnaires may provide useful pointers, but many users do not take the trouble to complain, they just turn to alternative products. In any case, productive feedback presupposes that you have asked the appropriate questions in the first place.

that's just how it is, isn't it? Another drawback to written or spoken feedback is that users develop work-around solutions which become so automatic that they become unable to articulate the original problems. If all the members of a product category typically present a particular failing, consumers often assume that they have to put up with the product as it is and perhaps never think to challenge its limitations.

Marks & Spencer recognised that flat-pack furniture right across the industry had an unpleasant habit of reducing otherwise sane and reasonably well-adjusted adults to sobbing, pitiful wrecks.[58] The company achieved differentiation by acting on this recognition, recruiting a company specialising in writing assembly instructions, who tore up the existing manuals and started from scratch in developing customer-friendly instructions in plain English.

actions speak louder than words A final drawback derives from individuals' economy with the truth about their own behaviour. While individuals may not actually lie, they may be unable to tell the exact truth – after all, how many senior directors have you met who publicly extol the virtues of the digital age in creating the paperless office, but in private have their e-mails printed off for them by others because they cannot operate their personal computer effectively?

All in all, it is always better to be guided by the maxim 'Do as users do' rather than 'Do as users say they do'. Getting right inside your home market is all the more important because of the high proportion of business ideas which originate from an individual's current work environment. Jack Kaplan reports research which shows that almost 50

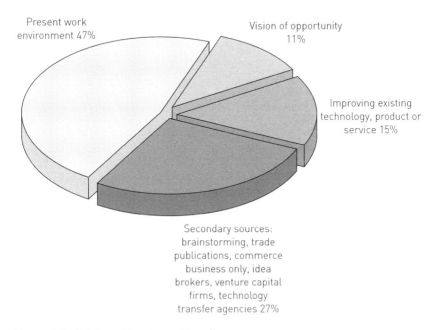

Figure 3.2 Origins of business ideas[59]

per cent of new business ideas originate from this source (see Figure 3.2).

First-hand observation of user behaviour is an excellent technique to reveal the information and insights which you need to get right inside your home market. User observation allows you to see at first hand areas of the market which the product or service intends, but fails, to reach; it can also reveal unexpected and initially unintended uses for the product. This holds true not only for existing products but also for new products and services, when prototypes come into their own, as we shall see in Chapter 5.

There are two discrete user groups whose actual behaviour should be observed in order to reduce your reliance on assumptions or third-party information on how existing products and services are currently used in the market. The first group comprises users at the heart of the conventional market (core users), while the second includes those at the edge of the conventional market (lead users).

the technique of observing core users
Patterns of usage among core users which run counter to conventional wisdom and to intended market positioning represent a potentially rich source of new business opportunities.

Harvard Business Review reports that when General Mills undertook a series of field visits in order to understand the market for Cheerios, it discovered that consumers were using its product not just as a breakfast cereal as it had imagined but as an easy-to-dispense snack for children throughout the day.[60]

The Lucozade brand was initially associated with illness and convalescence. SmithKline Beecham's observation that many consumers purchased the high-glucose drink as a pick-me-up as well as for illness prompted the company to develop a new positioning as an in-health product. This positioning was further reinforced when Lucozade was relaunched as a sports drink in the 1980s.

Kleenex was initially intended as a niche product, serving as a disposable cold-cream remover. Only when consumers started to wipe their noses with the product did the Kimberly-Clark Corporation see the additional opportunity and reposition the product as a disposable handkerchief.

The dangers of ignoring the core user are illustrated by Johnsonville Sausage Company before it was turned around during the 1980s by a new CEO, Ralph Stayer. So remote was the organisation from its products and markets that not only did the staff fail regularly to taste the company's products, they also defined the products purely in manufacturing terms, in other words according to how they were made.

Stayer's success in getting the company to explore how the customers actually consumed the products – pouring maple syrup over their breakfast frankfurters or drinking beer with their bratwursts at lunchtime, for example – highlighted opportunities for product developments which transformed the business.

exploiting personal experience Possibilities often present themselves as difficulties which you, or someone close to you, have experienced at first hand.

James Dyson translated the inefficiencies which he encountered in using a conventional vacuum cleaner into the Dual Cyclone. We have already seen how Anita Roddick had the insight on breaking bulk in the cosmetic sector while out shopping with her young family. Julie Pankhurst had the idea for the website Friends Reunited while she was pregnant, wanted to contact old school friends and found it difficult to do so. Scott Cook, founder of Intuit, whose Quicken software transformed how individuals and small businesses managed their finances, had the first insight into the possibilities of the personal finance software market when watching his wife managing the monthly bills by hand in time-honoured, but tedious, fashion.

possibilities often present themselves as difficulties which you have experienced at first hand

These examples provide credence to the assertion by Robert Epstein: 'Becoming more creative is really just a matter of paying attention to that endless flow of ideas you generate and learning to capture and act upon the new that's within you.'[61]

the lead-users technique While core users operate at the heart of the conventional market, lead users operate at the edge of the conventional market. Investigating lead users recognises that many products are initially thought of and even prototyped by users rather than manufacturers. This occurs because lead users stretch the capabilities of the product, want the product to achieve something which does not feature in the manual or see in the product a potential application perhaps unintended by the manufacturer. For the enlightened entrepreneur, these users can provide the seeds of innovative products or services, inspired by wishing 'if only . . .'

Positioned at the head of the market, and with needs which may extend beyond those of the typical user, lead users have developed solutions to overcome the existing product's limitations.

There are two steps in the lead-user process: the first is to identify lead users in a given market; the second is to use your creativity in identifying other markets which face similar problems in more extreme or sophisticated forms and, crucially, have solved them.

lead users see in the product a potential application perhaps unintended by the manufacturer

step one: identifying lead users In 1921, Earle Dickson was working for Johnson & Johnson and happily married to wife Josephine. Although married life agreed with Josephine, housekeeping did not – she suffered far more than her fair share of cuts and burns.

Dickson modified the large surgical dressings then available from Johnson & Johnson, fixing the small pieces of gauze which he cut from the large dressings with adhesive tape to whichever part of his accident-prone spouse had most recently been injured. Tired of creating these bandages on an ad hoc basis, Dickson started to make them in quantity, covering the adhesive strip with crinoline fabric so that the adhesive strip remained fresh.

James Johnson, the company's president, happened to see Dickson apply one of the home-made bandages to his own finger, and was so impressed by the product's simplicity and convenience that mass production of Band-Aids® soon followed.[62]

When Craig Johnston played professional football for Liverpool Football Club in the 1980s, he analysed the team's boots to identify how the design could be improved to enable the players to increase their control of the ball. On retirement from professional football, he became head of innovation at Adidas and developed the Predator, which is now the world's best-selling boot, worn by the likes of David Beckham and Zinedine Zidane. Johnston was also a runner-up of the Design Museum Designer of the Year 2004 competition for the design of his latest boot, The Pig, which resulted from ten years of research and more than 1,000 prototypes.[63]

moving the hookah from café to home One of the more unusual UK winners of the Queen's Award for International Trade in 2004 was Swift-Lite Charcoal of East Sussex. The company was established to sell charcoal to tandoori restaurants and then extended to making charcoal tablets for use in burning incense. During his sales promotion trips to the Middle East, Steve Barnes, the managing director, observed that consumers were also using the product for smoking hookah pipes. Cafés had always represented the traditional venue for the pastime of smoking hookah pipes, by virtue of providing a permanent source of heat to keep the pipes alight. Swift-Lite's charcoal tablets allowed individuals to smoke at home and in hotels rather than just in cafés.

From the 20,000 boxes of charcoal tablets produced in the company's first year, annual sales of boxes have expanded to 1.2 million, of which 75 per cent are exported.[64]

step two: identifying parallel and 'extreme' markets The second step in the lead-user process involves the creative identification of markets which face similar problems in more extreme or sophisticated forms and have solved them. Your task is then to identify what lessons you can learn from these parallel markets and apply to your own business idea.

Suppose we take the UK pre-university examination market system to illustrate the second step. In Chapter 2, we described how the average US student sits an average of 2,600 examinations during an academic lifetime. In the UK, a similar phenomenon generates some 25 million handwritten scripts each year which are distributed by mail to external examiners. It only takes a (statistically insignificant) handful of exam scripts to be delayed or lost in the post for individual academic careers to be blighted and for a PR disaster to be whipped up in the media for the examination board concerned.

the right questions for an examination board to ask In this market, step two of the lead-user process would prompt examination boards to explore the document transmission and tracking systems deployed in parallel and more challenging markets. Divergent thinking might suggest the market for time-sensitive financial documents as a good example. In turn, the tracking technology employed by operators such as Federal Express might well emerge as a natural candidate for further review.

The examination board scenario neatly illustrates the point that you should not to stop at the first solution to the first problem. Further exploration of the 'missing script problem', perhaps guided by the 'Why?' technique described earlier and stimulated by thinking around Federal Express's use of digital technology, might prompt the question: 'Why couldn't the handwritten scripts be scanned and then digitally transmitted?'

But even that does not go far enough. Further use of the 'Why?' technique might challenge the need for students to be handwriting scripts in the first place. Why couldn't online assessment replace handwritten scripts, for example? The joint creation in 2003 of London Qualifications by leading UK examination board Edexcel and publishing giant Pearson, whose American operations have developed leading-edge expertise in online assessment and document scanning, suggests that the days of pen, paper and postman may be numbered.

it wasn't just that drop goal England's 2003 World Cup-winning rugby team also exemplifies the use of this second step of the lead-user process. Manager Clive Woodward continually thought 'outside the box' to develop new facets to his team's performance – in particular, he imported a range of specialist experts from parallel fields who had solved the problems he faced.

Clive Woodward continually thought 'outside the box' to develop new facets to his team's performance

His formidable backroom team included nutritionists, chefs, a visual awareness coach, psychologists, experts in physical conditioning and a masseur. The defence coach had studied American football, Australian rugby league and Premiership football. A specialist video operator filmed not only the movement of England players but also the playmakers in the opposing team, providing the type of competitive insight which translated England into the best defensive team in rugby.

Favourite among Woodward's many gadgets was a computer program which the players came to respect and dread in equal measure. Pioneered by four leading Premiership football clubs, Prozone tracked every move and tackle and pass of every player from start to finish of a game, bringing unprecedented factual rigour to post-match analysis.[65]

the technique of seeking inspiration from the unfamiliar
It is important to keep a perpetually open and questioning mind so that you can take advantage of chance encounters, events and insights which arise from your own life. Remember Louis Pasteur's wise counsel: 'Chance favours the prepared mind.'

Sometimes, however, you just can't see the wood for the trees. Tom Kelley, general manager of IDEO, points out that in many parts of your life, you go through steps so mechanically that it becomes impossible to find inspiration for innovation by observing yourself. By going off the beaten track, however, you are much more open to discovery – it doesn't matter whether you're travelling to different places or experiencing new activities or just doing something differently; it is at those times that 'you are more open to ask the childlike "Why?" and "Why not?" questions that lead to innovation'.[66]

Sahar Hashemi, co-founder of Coffee Republic, took time off from her career as a lawyer in order to travel. She ended up in New York to visit her investment banker brother, Bobby. On the eve of their return to London, they started lamenting that they would miss New York's coffee houses. Coffee Republic was the product of that lament.

By the same token, Chicago-based Gordon and Carole Segal spent their honeymoon in Europe, where they saw and bought all kinds of unique, functional and affordable designs for their home. On their return, they discovered 'that no one in Chicago was selling great design without charging the equivalent of a mortgage. Not being able to afford much of a mortgage themselves, the Segals decided to lease an abandoned elevator factory . . . in Chicago to showcase the finds they were finding all over the world'.[67] Created specifically to capitalise on the product's proven success in another market, the Crate and Barrel concept now boasts 115 stores throughout the United States.

There is every reason actively to seek out problems, opportunities and solutions from other markets and other areas of endeavour without feeling any shame. As arch-inventor Thomas Edison himself said: 'Make it a habit to keep on the lookout for novel and interesting ideas that others have used successfully. Your idea has to be original only in its adaptation to the problem you are working on.'

your idea has to be original only in its adaptation to the problem you are working on

boundary-examination technique

The expression 'pushing back the boundaries' is known to everybody. The visual exercise in Chapter 2 of the vase, human profile and other perspectives was an exercise in just that – examining the boundaries of a situation rather than accepting your first interpretation of that situation as being the only valid interpretation.

Boundary examination provides a structured technique to explore the emerging business opportunity. Its particular value lies in its ability to challenge what you consider to be part of the opportunity and, by extension, what you exclude from the opportunity because you assume it lies outside the boundary.

A classic corporate example of accepting conventional boundaries is offered by IBM, which took the view until well into the 1970s that the computing market would continue to be dominated by centralised mainframe computers, with ever-increasing memories and calculating capacities. Its efforts and resources were devoted to maintaining leadership in the mainframe market rather than engaging at a very early stage in the emerging personal computer market. Exploiting the intrapreneurial skills of an autonomous business unit fuelled by an apparently blank cheque, IBM recovered to produce its first personal computer in 1980, gaining market leadership in the category by 1983.

The salvage industry provides a brilliant example of redefining the boundary. Rather than frame the problem of salvaging sunken boats in terms of lifting sunken ships to the surface, Danish entrepreneur Charles Kroyer came up with the idea of pumping polystyrene beads into the wrecks, thus allowing them to float to the surface.[68]

When Charles Dunstone launched the Carphone Warehouse in 1986, the company was not just providing economical mobile phones, it was also demystifying the massively complex and opaque charging structures operated by the telephone networks. Rather than accept the conventional boundary represented solely by the product, Dunstone pushed back the boundary so that it included the product's subsequent economical use.

IKEA redefined the boundary of its flat-pack furniture offering in order to penetrate the Japanese market – the boundary was extended to include an assembly service. As we saw above, this boundary redefinition found a recent echo in the UK, where Marks & Spencer invested significant funds in user-friendly instruction manuals to accompany the launch of a flat-pack furniture range – it extended the boundary beyond the raw disassembled product to include its subsequent easy assembly.

boundaries can keep good ideas out Defining an opportunity necessarily puts boundaries on it. The opportunity's boundary is the notional 'container' which separates highly relevant features inside the boundary from apparently less relevant ones outside the boundary.

Just as with core users, your first definition of the market opportunity is likely to reflect your own assumptions, preconceptions and concerns, and quite possibly those of others. This means that potentially productive areas to explore may remain hidden in the background.

The following simple four-step method is very effective for bringing potentially relevant aspects back into awareness by examining each element of the problem definition for its hidden assumptions.

step one: write down an initial statement of the opportunity Imagine that you are Steve Millar, managing director of BRL Hardy, the Australian wine company which in the early 1990s was exporting $31 million sales, predominantly in bulk for the own-label ranges of retailers such as Sainsbury's. Such own-label activity capitalised on consumers' confusion in the face of a tantalising choice of *appellations contrôlées*, regions, grape varieties, vintages and so on.

Anxious to grow the overseas business, you might define the initial opportunity as: 'How to increase the sales through overseas branded retail of our Australian wine?'

step two: underline key words Underline each key word so that you can examine each in turn for hidden assumptions. Key words in the BRL Hardy example might be as follows: 'How to <u>increase</u> the <u>sales</u> through <u>overseas branded retail</u> of our <u>Australian wine</u>?'

step three: challenge each underlined key word Without considering the validity of each assumption, identify any important implications which they suggest. An effective way of doing this is to see how the meaning of the statement changes if you replace a key word by a synonym or near synonym. For example, why should sales be *increased*? Would the company actually make more money on fewer sales which produced a higher margin? Why could sales not be *improved* or *developed* in additional geographic markets, or *augmented* with other product ranges or *widened* with product extensions?

Why just *sales?* Why not marketing effort, physical presence or own distributor networks? What does *overseas* mean? Countries with a highly developed consumer market for wine? Countries without such a market or perhaps ones which do not produce their own wine? What do we mean by *branded*? Branded by country of origin, by producing village, by the type of food with which it should be drunk, by retailers' brands or by our own Hardy brand?

Why *retail*? Why not through wholesale or direct to intermediaries such as pub and hotel chains? Why *Australian*? Why do we have to restrict ourselves to distributing home-produced wine? Why not Chile, France or Italy?

Why just *wine*? Why not other fruit-based drinks or low-alcohol varieties or beer? Could we promote or distribute other different but complementary products to enhance the wine?

step four: redefining the opportunity Having explored how the particular choice of key words affects the meaning of the original opportunity definition, try redefining the opportunity in a better way. The aim is not necessarily to change the position of the boundary but rather to ensure that you understand more clearly how the wording of the opportunity is affecting your assumptions about the boundary.

In the BRL Hardy example above, the core problem might now be better defined as: 'How might we develop our own international brand of wine which we source from around the globe?'

The very act of exploring the boundary has prompted further questions, insights and opportunities which you can return to later – after all, no work is ever wasted in the idea development process. Within the wine distribution example, you have now explicitly included not only the possibility of handling wine produced outside Australia but also the possibility of developing your own over-arching brand.

drinking to success With the helpful benefit of hindsight, this is what BRL Hardy did, of course. Within a decade, the company had developed a dominant global brand, with overseas sales of around $180 million, almost all of which carried the Hardy's brand. Its 24 per cent share of the Australian market by volume was matched by a 25 per cent share of all Australian wine sold in Britain.

The strategy of sourcing wine from around the world created the necessary scale to negotiate vigorously with retailers and to sustain a credible brand, capable of escaping from commodity pricing levels. The multiple sourcing also radically reduced the risks of vintage uncertainties and currency fluctuations inherent in dealing with a single country.[69]

Given that your market knowledge and insight will constantly evolve throughout the problem definition step, it is worth regularly revisiting the boundary examination exercise during this step.

boundary-hopping technique

The technique of boundary-hopping goes one stage further than stretching the boundaries. The technique acknowledges the danger that if you work within a market, you inherit a preconceived set of ideas of what the rules of the market are. When all market participants share a common set of beliefs concerning customer profile and the conventional product range, competition tends to be focused on the basis of incremental improvements in cost or quality or both.

if you work within a market, you inherit a preconceived set of ideas of what the rules of the market are

the paralysing power of preconception We saw earlier, for example, how the Swedish furniture market pre-IKEA was conditioned to thinking that the core market comprised the wealthy upper-middle class. Pre-Dyson, the conventional vacuum cleaner always included a bag with which to collect dust. The wine market before the success of BRL Hardy focused more on the vintner's craft than on market potential. Dame Stephanie Shirley started to sell software into a market which expected software to be given away free.

Until the arrival of Penguin Books's new American CEO Peter Mayer in the late 1970s, all UK paperback fiction books were one standard size. It took an outsider's challenge to create a larger size – affectionately known as 'B format' – to ensure that the books achieved greater prominence by having to be displayed away from the pack of 'A format' titles and that they could command a considerable price premium by virtue of their greater physical size.

Inspired by the value curve concept created by *Harvard Business Review* authors W. Chan Kim and Reneé Mauborgne, the technique of boundary-hopping provides you with a structured technique to hop over the conventional boundaries of how a given industry traditionally views itself to generate truly breakthrough opportunities.[70]

Figure 3.3 Boundary-hopping into different areas

Boundary-hopping is particularly effective at prompting insights into what is missing from a market, as opposed to what could be incrementally improved. It goes without saying that these breakthrough insights are especially hard to achieve in markets where the conventional industry mind-set is particularly powerful.

Boundary-hopping targets six discrete areas in which to seek opportunities, as shown in Figure 3.3. Each target area is discussed in turn.

boundary-hopping into area one: substitute industries Hopping over the conventional boundaries of your industry into substitute industries may allow you to spot an opportunity which will make a difference in your home industry.

It is a truism that companies often demonstrate silo thinking along functional lines. Entire industries sometimes fall into the same trap, with internal market statistics and competitive actions and reactions recorded and analysed to death,

but alternative markets failing to receive the same attention.

We saw earlier how personal experience prompted computer software specialist Intuit to recognise that the market for personal financial software which allowed households to manage their monthly accounts represented a vast potential market. Of the 42 relatively complex financial software packages then on the market, none had emerged as a user-friendly market leader. Conventional industry thinking 'required' the products to be replete with accounting jargon and over-complex but under-used features.

Intuit's founder, Scott Cook, had the significant insight that it was the pencil, rather than another industry player, which constituted the greatest competitor, because the pencil was such a resilient substitute.[71] Cook realised that the humble pencil offered two key advantages over computerised solutions, namely ease of use and low cost. He saw that an opportunity existed to combine the computer's distinctive advantages over the pencil – speed and accuracy – with those of the pencil over the computer – simplicity of use and low price. When this opportunity was eventually developed through to product implementation, the basic functions which remained allowed a significantly lower price than the conventional market players.

Scott Cook's insight finds an echo in Jeff Hawkins' description of the key insight which led his team to design the Palm Pilot: 'I realised that my competition was paper, not computers.'[72]

boundary-hopping into area two: alternative strategic groups within industries

Mapping a market or an industry along the conventional lines of price and performance tends to reveal a number of strategic groups, that is companies competing in the same sub-space within the total market. The car market is an obvious example, with high-performance/high-price cars such as BMW, Mercedes and Jaguar defining a clear group.

Price and performance are not the only dimensions against which to map a market. The UK newspaper market used to be analysed according to physical size of newspaper versus perceived editorial quality. Broadsheets formed a conventional cluster, so did the red-top tabloids, and the tabloid-format *Daily Mail* was positioned in the middle. The broadsheet *Times* and *Independent* hopped over the traditional boundaries defined by format and created a new opportunity by publishing tabloid editions.

The Sony Walkman represents a further example of how elements from different strategic clusters within a market can be combined, in that the Walkman brought together the convenience and low cost of a portable radio with the sound quality and contemporary image of a conventional home stereo.

boundary-hopping into area three: non-conventional parts of the buyer chain

The concept of the buyer chain recognises that a number of different people are directly or indirectly involved in the purchase decision. While individuals may overlap, the typical roles include influencers, such as finance directors; specifiers, whose expertise guides product selection, such as architects, engineers or doctors; purchasers, who actually conduct the transaction; and finally the end-user. Each role will define value differently – an end-user may favour expensive functionality whereas the influencer may be more interested in the total product life-cycle cost.

Industries typically draw their boundaries around a particular element of the buyer chain – pharmaceutical companies traditionally target doctors, for example.

The merits of hopping over the boundaries created by the conventional buyer chain are well illustrated by the US market for online financial information in the late 1990s. Dominated by Reuters and Telerate, the industry focused its selling efforts on the information technology managers in their capacity as purchasers rather than on the end-user investment analysts. As we saw earlier, new market entrant Bloomberg spotted the opportunity to target the investment analysts themselves. Identification of this opportunity eventually led Bloomberg to create product features of particular value to the analysts, not only to help them to do their job better (with enhanced analytical features) but also to manage their cash-rich/time-poor lifestyle better (with travel and shopping channels).

Digital technology has allowed the buyer chain to be completely reconfigured in a number of industries. Direct Line Insurance, for example, revolutionised the personal insurance market by focusing on the end-user and eliminating the need for intermediary insurance agents, who both influenced and specified the insurance products. First Direct and Egg have created a similar model within the UK personal banking market, while the high-street travel agency business has been almost entirely replaced by online selection and booking. We will meet Travel Counsellors, a company which in turn has hopped over this 'new' conventional boundary, in Chapter 6.

boundary-hopping into area four: complementary products and services
It is rare that products or services are used in isolation.

We saw earlier how Johnsonville Sausage Company identified that customers combined their sausages with different drinks and other foodstuffs, depending on which

it is rare that products or services are used in isolation

meal was being eaten – maple syrup at breakfast, beer at lunchtime. This insight revealed the opportunity to create sausages which bundled together different elements from how the original products were consumed in practice, such as frankfurters flavoured with maple syrup.

Observing users in order to analyse how a total product or service is consumed from start to finish can often reveal useful opportunities to explore. Virgin Airways, for example, pioneered airline tickets which included limousine transport to and from the airport for business customers. Müller yoghurts come complete with a separate serving of fruit jam. Procter and Gamble extended its successful Pringles brand to include Pringles Dippers, a new range of crisps whose profile made them even easier to use with savoury dips, which research showed represented a growing usage for the original product.

When Tim Waterstone analysed the consumer's experience of book retailing, he imitated Jeff Bezos in hopping over the traditional boundary of book selling, which held that book buying was no more than implementing a previously planned transaction. He recognised that a large part of the joy of book buying lay in browsing, seeking alternatives, sampling your selection, seeking advice from others, gaining new and unexpected information and ideas. Tim Waterstone identified the opportunity for a physical book-selling model which raised the size and qualification level of its staff, widened the product range and created additional physical space in which to browse, including retailing innovations such as in-store coffee shops.

boundary-hopping into area five: functional and emotional appeals to buyers

We saw earlier how markets can be mapped against the dimensions of price and performance. Clearly these are not the only parameters which can be used; mapping markets along functional and emotional lines to help spot opportunities can also be highly effective.

Although the two parameters are not intrinsically exclusive of each other, experience has educated consumers to expect rational decision-making to inform industries where function is predominant, and emotional decision-making to characterise those industries where feelings predominate.

Hopping over the non-emotional boundary of a functionally oriented market may create the type of opportunity exemplified by Guinness. It is hard to consider that Guinness was once perceived primarily as a working man's drink. It also offered excellent nutritional properties for expectant mothers. The creation of an emotional component to the brand through distinctive advertising, the elevation to quasi-religious levels of 'the pour and the settle' process, the linkage to sporting events and health have created a distinctive lifestyle brand, whose premium pricing belies the fact that the basic product is effectively unchanged since its unassuming origins.

it needn't be a dog's life You might think that there is nothing more functional than a boarding kennel for cats and dogs. This is not a sentiment shared by Best Friends Pet Resorts and Salons, an American company which hopped over the boundary of providing functional accommodation to small animals.

The company's founders spotted the opportunity to give full rein to the emotional component of pet ownership, noting the research finding that more than 90 per cent of pet owners view their pets as family members. The resultant business now offers facilities which more closely resemble a five-star hotel for humans than a kennel. Personalised pet services include grooming, supervised playtime, tailored diets and odour-free suites. The emotional bond between pet owner and staff is fostered through hospitality industry-level customer service, including state-of-the-art customer relationship management software which tracks the pet guests' every trait, need and preference.[73]

from time-piece to fashion accessory In the days before Swatch, the traditional watch market represented the ultimate functionally oriented market, where the likes of Citizen and Seiko competed through such functional improvements as quartz technology or easier-to-read digital displays. Swatch transformed budget watches into fashion accessories. With a design laboratory based in Italy, the company vindicated the belief of its chairman, Nicholas Heyek, that 'if we could add genuine emotion to the product and a strong message, we could succeed in dominating the industry' by making repeat purchases the norm.[74]

unbundling the benefits Conversely, opportunities may exist to create simpler lower-cost business models in emotionally oriented industries which traditionally provide many extras which add cost without increasing functionality.

Conventional airline travel, for example, carried social and emotional cachet, with the trappings of customer service helping to command premium prices. easyJet dispensed with all the emotional trappings of airline travel – (ostensibly) free meals and drinks, high levels of customer service – to create one of the first no-frills airlines. Having observed the high proportion of customers who travelled extremely light for their weekend trips, competitor Ryanair researched whether to introduce a price premium for luggage which had to be stowed in the hold (and thus increased fuel cost through additional weight and extended turnaround time on the tarmac).

The cosmetics industry is typically viewed as a high-emotion market, where high levels of advertising and packaging expenditure sell hope rather than the physical products. Anita Roddick hopped over the emotional boundary by increasing the functional component of her Body Shop cosmetics – against industry convention, she focused on natural ingredients, healthy living and a positive environmental message and avoided the significant expense of paid-for advertising and non-reusable packaging.

boundary-hopping into area six: time

Hopping over the boundary of time in order to spot trends and take immediate action in order to secure future benefits is exemplified by Bernie Ecclestone of Formula One fame. He spotted the potential of digital television ahead of the pack and invested heavily in sophisticated systems

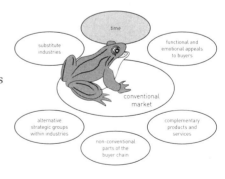

which would create a worldwide spectacle capable of commanding premium television transmission rights.[75]

Sony provides an interesting perspective on boundary-hopping because the company recognises that certain early-adopter markets represent a window into the future. Nobuyuki Idei, president of Sony, recognises that Tokyo has created a society which is completely different from other regions of Asia. Accounting for a quarter of Japan's gross domestic product (GDP), Tokyo has created its own, totally different lifestyle. As a result, companies such as Sony regard Tokyo as an undisputed lead market for product planning: 'Devices that work here are forerunners for the rest of the world.'[76]

A more transient example of using trend-spotting to secure early advantage was demonstrated in the very early days of the internet. A number of entrepreneurs recognised not only that most major companies would eventually be forced by market pressure in the medium term to register their domain names, but also that many companies lacked the technical awareness or belief in the internet's potential to do so immediately. These entrepreneurs bought up domain names which they considered likely candidates for the major players and commanded high fees for subsequently selling them on.

companies such as Sony regard Tokyo as an undisputed lead market for product planning

Hopping back in time, finding new expression for old concepts, can be equally valuable. Trevor Baylis, for example, made brilliant use of old technology with his clockwork radio, whose stunning simplicity in not needing batteries or electricity revolutionised the lives of millions.

moving to step two – acknowledging Catch-22

All the techniques discussed above will help you to produce new definitions of the embryo business opportunity. They will also help you break down your initial business idea into its essential elements. All the data which you have generated will contribute to a wider and clearer view of your business opportunity and provide you with the cool detachment you need to stand back from the enthusiasm of your first definition.

This first step should have moved you from a fuzzy sense that a market opportunity might exist to a series of clearer definitions of that opportunity.

identifying the 'hot-spots'

You must now prioritise the opportunities so that it is the most promising ones which you take forward first to the next step of creating business solutions to seize those opportunities. If you have managed to generate a substantial number of definitions of where the opportunities lie, it pays to identify clusters or 'hot-spots' of similar definitions. Clustering does not lose any opportunities; you are merely prioritising them for further work.

Having created a long list of 20 possible product areas, Jeff Bezos identified a cluster of two – music and books – which presented the characteristic which he regarded as key, namely more individual products than the largest physical retailer could possibly stock.

This need to prioritise reveals that you are in a Catch-22 position – in order to prioritise rationally the opportunities for refinement and evaluation at steps two and three of the idea development process, you need to have already undergone the second and third steps.

adopt a whole-brain approach

The best way for you to break out of the impasse of prioritising from among multiple opportunities is to use a whole-brain approach. You may have discovered market data which allows your left-brain to influence the decision – some market opportunities may appear significantly more attractive from a financial perspective than others. You may also reflect whether the opportunity appears durable, timely and capable of sustaining a product or service which creates or adds value for its buyer or end-user.

In large part, however, you will have to rely on your gut-feel and intuition to make your decision. Having been through the techniques explored in this chapter, you are probably the person best placed to make that subjective judgement. After all, Jeff Bezos was a book industry outsider before he founded Amazon.com.

At all times, maintain sufficient emotional detachment from your ideas so that you can avoid the catastrophic crash to earth described in the following case study of Iridium, the global telephone service which did not work and no one wanted.

in large part you will have to rely on your gut-feel and intuition to make your decision

Iridium – the imperfect solution to an opportunity which never existed?[77]

Iridium highlights the double-whammy danger of incorrectly defining the opportunity and then selecting, and persevering with, an unworkable solution.

In the late 1980s, cellular phone technology was in its infancy. Technology focused on radio towers to provide coverage for a limited geographical area, the cell. Where there were no towers, there was no reception – effective operation was limited to a few high-density urban areas.

Legend has it that in 1987, the wife of the chief engineer in Motorola's Space and Systems Technology Group refused to go on holiday to the Caribbean because she feared that she would be unable to keep in phone contact with her Arizona property company in order to close a particular property deal. 'Why couldn't her husband create a global telephone system which worked?' asked Karen Bertiger.

This real-life challenge to Barry Bertiger was extremely timely for Motorola, a leading player in the satellite and telecommunications business which was suffering from the down-turn in government defence spending caused by the end of the Cold War. Bertiger's boss established Bertiger and a small number of colleagues in a covert bootleg operation within Motorola, invisible to other projects competing for limited research funds and hidden away from general management scrutiny.

The small bootleg group defined the market opportunity as how to create a global telephone service which worked. They appeared not to explore or challenge the need for the service to be truly global, available absolutely everywhere, despite the fact that the majority of the earth's surface is uninhabited or poor. Even when the bootleg group turned their attention to creating a satellite-based solution, the fact that satellite-based competitor Globalstar retained blackspots over the oceans and poles and that Ellipsat (a potential competitor) skewed coverage to more populated areas did not lead them to challenge their global definition.

In addition, their definition of the opportunity was framed by reference to existing cellular phone systems. This created the artificial constraint that their solution had to compare favourably to a conventional cell phone in terms of size, voice delay and overall quality of experience. ▶

The bootleg group devised a technically brilliant solution to the problem as they defined it. Instead of creating a telephone network on the ground, they elected to put it in the sky. And instead of using conventional system architecture, they created their own.

Convention favoured what was known as 'bent-pipe' architecture. This meant that when a telephone handset sent a signal to a satellite, the satellite bounced the signal straight back to a land-based 'gateway', which then routed the call into a land-based telephone system. Global coverage required 40–70 such gateways, each costing around $25 million.

Motorola's technically ingenious solution was based on a 'bypass' system, which meant that when a handset sent a signal to a satellite, the call was re-routed in the sky between the other satellites until it reached the satellite orbiting above the system's single gateway into the land-based telephone system. This saved the capital cost of constructing gateways, increased operating margins by cutting out the local land-based operators and provided true global coverage.

While technically brilliant, the solution betrayed the weakness of an ineffective fact-finding stage. Numerous national governments would be required to provide licences for Motorola to operate its system. Given that the 'bypass' system circumvented the use of landline systems which national governments tended to own and from which they derived considerable income, it was naive to expect universal political support in the licence negotiations. When Motorola weakened its already fragile negotiating position by announcing the Iridium project to the world in 1990 before even embarking on these licence negotiations, *Wired* magazine was moved to criticise Motorola's actions as 'a case of geekish can-do enthusiasm getting ahead of the plodding nuances of global lobbying and diplomacy'.[78] *Realpolitik* meant that the technical solution as initially devised was literally never going to fly. The fact-finding homework had not been undertaken.

Only when Motorola had created the solution in the form of Iridium – the project took the name of the 77th element of the periodic table to reflect its 77 proposed satellites – was market research undertaken. To compound matters, the project engineers led the market research themselves, making it likely that they would be more receptive to information which confirmed their assumptions rather than feedback which challenged them.

By the same token, Iridium did not undertake extensive technical testing which would have provided feedback earlier than the big-bang launch in 1997. It did not launch a single 'stripped-down' satellite to evaluate technical performance to and from a ground-based user. The actual launch revealed humiliating technical problems, such as weak signal strength which prevented the telephone from being used from inside buildings or on the streets of cities with tall buildings. Nor was a second satellite launched to test inter-satellite communication.

By developing a life of its own from an imperfect beginning, the Iridium project illustrates the dangers of following the stage-gate process for developing products which we discussed in Chapter 2. This process accepts that the optimal product has been correctly developed early on in the cycle. As a result, the subsequent highly focused execution strategy fails to review regularly the assumption that the initial design continues to represent the best option.

Unshakable belief in the original definition of the opportunity and in Iridium's technical solution, together with the difficulties encountered by external stakeholders in evaluating such new-to-market technology, meant that a number of external triggers which might have led Iridium to be aborted were ignored or down-played.

In the early 1990s, market forecasts had universally underestimated the growth and improved functionality of cellular phones. But by 1995, a full two years ahead of Iridium's initial service launch in 1997 with 47 of the eventual 66 satellites, improved forecasts had highlighted that enhanced cell phones, together with the internet, were rapidly making alternatives to cell phones when travelling considerably less attractive.

Even when *Realpolitik* forced Iridium to create regional gateways, sacrificing two of the three benefits of the initial solution – no capital costs to establish land-based gateways and no loss of margin to the government-owned landline systems – the need to be truly global was never challenged. Despite the incremental cost of achieving total global coverage having become massive, Iridium did not return to the original definition of the opportunity to ensure that it was still valid.

Iridium filed for bankruptcy in 1999 and ended commercial service in 2000. ▶

Little wonder that John Richardson, parachuted into Iridium as trouble-shooting CEO in 1999, commented: 'We're a classic MBA case study in how not to introduce a product. First, we created a marvellous technological achievement. Then, we asked the question of how to make money on it.'[79]

key points

- Avoid rushing into action with the first apparently feasible business idea you create

- Decide when to decide on what action is required, exploiting the 'creative procrastination zone' to explore fully the opportunity to which your business idea appears to present a solution

- Immerse yourself in the market, collecting and structuring a wide range of facts, figures and observations from the widest range of sources

- Choose from among the wide range of predominantly divergent tools to seek and shape market opportunities

- Include your gut-feel and intuition in prioritising which definitions look most promising to pursue

four

step two- generating new ideas

- Howard Head – an analogical approach to business success
- Eureka?
- The Mind Gym: six mental workouts and their related routines
- ground-rules for productive mental workouts
- mental workout one – checklists
- mental workout two – stimulus materials
- mental workout three – combinations
- mental workout four – free association
- mental workout five – analogical thinking
- mental workout six – upside-down thinking
- moving to step three
- Thomas Alva Edison – idea generator *par excellence*

Where do good ideas come from? Should you lie in the bath like Archimedes? Should you sit under a tree waiting for the proverbial inspirational apple to fall? Or should you work with what you've already got, using a range of idea-generating techniques to shape, challenge, overturn, shock and surprise your way to new insights and ideas?

This way is certainly hard work – it's the 99 per cent perspiration and 1 per cent inspiration evoked by arch-innovator Thomas Edison. But it's certainly effective.

Do you know what the similarity between an aircraft wing and a ski is? Or between a ski and a tennis racket? Howard Head did. His use of the idea-generating technique of analogies allowed him to revolutionise two industries with his Head skis and Prince tennis rackets respectively. Head's revolutionary products opened up these markets to individuals who thought that they could not participate. Structured idea-generating techniques can enable you in exactly the same way.

Howard Head – an analogical approach to business success[80]

Howard Head epitomises the entrepreneurial skill of seeing analogies between elements which are similar but different. This facility to perceive patterns between related ideas applied to his whole life path, since he realised that his great transferable skill lay in debugging and perfecting things. He had the ability to spot similarities between apparently quite different user markets and a gift for spotting how to transfer technologies between apparently quite different applications.

During World War Two, Head worked as an aircraft engineer and developed expertise in the various uses of aluminium. After the war, Head took up skiing. He was massively incompetent. Whereas most amateurs would have wished to avoid the charge of being the bad workman who blames his tool, Head was quite happy to reverse this assumption. He was convinced that the problem lay in the skis, not in his ability. 'I was humiliated and disgusted at how badly I skied, and characteristically, I was inclined to blame it on the equipment, those long, clumsy hickory skis.'[81] That is not to say that this blame was completely unjustified, however. In 1947, skis were made of wood, which quickly lost its shape and thus left the skier with little control. Head was also convinced that if he was experiencing problems, then others would be as well.

Head's first great insight was to perceive how the design, materials and construction processes used in aircraft manufacture could be applied to the design and manufacture of metal skis. His ski idea drew on the analogy of the structural principle common in the aircraft industry: metal-sandwich construction. This analogy from aircraft design and construction allowed Head to imagine a ski made of two light layers of aluminium bonded to sidewalls of thin plywood, with a centre filling of honeycomb plastic.

A lesser man would have been crushed by the fate of the first six prototypes which resulted from Head's right-brain doodles on his drawing board. The professional ski instructors at Vermont managed to break all the skis within the hour. Undaunted, Head took $6,000 in poker winnings from under his bed to fund development work in earnest, becoming in the process an early exemplar of so-called 'bootstrap financing' – launching ventures with modest personal funds.

a lesser man would have been crushed by the fate of the first six prototypes

Exhibiting the persistence required of every successful entrepreneur which we identified in Chapter 1, Head persevered for two more years through 40 different designs. Each time he completed a pair of skis, he sent them immediately to professional ski instructor Neil Robinson, who trialled them on the slopes, broke them and sent them back. Each time, Head worked out why the ski had broken and made appropriate changes.

By 1951, Head had created an aluminium ski which had a plywood core for strength, steel edges for turning and a plastic running surface which slid easily over most snow surfaces and took wax well. Not only did the ski not break, it also delivered such outstandingly forgiving performance that the public soon dubbed it 'the cheater', acknowledging that even novice skiers could carve through turns with little effort. The Head ski transformed the sport from one for very skilled athletes to one capable of mastery by millions.

Having sold Head Ski Company, Head went into supposed retirement and took up tennis. He was as inept at tennis as he had been at skiing. Legend has it that his professional coach became so tired of being blamed for Head's shortcomings that he suggested Head should buy a tennis ball machine to practise against. Head duly made the purchase from the Prince manufacturing organisation and took delivery of the machine, only to find that its performance was as lamentable as his own. Acting on the realisation that his gift lay in debugging and perfecting pieces of equipment, Head swiftly joined Prince as chairman of the board and acting chief engineer.

Head was a great exponent of the 'Why?' technique, continually asking the Prince engineers 'Why?' when they claimed that something would ▶

not work, often leading them to accomplish things which they had thought impossible. Within 18 months, Prince had volleyed its way to a 50 per cent share of the tennis ball machine market.

Head was a great exponent of the 'Why?' technique

Involvement in the tennis-playing world led Head to perceive the analogy between the world of skiing and that of tennis. Both markets were overflowing with amateurs who would do almost anything to improve their ability, gravitating without fail towards products which worked better. That their ability required improvement is evidenced by a 1974 *Sports Illustrated* article, which noted that 21 million Americans, drawn like fruit flies to a vast ripening vine, were now playing tennis at one level of incompetence or another. As the article pointed out: 'Unlike golf, tennis has no par to alert man to his inferiority. He can reach new depths without the need of a 19th-hole elixir to ease the pain.'[82]

Head saw it differently: 'I saw the pattern again that had worked at Head Ski . . . I had proven to myself before that you can take different technology and know-how and apply it to a solution in a new area.'[83] In other words, his right-brain insight spotted the analogy, highlighting a different but similar opportunity to empower sporting amateurs to perform like champions by transforming their sporting equipment.

'I saw the pattern again that had worked at Head Ski'

In accordance with whole-brain thinking theory, he then had to set about the highly rational and convergent task of learning the physics of tennis rackets, surfaces and string tensions before he could successfully develop the oversized Prince tennis racket. To understand the intricacies of stringing rackets, for example, Head and his manufacturing director immersed themselves in the market by buying every single stringing machine available in order to understand how each individual machine worked.

After a period of persistent trial and error, and having overturned conventional industry thinking on the 'correct' size and shape of a tennis racket, Head reached his final design. Head's oversized racket offered much greater stability for the off-centre shots which are the hallmark of the true amateur. The hugely enlarged 'sweet spot' of the racket improved the performance of rank amateurs to such an extent that initially some professionals would not use the product on the grounds that it was an admission of technical weakness. Nevertheless, the commercial power of the patent which covered the invention led one competitor to observe acidly that it was akin to securing a patent on a size nine shoe.

So important are Howard Head's entrepreneurial achievements that his first metal skis and his Prince Classic racket are now permanently displayed at the Smithsonian Museum in Washington.

Eureka?

As with Howard Head spotting that the tennis racket market presented an analogy to the skiing market, this second step seeks to generate a range of alternative ideas which can capitalise on the business opportunity defined and redefined by the first step.

It may well involve creating ideas way beyond your original concept. Thomas Edison, for example, went beyond the development of a practical and affordable light bulb to create an entire infrastructure for the electrical industry. As we shall see in the case study at the end of this chapter, Edison repeated the same feat within what was to become the recording industry, widening from the development of the phonograph to the creation of an industry infrastructure.

This step is one of the most exciting because it is when the ideas which you were seeking start to emerge. Many people associate idea generation with the Eureka moment, the sudden single moment of inspiration beloved of myth. Archimedes heads the bill of these dramatic moments. He took a bath as a refuge from wrestling with the problem of how to establish whether a gold crown was counterfeit. The experience of bathing led him to the analogical insight that he could use water displacement to measure the cubic area of the gold crown. This would allow the correct weight of the crown to be calculated as if it were pure gold and then compared against the crown's actual weight. 'Eureka – I have it!' he shouted as he leapt out of the bath.

many people associate idea generation with the Eureka moment, the sudden single moment of inspiration

perpetuating the myth Other dramatis personae in the Eureka series include Samuel Taylor Coleridge, whose epic poem, *Kubla Khan*, appeared to him in a single dream, and Isaac Newton, on whose head the apple fell, thus inspiring his insight into gravity.

Andrew Palmer, founder of the New Covent Garden Food Company, has laid recent claim to the Eureka mantle. As his company website puts it:

'The idea came to us – like so many good ideas – in the bath. Our founder, Andrew Palmer, was winding down after a day's sailing and fancied some of his mother's delicious home-made soup. Alas, his mother had prepared salad. The shock set Andrew thinking about why his local supermarket stocked nothing but tinned or dried soups.'[84]

While dramatically uplifting, these stories of almost magical inspiration belie the preparation, introspection, research and analysis which allow the apparently random Eureka moment to happen. As the French mathematician, Henri Poincaré, wrote:

'These sudden inspirations . . . never happen except after some days of voluntary effort which has appeared absolutely fruitless and whence nothing seems to have come, where the way taken seems totally astray. These efforts then have not been as sterile as one thinks: they have set going the unconscious machine, and without them it would not have moved and have produced nothing.'[85]

Or as top golfer Arnold Palmer expressed it more prosaically: 'The harder I practise, the luckier I get.'

don't wait for inspiration Creative ideas are not the inevitable result of bathing, dreaming or sitting under trees, waiting for the muse to deign to alight. Creative ideas are more likely to result from pure hard work and concentration, the 1 per cent inspiration and 99 per cent perspiration evoked by Thomas Edison.

The message is that you can, and indeed must, apply divergent and convergent thinking styles in order to generate creative product, process and service ideas.

The structured techniques which follow represent your personal workout routines which will allow you to perform the type of creative gymnastics which you probably thought you could never do yourself. How do these structured creativity techniques work and what are the principles which underpin them?

why bother with idea-generating techniques? It is very

easy to become stuck in given ways of thinking and acting. This is as true for everyday life as it is for business. Faced with cooking for a dinner party, most hosts will opt for tried-and-tested favourite dishes which they know will work rather than experiment with exotic dishes which may go badly wrong. It is often the same in business, where individuals and companies develop a successful way of doing things, a 'winning formula' which works and which they will often then apply routinely in different situations.

That is not to say that the application of a winning formula to a similar but different opportunity cannot be highly effective, especially if the similarity between the opportunities is not immediately apparent. The case study on Howard Head demonstrated his brilliance in perceiving similarities both between aircraft manufacturing and the production of wooden skis, and between the skiing and tennis markets.

unquestioning repetition Problems can occur when the

supposedly winning formula is applied unchanged or unchallenged to a market opportunity which perhaps does not represent a satisfactory analogy. Having successfully applied the winning formula of the original Californian Disneyland to Florida and Tokyo, for example, Walt Disney attempted to replicate an unchanged formula outside Paris. Cultural differences, including an unwillingness to queue and a propensity to visit for the day rather than stay for the predicted three days in the huge hotel complex, together with the cold and damp Parisian weather, made the project more cultural Chernobyl than Magic Kingdom. Only when the formula was adapted to acknowledge specific European needs and tastes was Eurodisney able to survive.

It is all too tempting to rerun the same formula and to replicate 'me-too' products or services. It increases the mileage to be obtained from an initial creative idea. It avoids having to rethink a new strategy. It can represent the type of safe choice typified by the 1980s' adage that 'you'll never get sacked for buying IBM'. All these aspects can be very attractive, especially when you are under pressure for rapid and decisive action or are facing the fear of failure. In addition, the formula may be all that you think you know because you lack the confidence, or believe that you lack the skills, to think innovatively.

Convergent and divergent idea-generating techniques are therefore extremely valuable in helping us break out of these self-imposed blocks to challenge tried-and-tested formulae in order to arrive at innovative ideas for new products, services and processes.

Convergent and divergent idea-generating techniques are extremely valuable in helping us break out of these self-imposed blocks

the mind gym: six mental workouts and their related routines
The Mind Gym provides a clear structure to allow especially your divergent thinking to work out fully and to escape from the mental straitjackets imposed by your experiences, assumptions and external pressures. The Mind Gym also ensures that whole areas of potential importance are not overlooked.

You will find that each of the six types of mental workout, and the specific techniques within them, will liberate your thinking rather than confine it. Literally hundreds of techniques exist within these six distinct workout types to assist you in generating innovative business ideas. We have highlighted just 16 of these techniques, basing our selection on those which our experience and research have shown to be the most effective.

A further benefit of our selection is that all the techniques can be used by individuals on their own, as well as in groups. Experience shows that this aspect is critical to anyone setting up a new business, since it often is done either alone or with one or two other additional partners at most.

We also recognise that cash and time are scarce resources for the budding entrepreneur. We have therefore selected techniques whose application requires no special training other than the guidance offered in this book. The techniques are united by the shared theme of drawing heavily upon right-brain divergent thinking – the process of generating many different types of ideas. Table 4.1 below identifies the different routines within each type of mental workout.

Table 4.1 Types of mental workout and associated individual routines

Type of mental workout	#	Individual routine
Checklists	1	Davis
	2	Osborn
	3	SCAMPER
	4	The big four
	5	Mapping the customer journey
Stimulus material	6	Pictures/objects/words
Combinations	7	Morphological analysis: ● Four on the flat ● Four + on the flat ● Cube-crawling
	8	Force-fitting
Free association	9	Brainstorming
	10	Mind-mapping
Analogical thinking	11	Transferring an underlying principle
	12	Transferring a business process
	13	Transferring sub-systems and components
	14	Bionics
Upside-down thinking	15	Rule reversal
	16	Assumption reversal

ground rules for productive mental workouts

Chapter 2 touched on the ground rules for divergent thinking. Four of these ground rules are particularly helpful as you attempt each of the mental workouts. Let's explore each of these in turn.

ground rule 1: defer immediate judgement and evaluation
Put your left-brain logical and analytical thinking to one side. Successful right-brain divergent thinking relies on your ability to suspend analysis and judgement. If you immediately evaluate and criticise every idea as you generate it, you will automatically limit the number of ideas you produce and so reduce your chances of generating a unique solution. It is far more productive to list every idea no matter how foolish or impractical it may seem at first. There will be plenty of time later to apply rational judgement and convergent thinking.

ground rule 2: quantity breeds quality This principle

develops naturally from the preceding one. The more you defer judgement, the more ideas you are likely to generate. The more ideas you generate, the greater the likelihood that some of the ideas you develop will be of good quality. Experience suggests that on average, out of every 60 ideas only one will be a true winner. So always try to generate as many ideas as possible to increase your chances of developing good ideas.

You should also try to build on as many ideas as you can, creating associations and developing links wherever you can.

Alex Osborn tells the story of a brainstorming session undertaken with helicopter pilots in order to address the problem of rapidly unfreezing 700 miles of outside telephone cables which were so coated in frost that long-distance calls could not be made. The idea which was selected for implementation, and which you might have thought would have been the most 'natural' for the pilots to identify, presented itself only as idea number 36. The solution involved flying helicopters over the telephone cables so that the blades' downdraft dissipated the frost.[86]

ground rule 3: the wilder the idea, the better You must

be prepared to take a certain amount of risk in what you propose if you want to be truly productive. If you start with 'safe' ideas based on cautious rationality, you are unlikely to achieve real breakthrough ideas.

The discipline of business process re-engineering provides many examples of this. The cautious approach would be limited to asking how to make a given process 10 per cent more efficient, whereas the breakthrough ideas which are the essence of business process re-engineering result from the question: how could we eliminate the process completely?

Although a wild idea cannot always be implemented exactly as proposed, a subsequent modification to one of these so-called 'intermediate impossible' solutions frequently can be. So a particular value of wild ideas lies in their ability to provoke, and to act as stepping stones to, highly innovative and workable follow-up ideas.

A brainstorming session at a chemical company produced a startling question from an engineer: 'Why don't we put gunpowder in our house paint?' The background to his question was the difficulty home owners encountered in trying to remove old and cracked paint prior to repainting their homes. Rather than dismiss out of hand his idea of using gunpowder to literally blow the paint off houses, his brainstorming colleagues used this wild idea as a stepping stone to considering how to create a chemical reaction to remove old house paint. Their creative practical solution introduced additives into the paint which remained inert until they came into contact with a solution containing other additives which was applied prior to repainting. The contact caused a reaction which stripped the old paint right off.

a particular value of wild ideas lies in their ability to provoke, and to act as stepping stones to, highly innovative and workable follow-up ideas

If you enter the idea generation step believing that you need to produce nothing but rational and practical ideas, that is probably the type of idea you will get. Although such ideas frequently will be workable, they may fall into the 10 per cent process improvement category which is no match to the higher-quality process-elimination category which might have been stimulated by a wild initial idea.

ground-rule 4: take a break from the problem It is

good practice to take routine breaks from creative idea generation. It is all too easy to become so immersed in the process that without realising it our minds tire and inhibit us from thinking freely. Alongside 2,500 bottles of chemicals, the laboratory in Thomas Edison's 'Invention Factory' included a pipe organ which was the focal point for singing and beer drinking during breaks from late-night working sessions.

Individuals generating ideas on their own should take a break every 15 minutes. For a group, around 30 minutes is the recommended period, although if the group dynamics are working really well, you may on some occasions want to exceed this norm.

So with these principles in mind, let's start our creative workout.

mental workout one – checklists
Checklists provide an effective way to get started with innovative idea generation. As their name suggests, checklists provide structured prompts to generate business ideas by highlighting areas to investigate and explore. They are great confidence-boosters because they help prevent obvious solutions being overlooked and are also easy to use.

Many different forms of checklist exist. Very few of them would claim to be rocket science. As is often the case with the best management tools, they represent organised common sense. However defined, all serve a common purpose, namely to apply a structured approach to generating ideas and new perspectives on products, services and processes.

The following section highlights five of the most frequently used.

Davis product development list
The possible solution checklist for product improvement developed by G. A. Davis and others uses seven items to stimulate idea generation.[87] Table 4.2 shows recent examples from the camera world to illustrate each item of the checklist category.

Table 4.2 Davis product development list applied to cameras

Checklist item	Camera example
Add and/or subtract something	Add on motor drives to achieve more frames per second; introduce digital technology to allow image manipulation
Change colour	Different camera body colours
Vary materials	Plastic lenses to replace glass; metal or plastic camera body
Rearrange parts	Integrated or external flash
Vary shape	Movie-camera style with single grip
Change size	Compact; disposable; conventional
Modify design or style	Combine digital camera with mobile phone; replace manual focus with auto focus; weatherproof and underwater cameras

osborn product and service development list
Creative problem-solving pioneer Alex Osborn developed an extensive list of idea-spurring questions to stimulate the development of a new product or service by altering an old one. The eight questions in Table 4.3 are particularly helpful and possess the advantage over the preceding Davis list of being as relevant to services as they are to products.

Table 4.3 Osborn product and service development list

Checklist statement	Key word
● What other product or service could I adapt to my opportunity?	adapt
● How could I change the existing product/service?	modify
● How could I add to this product/service?	magnify
● What could I take away from this product/service?	minify
● What could I use instead of this product/service or a portion of it?	substitute
● How could I alter the composition of this product/service	rearrange
● How could I turn the problem/service around?	reverse
● What could I put together to make a new product/service?	combine

Imagine how the founders of low-cost airline easyJet could have applied this technique as they assessed how to break into the low-cost end of the air travel market – see Table 4.4.

Table 4.4 Osborn product and service development list applied to easyJet

Adapt	Apply the principles of the economy-class segment which exists within conventional full-service airlines to an entire fleet; mimic the no-frills concept from American pioneer Southwest Airlines; apply the lowest-cost self-serve marketing principles of discount stores such as Aldi to the airline business
Modify	Sell tickets direct to the customer and create cost savings through eliminating travel agents; eliminate meals from the service offering
Magnify	Extend the time spent flying by aircraft with full passenger loading by minimising turnaround times at airports, by maximising pilot flying hours within legal requirements, by eliminating the need to load the planes with pre-prepared food at every stop, by discouraging customers from bringing baggage which requires storage in the hold, by heavy discounting to ensure that flights are always full
Minify	Offer price discounts to passengers carrying hand luggage only; eliminate system of pre-allocating seats; reduce customer service to bare minimum; do not offer refunds for delayed flights; minimise the number of routes offered; minimise the different types of aircraft flown to optimise aircraft maintenance arrangements
Substitute	Purchase second-hand aircraft with low depreciation; fly to out-of-town airports
Rearrange	Focus flights very early and very late during the day
Reverse	Unbundle the service so that customers are charged for all baggage stored in the hold (which incurs handling cost for the airline and impinges on turnaround time) rather than charge customers only for excess baggage
Combine	Establish in-house car rental service for easy onward transmission for customers from airports; multi-skill the staff to maximise productivity

SCAMPER product and service development list

A memorable variant on Osborn's theme is Eberle's SCAMPER checklist, an acronym for:

Substitute
Combine
Adapt
Magnify (or minify)
Put to other uses
Eliminate (or elaborate)
Rearrange (or reverse)

The approach to using SCAMPER is clearly similar to that required for the Davis list.[88]

the big four industry-level checklist

An even more focused list is suggested by *Harvard Business Review* authors W. Chan Kim and Reneé Mauborgne. Writing in relation to the value curve concept which inspired the boundary-hopping technique described in Chapter 3, they propose that attention should be focused at the industry level on just four questions:[89]

1 What factors could be *reduced* well below the industry standard?

2 What factors could be *eliminated* which the industry has taken for granted?

3 What factors could be *created* which the industry has never offered?

4 What factors could be *raised* well above the industry standard?

We saw in Chapter 3 how Intuit answered these four big questions in the market for personal finance software with its mould-breaking Quicken product. By eliminating all unnecessary accounting functionality and jargon which the market had previously taken for granted, the software retailed at a price reduced well below the industry standard.

The big four technique's strength lies in the provocative extremes of its focused questions which force you to challenge conventional industry thinking head-on.

mapping the customer journey
A final valuable technique in this checklist section involves mapping all stages of the customer journey with the product or service, from the first stages of pre-purchase right through to disposal.

As with all these idea-generation techniques, the customer journey technique builds on the in-depth information about actual, rather than presumed, customer usage which you will have developed during the fact-finding phase of Step One of the idea development process. The technique's strength lies in making you consider the product or service from the customer perspective and in relation to every stage of the customer's contact with that product or service. It widens the focus away from the product or service itself, particularly at time of consumption.

the customer journey technique builds on the in-depth information about actual, rather than presumed, customer usage

As with so many creativity techniques, it is best used in combination with other tools such as the '5 Ws plus H' (discussed in Chapter 3), the Osborn product and service development list (outlined above) and brainstorming (described in a later section in this chapter). And in common with the best creativity techniques, it involves a combination of convergent and divergent thinking.

The first stage is to identify every single phase in the customer's total experience of a product or service, the so-called customer journey. Having identified the various phases, the next stage is to use one or a permutation of the three techniques listed above – '5 Ws plus H', brainstorming or Osborn's list – to develop ideas for innovation and differentiation.

While every product or service will lay different emphasis on particular phases, the underlying phases are likely to be broadly similar. Table 4.5 lists the typical phases of a customer journey and offers examples of innovations achieved at each phase across a variety of sectors.

Table 4.5 Cross-sector application of customer journey technique

Phase in the customer journey	Product/service example
Awareness of need	Oral-B toothbrush, which includes the innovation of a patented blue dye in the central bristles whose fading indicates when the toothbrush requires replacing; household batteries which allow you to measure how much residual charge they contain; Hallmark Cards' reminder to customers when and to whom they want their online cards to be sent
Distribution	Actors bringing performances to people's homes; Cadbury creating scarcity value for its Chocolate Creme Eggs by removing them temporarily from distribution (the so-called 'strawberry syndrome'); The Book People company, focused entirely on selling books direct to people who would never normally visit a bookshop – distribution is typically via factories and offices; Haines & Bonner, traditional English shirt makers since 1865, who deliver brand new hand-pressed shirts direct to the desks of City of London-based executives
Selection	Amazon.com's bespoke software to prompt intelligent suggestions online for additional purchases; major retailers such as Harvey Nichols offering 'personal shopping' services
Ordering and purchasing	Dell Computers, Direct Line Insurance and easyJet, all establishing direct sales links with customers in their respective markets
From delivery to installation	Marks & Spencer's investment in user-friendly assembly instructions for its flat-pack furniture
Payment	Blockbuster Video, which changed the industry pricing model from selling to renting; Ben & Jerry's, the ice-cream manufacturer, which donated 10 per cent of its profits to charity; Student Loans Company, which requires loans to be paid back only when a graduate's income has exceeded a certain level
After-sales service	Customer dissatisfaction with 'revolving door' outcomes of anonymous call centres has prompted certain banks to differentiate themselves on the basis of availability of local managers, including mobile and direct line numbers; FirstDirect Bank, open for human contact 24/7
Repairs and service	Replacement service for travellers offered by credit card providers and spectacle manufacturers
Disposal	Lexmark printer cartridges, which can be collected and recycled at manufacturer's expense once exhausted

mental workout two – stimulus materials

The risk of becoming stuck in mental ruts, always thinking along the same lines, cannot be exaggerated. Stimulus material, whether pictures, words or objects, is ideal for helping you reach ideas which you perhaps already had in your subconscious but could not express. Pictures, words or objects can all stimulate you to free-associate around your idea and they can suggest different angles from which you can approach your business opportunity.

keep seeking new materials

Because the materials are designed to stimulate your subconscious in new and unexpected ways, you should continually update and refresh your stock of them. As Thomas Edison is alleged to have once said: 'To invent, you need a good imagination and a pile of junk.'[90]

> to invent, you need a good imagination and a pile of junk

Part of this involves keeping your mind constantly alive to the potential value of what you see as you go about your everyday business – remember the old dictum that your mind is like a parachute, only of any use when it is open. Part of it involves actively seeking out new experiences and insights to add to the stimulus stock-room – it could be visiting an art gallery or toy shop, browsing the sections of bookshops you would not normally visit or surfing the internet. And part of it involves keeping a record of the various stimuli, however informal, to which you can return when needed.

the science of collecting junk

It often helps to keep a scrapbook or box of useful ideas or articles to which you can refer when you need inspiration. It may be that you see a snippet in the newspaper which makes you think 'That's clever' or 'I could use that'; it may be that you spot an elegant application of technology in a product when you are browsing through a store. It's important to keep track of these ideas so that you can apply them directly to your own opportunity or use them as a springboard to create further innovative ideas.

IDEO, for example, has made a science of collecting junk. The company maintains a continually updated 'Tech Box' which it treats as its corporate lending library of innovation ideas. Described by CEO

Tom Kelley as the 'corporate spark plug' for new ideas, the Tech Box has been adopted at all IDEO offices worldwide.[91]

Famous for his BBC TV series *Changing Rooms*, Laurence Llewellyn-Bowen highlights the importance of continually seeking, and keeping, images and designs to inspire him with ideas for potential room make-overs. As the flamboyant designer puts it: 'In much the same way that we visit our hairdresser clutching a picture of Kylie, magazine "tear sheets" are a prize jewel in our design treasure chest. No matter if you aren't planning a room at the time – if you see an idea you like, tear it out! Keep a big box full so that when it comes to the right time you will have great fun sifting through all the possibilities.'[92] He is a particularly ardent advocate of digital cameras to record ideas, whether seen in shop windows, friends' houses or holiday spots.

jolt yourself out of the rut

Some companies deliberately go as far as regularly changing the décor of their environments to expose their staff to new stimuli and to avoid them becoming stuck in routines.

Creative communication company St Luke's, for example, employed an artist-in-residence with only one brief, namely to surprise the company with art. As chairman Andy Law noted in his account of the company's early years: 'We loved the thrill of this kind of constant change and enjoyed seeing ourselves provoked into a debate by the arrival of an army of tiny mice that appeared painted everywhere and which, when looked at closely, built up through clues a picture and view on the role of modern art.'[93]

structured use of unrelated stimulus materials

There are a number of ground rules which you can follow to make the most of unrelated stimulus materials, particularly pictures. These are based on the principle of placing diverse or unrelated elements together in order to provoke different insights into an issue or opportunity.

The ground rules are as follows:

1   Select from a variety of contexts pictures which contain a range of objects, actions, textures and other stimuli.

2   Begin by focusing on a picture unrelated to your problem. Describe the picture in detail, noting any relationships, concepts and principles present. In particular, describe whatever action you see, actual or implied. The purpose of this stage is to stimulate ideas, not to achieve

correctness; the precise accuracy or otherwise of the descriptions is completely irrelevant – you are seeking to create a set of descriptions to spark off unexpected and unpredictable associations, so remember to put your left-brain concerns to one side.

3 Look over all your descriptions and see which ones might stimulate ideas. Use your selection to free-associate.

Here is an example of how to use a picture as a stimulus to finding solutions. Imagine that you working in a large stationery wholesaler and that you are considering establishing your own stationery retail outlet. You happen on a photograph of a large country house – the image is completely unrelated to your business opportunity, so is ideal for this purpose.

You might describe the image in the following terms:

'This is a large country house. It has a large and imposing external staircase which leads to the main entrance, over which is inscribed the date 1746. The house can be accessed by a number of avenues, one of which has just been planted with young trees. The surrounding lawns have been cut very close. The house has a multitude of windows, all of different sizes; the below-stairs servants' windows are particularly small. The wind and rain have cracked a number of windows and have dislodged some tiles off the roof. Although the sun is shining, smoke is coming out of the chimneys – all the barley-sugar chimneys have a slightly different decoration.'

Next, you can use the descriptions to spark ideas:

- Introduce an element of personalised stationery, perhaps by linking with a local printer (from 'chimneys have a slightly different decoration')

- Include hand-crafted traditional papers in the product range (from 'the main entrance, over which is inscribed the date 1746')

- Promote your company on the basis of low cost (from 'the surrounding lawns have been cut very close')

- Include in your product range stationery products which you can promote on environmental grounds (from 'just planted with young trees')

- Segment your market into different customer types and sizes – perhaps home office, small businesses, school segment, as well as general retail customers (from 'the house has a multitude of windows, of different sizes') – and devise a strategy to grow your customers (from 'large and imposing external staircase')

- Position your company on the basis of attention to detail and quality (from 'the wind and rain have cracked a number of windows and have dislodged some tiles off the roof')

- Promote your company on the basis of efficiency (inverse insight from 'although the sun is shining, smoke is coming out of the chimneys')

- Create alternative distribution strategies – e-mail ordering and selection for local offices, backed up by delivery to individuals' desks; perhaps link up with other suppliers who target the same market with regular deliveries, such as sandwich providers (from 'the house can be accessed by a number of avenues').

mental workout three – combinations

A number of the checklist techniques discussed earlier included the active combination of products or services as an idea-generation tool. Sometimes the inspiration for such combinations can result from one's own experience, such as Benjamin Franklin combining long- and short-distance spectacles into bi-focals, or Earle Dickson combining gauze and adhesive tape to inspire Band-Aids®.

the accidental product developer

More recently, Darryl Lenz, a working mother who was a stewardess with American Airlines, strapped a child's folding beach chair to her suitcase to make air travel with her young son less of an ordeal. Having discovered that she could not get through an airport without people stopping her asking where they could buy the product, Lenz commercialised the Ride-On Carry-On as a detachable child seat to fit on roll-aboard luggage.[94]

Sometimes the inspiration will derive from observation of customer usage, such as the power drill which includes an integrated dust-collector, or the Sony Walkman which combines transistor radio with a high-quality stereo system. High-profile entrepreneur Michelle Mone combined the liquid silicon gel used in cosmetic surgery with the conventional bra concept to produce the award-winning, figure-flattering Ultimo brand of bras and swimwear.

At other times, inspiration can come from considering all phases of the customer journey, such as Charles Dunstone's Carphone Warehouse, which combined the service of providing information on complex phone tariffs with a wide range of mobile phones.

We will see later in this chapter how analogical thinking, among other techniques, has contributed to such other long-lasting combinations as Gutenberg's printing press (which combined the grape press and the coin punch), the military amphibious landing craft (combining a boat with a lorry), the world's first 'Pleasure Wheel' in Chicago (combined by George Washington Gale Ferris Jr in 1893 from the chair and the wheel) and resealable food storage bags (combining the concept of a zip with the humble plastic bag).

focus on the process The technique of combinations focuses on the *process* of combining things to suggest new product ideas. We explore two types of technique in particular – morphological analysis and force-fitting.

the technique of combinations focuses on the *process* of combining things to suggest new product ideas

Morphological analysis offers structured methods of ensuring that you systematically consider all possible angles within a market as currently defined. It is an excellent technique for spotting market gaps and for generating ideas for product and service extensions. It sits well alongside analysis of the customer journey and observation of user behaviour.

Force-fitting, on the other hand, is a more provocative and right-brain way of juxtaposing apparently unrelated items to spark off completely new and unexpected directions. It is similar in principle to the use of stimulus materials, which allow elements which may or may not be related to be 'interrogated' for innovative solutions.

We will deal with each of the two types in turn.

morphological analysis Despite its daunting name, morphological analysis is an important element in the range of mental workouts. It involves structuring markets or opportunities into a clear graphic representation so that you can study their composition, consider all the options and identify possible market gaps. Its systematic and searching nature will undoubtedly appeal to left-brain thinkers.

This type of analysis is particularly effective at generating new combinations of existing products or services. It is often best complemented by divergent techniques such as boundary-hopping (see previous chapter) or brainstorming (discussed in a later section in this chapter) because the technique's strength lies in its exhaustive exploration of all conventional dimensions of a market rather than in generating completely new dimensions.

It can be used with increasing degrees of sophistication, from a four-box matrix in two dimensions to the equivalent of a Rubik's Cube. We will look at the varying degrees of sophistication in turn.

four on the flat In its most simple form, two independent variables within a market or situation can be plotted against each other to form a four-box matrix. We saw an example of its usefulness in the previous chapter, where the 'creative procrastination zone' could be plotted along the two axes of timing and analytical depth. The graphic representation of the concept promotes a speed of understanding, together with a facility to consider the different behavioural options, which words alone would struggle to achieve.

the Ansoff Matrix The Ansoff Matrix is one of the best-known structured guides to product and market development (see Figure 4.1).[95] Business opportunities can be reduced to the two dimensions of markets and product concepts. The technique has merit both for existing businesses which wish to identify growth opportunities and for individuals seeking to break into a market area.

	PRODUCT	
	Current	New
MARKET Current	Market penetration	Product development
New	Market extension	Diversification

Figure 4.1 Ansoff Matrix for product and market development

The matrix helps structure your thinking by identifying four different growth strategies for an existing operation or launch opportunities for new entrants:

- Achieve additional sales of existing product concepts in existing markets
- Extend existing product concepts to new markets
- Develop new product concepts for existing markets
- Develop new product concepts for new markets.

Each box in the matrix has a different significance, which will also vary depending on whether you are already in business or are seeking to enter. From a new business perspective, there is a particular risk in focusing on the existing combination of product concept and market if you do not give sufficient thought to how you will differentiate your offering.

no differentiation, no future The previous chapter highlighted the recently published study of three decades of enterprise policy in the Tees Valley. This study identified the danger of confusing the quantity of new business start-ups with the differentiated quality of those start-ups. It noted the law of unintended consequences at play with government initiatives targeted at relatively poor areas to subsidise enterprise. The new businesses which resulted from this government pump-priming were often clustered in low entry-cost activities, focused on the immediate locality.

The study found that in the 1980s almost 25 per cent of new business start-ups in Cleveland, excluding retail, were in motor vehicle repairs, hairdressing and beauty salons. The subsidised start-ups often undercut existing companies to the point of putting them out of business, only to go out of business themselves once the pump-priming has been exhausted. The killed-off competitor resuscitated itself, giving an illusion of real economic activity to what was actually just zero-sum 'churn'.[96]

the death of the 'butt-crack' plumber Occasionally, there is such a shortage in the market that the aspect of differentiation becomes less important. Plumbing is currently just such a market, characterised by huge waiting times for getting hold of a plumber and abundant stories of white-collar professionals retraining in order to participate in a highly lucrative and allegedly fiscally efficient market sector. Recent students on plumbing courses at Colchester Institute, for example, include a city executive, a computer engineer with a Masters degree and a £750,000 house in Ealing, and a redundant jet pilot.[97]

Despite the plumbing market being a seller's market, a growing segment of new entrants to the industry are women who differentiate themselves by targeting women customers. As the Institute of Plumbing, the main UK industry body, reports: 'Quite a few of our female plumbers don't have to advertise at all. They get all their work from the other mums at the school gate and they do their jobs while the kids are at school.'[98]

The UK experience is mirrored in the United States. Stephania Alexander moved into the plumbing service business in the early 1990s when the collapse of the Californian economy forced her to leave her plumbing materials shop. In her first year alone of operating the Mr Rooter plumbing franchise for Dallas-Fort Worth in Texas, Stephania achieved sales of over $1 million.

A large part of her success comes from differentiating her business to meet the specific needs of women customers. This means that when her employees come to a customer's door, they wear crisp, clean uniforms and bring with them a Mr Rooter doormat to wipe their feet. Protective equipment includes booties to wear over their shoes, carpet protectors and work-mats. Her staff are trained to enter only the room which needs attention, always following the same traffic pattern to and from their truck, so that they do not interfere with other rooms. The package is completed by up-front menu pricing to avoid any stressful quibbles over mysterious 'extras', together with a guarantee on workmanship.

Stephania Alexander provides a good example of innovative differentiation in a highly conventional industry sector. As she vividly puts it: 'Our attention to detail coupled with our sensitivity to the needs of the customers give us a definite advantage over the stereotypical "butt-crack" plumber.'[99]

market mapping Market mapping is a useful technique to examine how competitors shape up to each in other in a market and to reveal possible market gaps.

The market map in Figure 4.2 shows how the UK lunchtime eating and drinking market might have looked to Pret a Manger's founders, Julian Metcalf and Sinclair Beecham, in the mid-1980s. The analysis describes the market along the dimensions of eating in or out, and quality levels.

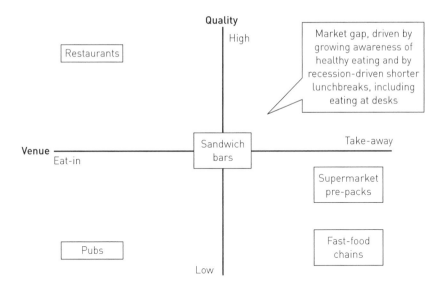

Figure 4.2 Map of UK lunchtime eating and drinking market in the m, _-1980s

Mapping the market along these dimensions shows graphically that a gap existed for a high-quality offering for the take-away market. The founders' market research identified that the growing interest in healthy eating, together with an increasing propensity for workers to eat at their desk, supported the existence of this gap. All elements of the resulting Pret a Manger offer contributed to this high-quality positioning, from choice of ingredients, freedom from preservatives and additives, through to the freshness of the product and its environment-friendliness.

four + on the flat A refinement of the four-box matrix is offered by the multi-box matrix. This technique is designed to generate multiple different permutations of the major attributes of a product or service.

The first stage of using this more sophisticated type of morphological analysis is to identify the major attributes. Its usage is perhaps best explained through example. Suppose that you work for a stationery manufacturer such as Berol and have been charged with generating some new product ideas for Berol's pencil range. In the pencil example, you might identify the following attributes: material, finish, profile, lead, pencil top and packaging. The next stage is to list as many attributes as you can under each dimension, as shown in Table 4.6.

Table 4.6 Attribute analysis for new pencil range

Material	Finish	Profile	Lead	Pencil top	Packaging
Wood	Natural	Round	Black	With eraser	None
Plastic	Painted	Square	Coloured	Without eraser	Tin
Rubber	Transparent	Elliptical	Eraser	Square-cut	Cardboard
Metal	Textured	Hexagonal	Water-soluble	Chamfered	Plastic
Foam	Striped	Triangular	Erasable	Pointed	Wood
Paper	Printed		Non-erasable	With toy	
Cloth	Die-stamped		Scented		

By selecting one entry from each column, you can create an extremely diverse range of new product possibilities from an apparent commodity product. A particular attraction of the technique is that by forcing you to break the product down into its constituent parts, you avoid viewing the product as a solid single entity, creating instead a range of avenues to explore.

One of the new products developed by Berol from exercises such as this was the Karisma colour pencil range. Aimed at artists, this high-quality range was finished in natural wood, with a chamfered top to maximise the impact of the lead's colour. The top-quality positioning was further accentuated by the brand logo hallmarked on to the casing and by the highly textured environmentally friendly cardboard packaging, which came complete with velvet cloth to safeguard its precious products, which were commodities no more.

'cube-crawling' Three-dimensional models are even more powerful than their two-dimensional counterparts. A classical application of a three-dimensional model is the Scimitar (Systematic Creativity and Integrative Modelling of Industrial Technology and Research) approach to new product invention and implementation, whose original application in the Steetley Organisation by new products manager John Carson is recorded by Tudor Rickards.[100]

Carson created a physical three-dimensional model, made of perspex sheets supported by perspex rods, as a means through which to develop new product ideas for the chemical industry. The model's three dimensions were the company's raw materials, processes and markets (see Figure 4.3). Calling to mind the multi-coloured Rubik's Cube may make it easier for you to imagine that each filled-in cube of Carson's model represented an existing combination of raw material, processed in a particular way, promoted to a specific market and uniquely defined as a distinct product. The gaps represented opportunities for new products.

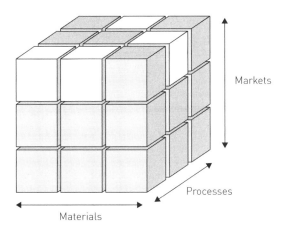

Figure 4.3 Carson's three-dimensional model

Carson had the wit to term the process of systematically examining the model for new products 'cube-crawling'. His approach was to take a slice across the model, such as a particular market sector, and then analyse each cube within the slice – the empty cubes automatically represented a potential product, which could subsequently be evaluated and refined further.

'Cube-crawling' represents an elegantly simple framework to structure creative thinking. In the model shown in Figure 4.3, the grey cubes represent existing products. The white cubes represent opportunities within a given market sector to create new process/material combinations.

Clearly the axes do not have to be restricted to markets, materials or processes. You should use any dimensions which help you interrogate a market.

taking Swatch to the slopes Swatch, for example, could have mapped out the conventional watch market along the dimensions of price, technical performance and market type, including fashion. A systematic analysis such as this cube-crawling would have created the potential combinations of high technical performance and high fashion across a range of prices. This might seem counter-intuitive to Swatch's predominantly fashion-conscious accessory positioning.

Significantly, however, the recently launched hi-tech Swatch Access watch targets the fashion-conscious skiing community by incorporating a microchip and antenna. Once 'charged', it allows contactless access to the slopes through lift turnstiles. Not only does the skiing-specific product range make 'lengthy queues and lost lift passes a thing of the past . . . it eliminates the horror of removing gloves or undoing zips'.[101]

force-fitting unrelated elements

The morphological analysis described in the previous sections tends to combine related elements in unexpected ways, create market insights and powerfully investigate the permutations which could be created of the major attributes of a product or service.

shock effects In contrast, the technique of juxtaposing deliberately unrelated elements seeks to provoke unexpected and innovative ideas. This force-fitting is designed almost to shock you out of conventional thinking into new approaches to the opportunities which you are considering.

> the technique of juxtaposing deliberately unrelated elements seeks to provoke unexpected and innovative ideas

Suppose that you run a small book-publishing operation aimed at the traditional children's market. Your challenge is to generate ideas to increase sales. You might prepare two lists – one which itemises the constituent elements of a physical book, one which lists the signage in your local supermarket. If you chose one item from each list at random, you might come up with the book's printed text and the supermarket's guarantee of customer satisfaction. Force-fitting these two items provokes the question – how could I improve the sales potential of the book's contents by offering something like a customer guarantee? Possible solutions might include using children as editorial readers to ensure at first hand that the content was appropriate to the target market, and publishing an internet site with peer group reviews of the various titles you offer.

You might match up the book's contents with the supermarket's home delivery sign. This might prompt you to consider making the books downloadable from the internet or perhaps available in taped talking-book versions. You might want to match the customer guarantee angle with the book's cover. This might lead you to consider signposting clearly on the cover the similar titles which would most appeal to particular readers. Or you might want to print an endorsement from children's current role models.

what does a book jacket have in common with a delicatessen? In addition, you could stick with the book's jacket, but match it against the supermarket's delicatessen. How could you improve the marketing potential of the cover by making it more like a delicatessen? This forced association might lead you to applying the numbered ticket system used in the delicatessen to the launch of a numbered, limited edition print run of a particular title or series, all of them with an added-value element such as the author's signature or a free prize entry. The forced association might also lead you to consider whether you could personalise the book's cover at point-of-sale.

The possibilities really are endless. The tasters on the delicatessen counter might prompt you to provide a sample chapter to allow parents to try out the book on their children at home. A sign for personal shoppers might prompt the idea for a telephone reading service.

go for quantity and don't judge You should work through all possible combinations from both lists. As the example above shows, the forced connection between two apparently unrelated elements can generate a significant wealth of first-level ideas which can be screened and developed further. As ever with divergent thinking, the intention is to generate ideas in quantity while suspending all critical judgement which inevitably inhibits the fluency of your idea generation. There is plenty of time left in the process for analytical left-brain thinking to perform its evaluative task.

mental workout four – free association

Free association is the most basic of all idea-generation techniques, with one idea being used to generate another, which then sparks off another and so on. In contrast to the earlier force-fitting technique, free association relies heavily on chance, together with your past experience and current frame of mind, for its effectiveness.

The success of this technique relies upon your ability to let go and allow one thought or concept to lead to another. It is important to indulge in one especially of the four Ps which we met in Chapter 1: playfulness. You must feel able to let your mind flit about. The more you let go, the more you will boost your right-brain thinking to produce innovative ideas. Put the left-brain analytical constraints to one side and give yourself time to sink into a 'deep think'.

It is important to get into the correct and relaxed state of mind-set before starting to use these techniques. The brainstorming room at the IBM Research Centre in Bethesda, Maryland, is said to be filled with a collection of metal-hinged puzzles, to allow participants to play with the puzzles before getting down to work. IDEO routinely engages in mental warm-ups, as well as encouraging 'content-related homework', to ensure the success of its brainstorming sessions.

> the more you let go, the more you will boost your right-brain thinking to produce innovative ideas

Individuals may have particular rituals for achieving a relaxed mind-set. Before starting to compose music, Gustav Mahler relaxed by stroking fur. Before starting to write, Samuel Johnson surrounded himself with a purring cat, orange peel and tea. Brahms is said to have received inspiration from shining his shoes, while Friedrich Schiller covered his desk with rotten apples. The rule is simple: do whatever does it for you.

brainstorming Brainstorming is a fabulously powerful technique for using free association to create a barrage of ideas, acknowledging Linus Paul's dictum that 'the best way to get a good idea is to get a lot of ideas'. The technique can be used by individuals as well as by groups.

While Alex Osborn is widely credited with developing the concept of brainstorming in the 1960s, leading-edge innovation companies such as IDEO have taken the idea on and often given it their own twist.[102] IDEO has gone as far as making brainstorming a central part of its modus operandi: 'Brainstorming is practically a religion at IDEO, one we practise nearly every day. Though brainstorms themselves are often playful, brainstorming as a tool – as a skill – is taken quite seriously . . . Brainstorming is the idea engine of IDEO's culture.'[103]

The power of brainstorming can be illustrated by the story of the plate manufacturer whose productivity was dropping because the packers were slowing down to read the old newspapers in which they were wrapping the plates. A brainstorming session to address the issue generated a number of ideas, including changing the language of the newspapers, using alternative packing materials and awarding incentives for the number of plates wrapped. Finally, and using the privilege of suspended judgement to be politically incorrect, one manager suggested a truly wild idea: 'Why don't we poke out the eyes of the packers?' Although the suggestion sounded ridiculous, it did eventually lead to the idea of hiring blind people. The blind packers did the job very effectively without being distracted and the company was able to provide a valuable service to the community.

There are a number of stages to achieve effective brainstorming, including:

- Stage One: if brainstorming in a group, circulate ahead of the session brief summary details of the issue or opportunity to be brainstormed

- Stage Two: use a warm-up activity ahead of the main brainstorm in order to create a playful and positive atmosphere to encourage divergent thinking

- Stage Three: state the problem in simple, clear terms with a single focus – as we saw with the boundary-examination section in the previous chapter (remember the sunken ship which was floated to the surface), ensure that the problem statement does not presume a particular solution

- Stage Four: this is the key phase – generate a fluent sequence of ideas, writing down each one, encouraging people to build on others' ideas, maintaining the pace. It is essential that no critical evaluation whatsoever is allowed. Numbering the ideas creates a sense of achievement and setting targets reinforces the quest for quantity – IDEO has a minimum speed limit of 100 ideas per hour, with a maximum of about 150

- Stage Five: expect to close the session after about 30 minutes, although a group in full song might stretch to up to 45 minutes

- Stage Six: select an evaluation group, present the ideas to it and ask the group members to pick the best ideas (we will cover evaluation techniques in the following chapter). Remember that if you have managed to generate 50–75 ideas in your 30-minute slot, probably only a handful will merit further detailed examination

- Stage Seven: 'go back for seconds' – present the selected ideas back to the original group and seek additional ideas based on this list. Not only will the original team have had a chance to sleep on the initial exercise, which may itself have suggested further ideas, reviewing the selected list may also prompt further refinements

- Stage Eight: carry the final list of possible ideas through to the evaluation process, which we will discuss in the next chapter.

If working in a group, Tom Kelley, IDEO's managing director, also suggests some additional rules for effective brainstorming:[104]

- Ensure that the session is entirely status-free

- Encourage spontaneity rather than allocate every participant specific air-time

- Do not restrict the group just to the recognised experts – in order to encourage insight and thinking outside the box, include free-thinkers who do not suffer from the mental stuckness which we discussed earlier. Remember that one of the troubles with experts is that they always know why things cannot be done

- Always schedule brainstorms in-house – brainstorming at external venues can encourage the perception that innovation and creativity are not your normal stock-in-trade

- Do not get bogged down in excessive note-taking – encourage all participants to engage in real time, without prompts and without keeping the score themselves, so that everybody is poised to contribute all the time.

one of the troubles with experts is that they always know why things cannot be done

mind-mapping Mind-mapping represents a good technique for tapping into your intuitive, holistic right brain in order to develop creative ideas for products and services. Originally developed by

Tony Buzan in the 1970s, mind-mapping is rather like a visual version of brainstorming.[105] It allows your ideas to run wild, feeding off each other, jumping around and creating multiple cross-references rather than being constrained by the sequential linear style of left-brain thinking.

When we think with our left brain, we tend to focus on logical sequences of ideas, with the sequence often taking precedence over the content. Crossword puzzlers recognise this when solving anagrams – rather than leave the jumbled-up letters in a straight line which might constrain thinking, successful anagram-solvers tend to arrange the letters randomly in a circle precisely to avoid any fixed pattern forming and to allow their imagination to have free rein.

Mind-mapping therefore focuses on generating content with the sequence of ideas taking second place. Ideas really can run wild, branch out in any direction, without the need to follow any predetermined direction. The key issue is that individual ideas and the developing branches of ideas should stimulate quantities of further ideas.

As with verbal brainstorming and all divergent techniques, remember to suspend your judgement – securing a significant quantity of ideas is the aim. It is often the case that the technique will unleash ideas which you never knew you had, such is the power of association and memory.

The basic stages for mind-mapping are as follows:

- Stage One: in the centre of a large piece of paper, write down the word or phrase which expresses the opportunity you want to explore

- Stage Two: produce a mind-map of ideas related to this starting word. Write down ideas as quickly as they come to you, adding to existing branches and starting new branches as appropriate. Engage your right-brain by using arrows, colour and other visual effects. The key point is to keep driving forward, seeking associations, without being overly reflective. You should keep jotting until your ideas are exhausted

- Stage Three: continue drawing lines and adding topics until you have run out of ideas. We used the mind-map in Figure 4.4 to visually brainstorm this chapter.

Figure 4.4 Mind-map of Chapter 4 – generating ideas

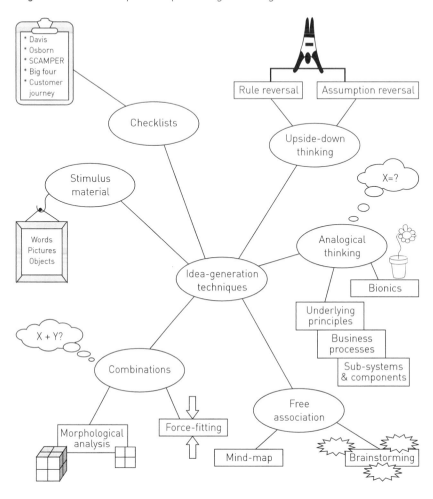

mental workout five – analogical thinking

A whole generation of secretaries owe a debt of gratitude to Bette Nesmith, an executive secretary with mediocre typing skills who worked at the Texas Bank & Trust in Dallas during the 1950s.

Why? Because while helping decorate the holiday windows at the bank, Bette Nesmith noticed that the artists corrected their mistakes by painting over the error. She had the insight to see that she could transfer the principle to her error-strewn typewriting and her first efforts with water-based paint soon turned into a cottage industry with quite massive potential. Within ten years, she had sold the Liquid Paper patent to Gillette for around $50 million.

Nesmith's skill lay in perceiving how an underlying principle, the essence of a process, could be transferred from one application to another which was 'similar but different'.

More recently, a senior Marks & Spencer director was wrestling with how to improve the massively inefficient process of buttering sandwiches by hand. When visiting a supplier who made bed sheets for Marks & Spencer, the director noticed that the supplier was using a silk-screen process to print patterns. Spotting the analogy, Martin van Zwaneberg, then head of home services and food technology, initiated an experiment to print butter on to cotton. As a result of this successful experiment, Marks & Spencer now silk-screens butter on to its sandwiches.[106]

The roll-call of analogically inspired products is impressive. Dietrich was inspired to create the Pritt Stick glue dispenser by watching a woman apply her lipstick; the roll-on deodorant was drawn from an analogy with the ball-point pen; and an engineer's ability to spot the analogy between a beer can and a low-cost disposable photosensitive drum contributed to the creation of the Canon Mini-Copier.

Clarence Birdseye, owner of an American produce business in the late 1890s, overturned the conventional business practice of the time of never leaving the store. Instead, he travelled frequently and widely. After observing the people of the Arctic preserving fresh fish and meat in barrels of seawater quickly frozen by the Arctic temperatures, Birdseye concluded that it was this rapid freezing in the extremely low temperatures that made food retain freshness when thawed and cooked months later. Birdseye saw how this principle could be applied to his own business and brought the analogy home.

In 1923, with an investment of $7 for an electric fan, buckets of brine and cakes of ice, Birdseye invented and later perfected a system of packing fresh food into waxed cardboard boxes and flash-freezing under high pressure.

similar, but different

There is nothing mysterious about analogies. An analogy is a statement about how objects, persons, situations or actions are similar in process or relationship to one another.

You make an analogy when you perceive that A is like B, only different. Perhaps you say to yourself: 'That reminds me of X' or 'I can see how I could usefully apply that to Y.' The exploration of the similarities can be a tremendous spur to generating ideas and to finding pre-existing solutions which have been created in other areas.

Once you have spotted a really good analogy, you often wonder how you missed it in the first place. You can take heart from the fact that steam engines had been used in mines for 75 years before Robert Fulton and others saw the analogy between their usage underground and as a means to propel boats. From this perception, they developed the first commercial steamboat.

'a minor invention every ten days'

Thomas Edison is generally credited with founding the original ideas factory, precursor to such organisations as IDEO. A feature of many inventions created at Edison's Menlo Park Research and Development base in New Jersey was that they used old materials, ideas or objects in new ways. The record player, for example, drew on analogies with existing technology in the fields of telephones, electric motors and telegraphs. The power of this technique among others allowed Edison to deliver on his promise of a 'minor invention every ten days and a big thing every six months or so'.[107]

applying old ideas to solve new problems

Analogies represent a powerful way of achieving different perspectives either on an overall opportunity or problem or on sub-systems or processes within them. Analogies can help you break away from your conventional routines, self-imposed constraints and 'mental stuckness'. Analogies can create links between opportunities in one type of business or area of activity and a proven solution in another. Analogical thinking allows old ideas to become effective solutions to new problems.

analogies can help you break away from your conventional routines, self-imposed constraints and 'mental stuckness'

Analogies can help in every area of life. A famous (and very thin) actor playing Shakespeare's larger-than-life character Falstaff observed that his infant son waddled in exactly the fashion that the actor wanted Falstaff to move. Realising that wearing nappies gave his son no option but to waddle, the actor bound his own legs in bulky cloth before each performance in order to achieve the Falstaff swagger.

natural solutions

Often nature provides the answer, or at least the inspiration, to problems and issues in real life because the underlying principle or approach can be translated across. This sub-set of analogical thinking is termed bionics. Nature's solutions have spurred products as diverse as Velcro, the heat-seeking technology of the side-winder missile, the Millennium Bridge in Newcastle and Pringles crisps.

Sometimes the analogy will just present itself by chance and then it is up to your open and receptive mind to perceive its value. More often than not, however, it will be up to you to undertake a structured search for analogies, following up the best with divergent exploration for further ideas.

We will discuss in turn a number of different techniques for actively exploiting the power of analogies. The techniques progress from a relatively high level of abstraction, investigating how underlying principles can be transferred, to a greater level of detail at the process or component level.

transferring an underlying principle

Computer expert Sir Godfrey Hounsfield was deployed in EMI Ltd on a computerised pattern-recognition project when he observed that if he were able to take readings which could detect the presence of materials from all angles through a box, in three dimensions, he would be able to determine what was in the box without opening it.

Hounsfield transferred the underlying principle of looking inside something without opening it to the human body. Using technologies including X-rays, which had been discovered in 1895, Hounsfield went on to create the computerised axial tomography (CAT) scanner. This device constructs a three-dimensional image of the human body, eliminating the need for much exploratory surgery.

A number of further analogical uses have been found for the CAT scanner, not least by Customs and Excise inspectors at ports of entry, who are able to restrict their physical search for contraband to those containers which scanning technology suggests merit closer inspection.

mapping the way to indestructible books for children A father of three young children, Simon Rosenheim had been in publishing for 15 years when he launched a range of physically indestructible children's books under an imprint of DC Thomson. As a motorcycle enthusiast, he had spotted an analogy between what did exist in a related field – waterproof and tear-proof roadmaps and road-users' atlases – and what could exist in the world of children's books. Reinforcement of the analogy of indestructibility came from his observation that ramblers and walkers also had strong but thin paper for their guides.[108]

how to transfer an underlying principle The spirit of the technique is to identify the essence or underlying principle of the opportunity which you are currently addressing to suggest analogies – situations or processes which are similar but different. These analogous situations or processes may help capture the opportunity which you are considering; alternatively, they may create new and unexpected perspectives on the opportunity which require further elaboration. Either way, seeking analogies is an excellent way of thinking outside the box.

seeking analogies is an excellent way of thinking outside the box

Good practice suggests that you should use animate analogies with problems involving non-living things and vice versa.

Once you have developed a list of analogies to the underlying principle, you select the most promising and describe it in detail, listing parts, uses and functions, taking care to include action-oriented phrases. You then examine each of the descriptions within the selected analogy, seeking stimuli for further ideas and refinements.

how a computer company learned from cooking The technique is best illustrated by a real-life example. In the early 1990s, Hewlett-Packard was struggling with inventory cost and product availability for its popular HP DeskJet printer. In order to maximise economies of manufacturing scale, production was centralised in a single 'global' plant. The three regional markets of North America, Asia and Europe all required the product to be regionalised in terms of power supply, documentation and packaging. Difficulty in accurately predicting demand resulted in significant region-specific inventories being maintained in the regional distribution centres (see Figure 4.5).

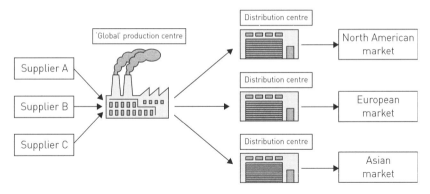

Figure 4.5 Initial supply chain for the HP DeskJet printer

The first stage for Hewlett-Packard was to identify other areas which involved the underlying principle of efficient modular processes. During the search, Hewlett-Packard came upon the restaurant analogy identified by leading-edge research into business processes such as supply chain management.[109] The researchers had highlighted that the basic food service transaction could be broken down into five core processes: order the food, cook the food, serve the food, eat the food, and pay for the food. They had also pointed out that the order in which the processes could be executed was variable, subject to the constraints imposed by the interdependencies – fast food requires 'cook, order, serve, pay and then eat' whereas full-service restaurant follows 'order, cook, serve, eat and then pay'. You cannot eat before the meal is prepared, but you can pay at any time, however.

challenging orthodoxy Having established that the food service business offered a powerful analogy because it challenged a fixed order of doing things, Hewlett-Packard started the second stage of exploring the analogy in more depth. The core activities could easily be transferred to manufacturing – 'cook' becomes 'manufacture', 'eat' becomes 'consume'. It enlarged the 'grammar' and 'lexicon', as it termed them, of the supply chain to include make-for-inventory as well as make-to-order, gateaux as well as freshly grilled steak, as it were. It acknowledged that inventory could include part-assembled materials, the equivalent of parboiled vegetables, and it included inputs from suppliers.

making the analogy work The final stage was for Hewlett-Packard to apply the restaurant analogy to the particular supply chain problem in hand. The outcome was significant. As shown in Figure 4.6, it modified the sequential structure of the supply chain so that the global plant produced a completely standardised product which did not include the region-specific components. The final assembly steps were moved to the regional distribution centres.

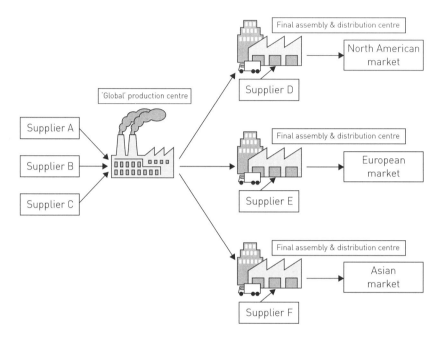

Figure 4.6 Reconfigured supply chain for the HP DeskJet printer

The business benefits included lower inventory levels at the global production centre because demand was smoothed across the whole global market, and increased market responsiveness because the regional plants could ship work-in-progress between each other to match the peaks in regional demand.

transferring a business process

Sometimes the approach to analogies will focus on a specific business process. We saw in the previous chapter how a services company had created a first-class luxury hotel environment for its demanding and pampered guests. The twist was that the guests were all pets. Best Friends Pet Resorts and Salons perceived an opportunity to offer first-class service to guests and had drawn a ready analogy between premium hotel service and luxury accommodation for pets.

inward transfer This searching for external analogies which you wish to transfer into your operation is very similar to the concept of process bench-marking. This involves seeking out best-in-class for a specific process, irrespective of the sector in which this expertise resides.

South West Airlines, for example, looked outside the airline business in order to perfect its refuelling processes. By adopting the turnaround processes used in Formula One pit stops, the company reduced the time required to refuel by 60 per cent.[110]

outward transfer Sometimes analogies work in the reverse direction – you operate a particular business process which you wish to transfer out and apply to other fields.

Stelios Haji-Ioannou is well known for his creation of easyJet, the low-cost no-frills model for air travel. He then sought other markets which were similar, but different, to the airline market and to which he could apply the easyFormula. It is generally accepted that easyRentacar has represented a satisfactorily analogous market. The jury is still out on whether the cinema market is sufficiently similar to sustain the easyCinema model, with its variable pricing and no-frills service – exclusively online booking has replaced the traditional box office; no food or drink is sold.

Providers of locum services in the UK medical market possess a particular expertise in high-volume, rapid-response matching of professionals to work opportunities. By identifying which other markets presented similar, but different, underlying characteristics, they have successfully moved into the supply of part-time teachers, for example.

serving God and Mammon In similar vein, Suffolk-based printing company Clays had developed over the years a specialism in printing the very lightweight papers used to produce high-quality Bibles. Seeking to expand the range of markets which it served, the printing company looked for markets which presented analogies to the Bible printing market. Clays succeeded in serving both God and Mammon when it realised that the market for computer games manuals, where high-pagination books had to be printed on very fine paper in order to occupy the small physical space defined by standard CD-ROM packaging, presented an analogous printing challenge to which it could apply its specialist expertise.

The key to using the technique at a business process level is to identify clearly the essence of the process which you wish to transfer out or transfer in. Then you should use your divergent thinking skills, whether through free association, mind-mapping or brainstorming, to generate ideas for the destination or source of the appropriate analogies.

transferring sub-systems and components

Analogies can sometimes be usefully applied to sub-systems or major attributes of the overall problem or opportunity.

When Edison's inventors were developing the light bulb, for example, they encountered the problem of the experimental bulbs continually falling out of their fixtures. One day a technician made the analogy between the thread cap which secured a kerosene bottle and the light-fixture problem. He mocked up the thread cap solution, discovered that it worked, and the so-called Edison Screw design has not changed since.

recognising the moment Professional footballer Craig Johnston reports how during his playing days he could not feel any tangible benefit of the new materials which certain manufacturers had incorporated into their football boots in order to improve their feel and touch. It was only later that his chance use of an analogy, and his immediate realisation of the powerful insight which the analogy revealed, led to a major breakthrough. As he put it:

'Years later I was coaching kids in Australia and I was telling them that they had to grip and bite into the ball like a table tennis bat to swerve it. "That's fine Mr Johnston," they said, "but our boots are made of leather and not rubber, it's raining and they are slippery." I went home and took the rubber off a table tennis bat and stuck it on my boots with superglue. Immediately I went outside again and kicked the ball, I could hear a squeak when the rubber engaged with the polyurethane of the ball.'111

everything and anything goes Medical engineering and children's toys would seem to make unlikely bedfellows, but in the world of analogical thinking, everything and anything goes.

Boston-based invention factory Design Continuum was involved in creating an innovative medical product for cleaning wounds with a flow of saline solution. Engineers made the analogy between the pressured flow mechanism of the desired medical product and battery-powered children's squirt-guns. This perception allowed them to incorporate the toy's low-cost electric pump and battery into the new design.[112]

no one gets ahead by copying the status quo Tom Kelley of IDEO is also a great exponent of seeking analogies in general and from toy stores in particular. Recognising that no one gets ahead by copying the status quo, as he puts it, his company has learned an enormous amount about how to do things simply and cheaply from toys, tearing apart the latest models to 'find out how the toy manufacturer did it with a few microchips and plastic'.[113]

The technique for generating analogies for sub-systems combines the attribute-listing technique with the technique for general analogies described earlier. The starting point is to break down the opportunity into sub-systems or attributes, as we saw with the morphological analysis technique of the 'four + on the flat'. You then develop analogies for each of the sub-systems or attributes. This technique is helpful in bringing alive the sometimes 'drier' techniques within morphological analysis.

bionics The term bionics has been used to describe the systematic use of biological and botanical analogies to solve novel engineering problems. Bionics uses stimuli from nature and biological and botanical systems to inspire ideas for products, services and processes. While it is a technique widely used in industry and private research labs to solve a variety of electronic, thermal, hydraulic, mechanical and chemical problems, it is equally valuable in more everyday situations.

bionics uses stimuli from nature and biological and botanical systems to inspire ideas

Joe Moya and Joe Raia, owners and founders of Joe Designer Inc., are eloquently aware of the power of the environment to stimulate ideas: 'There are beautiful things in nature that you can apply to products, especially with form. When we were developing [products with soft, rounded contours, such as the Betty Crocker Handmixer], we borrowed contours off everything from nature to classic cars.'[114]

nature's crisp solution Pringles Potato Crisps offer a particularly striking example of successful bionics. Consulting firm Synectics, Inc. was given the challenge of how to place more potato crisps on supermarket shelves. By containing significant amounts of air, conventional crisp bags occupied valuable space. If the product and its packaging could be compressed, the client company could increase its sales volume.

To solve this problem, Synectics, Inc. sought analogies from nature for the principle of compression. An example which leapt out was leaves. When crushed and mixed with water, the leaves would remain but would occupy much less space. The principle was applied across to potato crisps – water was mixed with dehydrated potatoes, the mixture was shaped, stacked and placed in the cylindrical packaging which has now become an integral part of the Pringles brand.

children's bubbles to underpin a building? Completed in 2001, the Eden Project created a living theatre of plants from a disused china clay pit in Cornwall. Because the pit was still being mined commercially during the structure's design phase, the architects were designing on a site which was constantly changing. It is never a good idea to build on shifting sand, but that is literally the problem which the designers faced.

The breakthrough came from watching soap bubbles. In his compelling account of the Eden Project, visionary founder Tim Smit recalls playing the children's game of blowing soap through a little hoop and noticing how the bubbles settled, adapting to whatever surface they landed on. The observation that where two or more bubbles landed adjoining each other, the line of join was always exactly perpendicular, provided the breakthrough which the project needed: 'By using this model, one can see that it is possible to develop a design that can adapt to whatever the surfaces beneath it are doing . . . Soon a model was created . . . The moment we saw it, we loved it, because it felt natural.'[115]

Cover the right-hand side of Table 4.7 and try to identify the products and artefacts which have been inspired by the natural phenomena listed in the left column.

Table 4.7 Man-made outcomes of inspiration from nature

Natural phenomenon	Outcome of inspiration from nature
Human arm	Anglepoise lamp
Swooping seagulls	The Spitfire fighter aircraft
Human eye	The Millennium Bridge in Newcastle, inspired by the blinking of a human eye
Beetle eye	Aircraft ground-speed altitude indicator
Humming bird	Harrier Jump Jet
Hollow tube of rye grass	Lemonade drinking straw, invented by Marvin Stone
Feline eye	Catseye road markings
Patterns on moth wings	US army camouflage
Bird feather	Airbus aircraft wings
Pea pods	Tube container for Pillsbury croissants
Rattlesnake temperature-sensing organs	Guidance system for Sidewinder heat-seeking missile
Bird's nests	New lining for furnaces – having considered how birds use mud to line their nests, a product development team decided on a clay lining for a new furnace

mental workout six – upside-down thinking

Sometimes known by the shorthand of 'reversals', this technique turns conventional logic upside down by reversing the direction of the issue or assumption under consideration. Such reversals are helpful in overcoming restrictions imposed by a fixed mind-set and conventional ways of thinking, whether on behalf of individuals or of entire industries.

Upside-down thinking is what translates a problem into an opportunity. It is what allowed Ingvar Kamprad to transform the blocking measures of the Swedish furniture retail and distribution cartel into an opportunity, identifying new sources of supply, establishing his own out-of-town distribution network and targeting a different market segment.

unable to see the wood for the trees
The natural temptation when you start to generate ideas is to dive right in and attack a problem from a fixed and pre determined perspective. By attacking problems head-on, it is all too easy to become too close to the problem and find yourself unable to generate new perspectives.

If you cannot see the wood for the trees, it often pays to enter the forest from a different direction. By changing direction, you change perspectives. Instead of being blocked by your initial, unproductive perspective, you will discover new ways of seeing your business opportunity, allowing new ideas to flow unfettered.

do not just wait for the muse You may be blocked or you may just be unable to get started. As de Bono elegantly points out: 'Unless one is going to sit around waiting for inspiration, the most practical way to get moving is to work on what one has.'[116] Upside-down thinking is an excellent way to start with what you have.

With rule reversal, you take the over-arching product or market situation as it is and then turn it upside-down in a provocative search for new ideas. Under the assumption reversal method, you overturn the key assumptions within a market to reveal new avenues to explore. We will discuss each technique in turn.

rule reversal

Rule reversal gives you licence to play the role of court jester, a historical role of such importance that British Airways offered BA insider Paul Birch the formal role of 'corporate jester'. A large part of his role involved turning reality on its head so that others might discover understanding and develop creative solutions.

Despite the venerable tradition dating from the 13th century that the court jester is immune from political punishment, the power of rule reversal to unsettle is revealed by the wry remark attributed to Birch that 'Whilst anyone can be a fool, it helps if you've a great future behind you'. The purpose of the rule reversal technique is quite literally to turn things on their head so that you escape from the conventional way of looking at a problem or opportunity. Birch is credited with challenging industry thinking on seat allocation, which led to customers who thought that they had pre-booked seats sometimes having to queue to get a seat on the plane alongside other customers who had paid less than them.

the purpose of the rule reversal technique is quite literally to turn things on their head

Sometimes the reversed approach is useful in itself. More often than not, the reversal creates an 'intermediate impossible' position which represents the stepping stone for a sound follow-up idea.

deliberately designing inefficiency Back in the 1870s, a leading manufacturer of manual typewriters, Sholes & Co., was grappling with how to solve the complaints which it frequently received about the keys sticking together when the typist was too fast. Having addressed the problem from the perspective of making the operation more efficient, it used rule reversal to consider making the operation less efficient.

The insight of slowing the typist down led to the design of the deliberately inefficient QWERTY keyboard, with the third and sixth most frequently used letters in the English language – 'O' and 'I' – being depressed by the hand's relatively weaker fingers. The power of conventional thinking is such that the QWERTY keyboard still persists, despite the physical requirement for it having been made redundant long ago by technological advance.

bringing the closed shop back into fashion Katharine Hamnett, fashion designer of the clothing range which bears her name, wanted to stimulate buyers' interest in her clothes at various trade shows. Rather than invite all the key buyers and distributors to her stand, she reversed the rules by barring some people from coming. She boldly let it be known that she was vetting people to see whether they were influential enough to come in and review her designs.

As she later commented: 'People got very wound up and were so grateful when I let them in because they had met the so-called criteria. It tainted their judgement in my favour.'[117]

mountain and mohammed A huge number of gyms were set up during the health and fitness craze of the 1990s. The 'rules' were that individuals came to the gym which was nearest to their work or home. By reversing the rule so that the 'gym' came to the individual, a massive industry of personal trainers was created.

killing with kindness A striking example of rule reversal in the field of human politics was provided by the Russians in their alleged treatment of Polish Solidarity leader, Lech Walesa. Desperate to be rid of a political trouble-maker, and anxious to avoid antagonising the West by being seen to kill him, the Russian authorities sought to look after him extremely well. It is widely thought that by making available inexhaustible quantities of high-fat food and high-tar cigarettes, the Russians hoped to trigger a heart attack in Walesa.

By turning this objective upside-down into how they would not kill Walesa, the Russians could discover the opportunity to exploit to their advantage his well-known penchant for life's good things.

what's waste to one is profit to another The application of the rule reversal technique to conventional waste products can be equally productive, as evidenced by the creation of Blu-tack, the all-purpose adhesive which began life as the dregs of a polymerisation process. By the same token, the Waterford Crystal Factory in Waterford, Eire, derives significant turnover from repurposing glassware with air-bubbles in it as novelty products.

the steps to reverse rules The simple steps for effective rule reversal are as follows:

1 State in clear and simple terms the market or product situation as is.

2 Reverse the direction of the statement.

3 Write down each reversal as a new opportunity statement.

4 Use each reversal as a stimulus for new ideas.

assumption reversal

A sibling of rule reversal, assumption reversal is also a distant relative of some of the boundary-examination techniques which we discussed in the previous chapter. Rather than reverse the current market situation, this technique reverses the assumptions underlying the current market situation.

This technique was developed by consultant Steve Grossman, who recognised that the assumptions we make about opportunities and problems often affect our ability to solve them.[118] Reversing these assumptions can sometimes produce unique perspectives which, in turn, can trigger creative ideas.

Dell reversed the computer market assumption that computers were packaged goods which could not be sold direct to customers. This assumption reversal led Dell to create a direct channel of communication to the consumer, offering reliable and customised products.

Ryanair and easyJet reversed the market assumption that airline travel must involve high service levels and airports close to major city centres.

IKEA reversed the assumption that pre-assembled furniture targeted at a middle-aged market should be distributed from city-centre sites. First Direct reversed the assumption that you have to meet your bank manager face to face to create a trusting and effective relationship. It recognised that perhaps the last thing on earth most people want to do is to meet their bank manager.

Jill Barker challenged the assumption that all modern nappies had to be disposable by launching her Green Baby shop in 1999 with a product range focused on washable chemical-free nappies. She reinforced her challenge to convention by painting her shop in north London bright pink, so that it would be noticed.

the steps to reverse assumptions

1   List the generally held assumptions about the particular product, service or marketplace, no matter how obvious or trivial they may seem.

2   Reverse each assumption in any way possible – there is no 'correct' way to do this, you are just on the look-out for all and any alternative options which may present themselves.

3   Use each assumption reversal as a stimulus for suggesting new ideas.

moving to step three
By working through this chapter, you will have built up a wide range of ideas around your basic business concept. Assuming that you have successfully deferred all critical judgement, your next challenge will be to evaluate and select from the range of ideas you have generated. In other words, you have used predominantly divergent thinking to generate the ideas; you must now employ predominantly convergent techniques for evaluation and selection, a process which involves converting ideas into practical and practicable solutions.

As we saw with the first step of seeking and shaping opportunities, it pays to identify clusters or 'hot-spots' of similar ideas if you have managed to generate a substantial number of them. Clustering does not lose any ideas; rather, the ideas are incorporated as sub-sets of the clusters and become more manageable.

it pays to identify clusters or 'hot-spots' of similar ideas

You must now prioritise the ideas so that it is the most promising ones which you take forward first to the next step of evaluating and selecting the business solutions to seize those opportunities. As with the previous step, this need to prioritise reveals that you are in a Catch-22 position – in order to prioritise rationally the ideas for evaluation and selection at Step Three of the idea development process, you already need to have gone through the third step.

The best way for you to break out of the impasse of prioritising from among multiple ideas is to use a whole-brain approach.

Your assumption reversal may have created perspectives which allow your left-brain to influence the decision – some ideas may appear significantly more attractive from a financial perspective than others, for example. This is well illustrated in the following case study on archetypal innovator Thomas Edison, whose left-brain business acumen allowed him to reject the technically superior option for his new light bulb filament in favour of a commercially less risky alternative.

You may also reflect whether the business idea appears durable, timely and capable of sustaining a product or service which creates or adds value for its buyer or end-user.

In large part, however, you will have to rely on your gut-feel and intuition to make your decision. Having been through the techniques explored in this chapter, you are probably the person best placed to make that subjective judgement. After all, Howard Head sensed the pattern between the ski market and the tennis racket market before he made himself a 'left-brain expert' in every area of conventional tennis racket manufacture.

Remember that there is nothing to be lost by this method – you are not screening out ideas, you are merely prioritising them for further work.

Thomas Alva Edison – idea generator *par excellence*[119]

in many ways, Edison is the archetypal successful innovator. With a record number of 1,093 patents for different inventions to his name, he combined right-brain imagination with left-brain business acumen to make things happen in a way that went far beyond the description of Edison as mere inventor. It is little wonder that British politicians so often enviously cite Edison when they bemoan the British inability to capitalise on ground-breaking invention.

Edison was born in Milan, Ohio, in 1847. His start in life was not auspicious. Born into a family of seven children, of whom only four survived, he received just three months of formal schooling. However, in addition to being taught at home by his ex-schoolteacher mother, he fed his inquisitive mind by reading voraciously and experimenting continually.

His innate and irrepressible commercial streak first manifested itself when at the age of 12 he started selling newspapers and journals from the Grand Trunk Railway. By the age of 15, he was publishing his own weekly, the *Grand Trunk Herald,* focused on local issues and railroad matters, which he printed in the baggage coach in which he had also established a chemical laboratory.

A fire which broke out in his travelling chemical laboratory led to Edison's permanent expulsion from the train. Matters took a turn for the better when Edison saved the child of a local station-master from walking in front of a slow-moving train. Edison's reward was to be taught all the intricacies of telegraphy: the Morse-code based communication method patented in 1840 which represented the 'information superhighway' of the day.

In pursuit of knowledge and experience, Edison used this new-found expertise in telegraphy to go 'on the tramp', working as an itinerant telegraph operator across the South and Midwest of the United States. Since telegraphers not only sent and received messages but also had to keep the equipment running, Edison learned a lot about practical energy – how batteries work, how to wire circuits and so on.

In 1868, at the age of 21, Edison secured his first patent, for an electrical vote recorder designed for the Massachusetts State Legislature. The politicians' failure to adopt the system meant that his first invention was not a commercial success. The experience led to two key realisations, however: firstly, never invent something which people don't want, and secondly, regard every wrong attempt discarded as a way forward.

Edison's in-depth knowledge of telegraphy led to his first successes. His 'Universal Stock Printer' for printing stock prices from the ▶

telegraph improved upon the so-called 'stock-ticker', the stock printing instrument first developed by Edward Calahan.

Edison's invention of the quadruplex telegraph system allowed more than one message to be sent in one direction over a single wire. Recognising the significant profit-improvement possibilities which the innovation offered to the telegraph companies, Edison approached the Western Union Telegraph Company. When the company asked Edison to name his price, Edison reversed the rules by inviting Western Union to make an offer. Its offer of $40,000 was in marked contrast to the figure of $2,000 which Edison had previously had in mind.

The $40,000 contract from Western Union allowed Edison to found a research and development facility in rural Menlo Park, New Jersey in 1876. Nicknamed 'the Invention Factory' by Edison, the Menlo Park complex housed a laboratory, machine shop, office and a library. With literally everything which could be needed for effective innovation available under one roof, it was the first facility of its kind in the world.

'The Invention Factory' was staffed by a large range of specialists who were often fresh from college or from technical training and became known as 'muckers'. The laboratory also included a pipe-organ, which Edison would play to accompany the singing, beer and sandwiches which were a feature of the regular late-night working sessions among the muckers.

Edison was always prepared to challenge conventional thinking with these 'muckers'. When he wanted Reginald Fessenden to work as a chemist, for example, Fessenden protested that he had been trained as an electrician. Edison replied: 'I have had a lot of chemists . . . but none of them can get results.'

Edison first became involved with telephones when Western Union retained him to circumvent some of Alexander Graham Bell's patents for the Bell telephone. Edison duly came up with a carbon button transmitter which formed part of the telephone's mouthpiece and which vastly improved the transmission of the speaker's voice across the wires.

While working to improve the efficiency of a telegraph transmitter, Edison noted that the machine's tape gave off a noise resembling spoken words when played at high speed. This analogy caused him to wonder whether he could record a message for the telephone system with which he was now familiar. In subsequently exploring the underlying principle of recording, Edison was led to consider recording any sound and playing it back as something separate. The resulting experiments led to the invention in 1877 of the tinfoil phonograph, by which sound could be recorded mechanically on a tinfoil cylinder.

Edison initially expected the phonograph to be of most use to businesses for dictating letters. In the *North American Review* of 1878, however, he published an extraordinarily prescient 'brainstormed' list of possible further applications for the product, including books for the blind, music, speaking clocks, elocution aids, the 'family record', including the last words of the dying, and the preservation of native languages. Edison can also lay claim to having invented the term 'distance learning', given the inclusion within the brainstormed list of 'educational purposes, such as preserving the explanations made by a teacher, so that the pupil can refer to them at any moment, and spelling or other lessons placed upon the phonograph for convenience in committing to memory'.

Edison demonstrated his ability to see the complete opportunity, to think outside the box, by effectively creating the recording industry during the subsequent process of making the phonograph practical. His company not only manufactured phonographs but also ran recording studios, produced cylinder recordings of some of the most famous talent of the day and produced the range of manufacturing equipment which the new industry required.

Although Edison's name is perhaps most closely associated with the incandescent electric light bulb, he did not in fact invent the lamp bulb; Humphry Davy had invented the first electric light in 1809 and Joseph Swan invented the first practical long-lasting electric light bulb in 1879.

Edison perceived the mass-market opportunity for refining the existing ideas to create a practical product which was safer and less flickering than the open-flame gas lights prevalent at the time and less intensely bright than the electric carbon-arc commercial and street lights also in existence.

The selection of the carbon filament was not the Eureka moment of myth. It was only after testing more than 1,600 materials to identify the correct filament, including coconut fibre, fishing line and even hairs ▶

from a friend's beard, that Edison and his muckers finally settled in 1879 on carbonised bamboo. It also benefited from a left-brain commercial decision. Working entirely separately, Edison and his British competitor Joseph Swan had both identified that platinum represented the best technological solution. Overturning Swan's assumption that the best technical solution was also the best commercial solution, however, Edison demonstrated his left-brain acuity by rejecting platinum because of its cost and the risk that continuity of supply could not be guaranteed.

Crucially, Edison realised that solving the issue of the bulb filament was only a small part of a far bigger jigsaw puzzle – the real opportunity lay in designing and delivering the electrical infrastructure to make the lights operate in a practical, safe and economical fashion. Edison clearly defined the opportunity when he stated that 'Electricity is not power – electricity is a method of transporting power.'

Edison combined what he had learned about electricity from his telegraphy experience with what he knew about gas lighting to create an electrical infrastructure. To achieve this, some seven system elements had to be developed, including improved dynamos for generating the necessary electric current; the underground conductor network; devices for maintaining constant voltage; safety fuses and insulating materials; and light sockets with an on-off switch.

Edison's marketing skills put those of Joseph Swan into the shade. While Swan demonstrated electric lighting in just one merchant's house, Edison's Pearl Street power station in New York City's financial district sent electricity to lights in 25 buildings in September 1882. This was a brilliant way to attract the attention, and the funding, of the Wall Street bankers whose support would be needed for rolling out the project. And while Edison realised that electricity was undoubtedly what would now be termed a disruptive technology, he positioned the product in terms which the consumer could understand, as an improved 'mimic' of the existing gas-lighting system.

Edison's left-brain business savvy extended to attacking Swan by suing the Swan United Electric Light Company for infringement of the Edison patents. Swan's backers joined Edison and a merger created the Ediswan Company which monopolised the British market until 1893. Edison's various electric companies were brought together into Edison General Electric in 1889.

Edison's ability to transfer the sound-recording analogy to the world of pictures was encapsulated in his 1888 submission to the Patents Office, describing his ideas for a device which would 'do for the eye what the phonograph does for the ear, which is the recording and reproduction of things in motion, and in such a form as to be both cheap, practical and convenient'.

Edison developed a motion picture camera called the kinetograph, as well as a projector called the kinetoscope, the first machine to produce motion pictures by a rapid succession of individual views. Like a phonograph without discs to play, or like a light bulb without power to light it, the kinetoscope lacked films to show. As ever, Edison literally saw the bigger picture and established a studio on the laboratory grounds. Given the technical limitations of the lighting systems at that time, the studio's roof opened to let in sunshine. The studio itself was mounted on a turntable so that it could rotate to follow the sun. Covered in black felt, the studio was nicknamed the 'Black Maria', contemporary slang for police vehicles. Edison later combined his phonograph and kinetoscope to produce the first talking moving pictures in 1913.

Edison had his share of failures, including talking dolls, whose tiny integral phonographs were too fragile for effective commercialisation, and concrete furniture. But the sheer volume of ideas generated, coupled with his ability to extract value from apparent failure, always kept him moving forward.

Although his efforts to extract iron ore from exhausted mines failed, for example, he saw how the milling machine which he had developed could be applied in another setting, namely to produce Portland cement, a new building material gaining favour around the turn of the 20th century. The original Yankee Stadium was constructed of Edison Portland cement, proving Edison's dictum that 'Just because something doesn't do what you planned it to do doesn't mean it's useless'.

In 1928, Edison received the Congressional Gold Medal 'for the development and application of inventions that have revolutionised civilisation in the last century'. By stressing both development and application, the combination of left-brain and right-brain thinking, the award paid a fitting tribute to perhaps the consummate innovator who went beyond mere products to create entire industries.

key points

- The 'Eureka' moment is a myth

- Getting started with idea generation is often the most difficult part, but don't be tempted just to wait for inspiration to occur

- Start with what is in front of you and then develop your angles of attack

- Choose from among the full range of structured idea-generating techniques to develop new insights and to escape from conventional thinking

- The best way to get a good idea is to get a lot of ideas

- Wild, impractical ideas are often the stepping stones to highly innovative and workable follow-up ideas – delay your judgement until later

- Be on a continual lookout for new ideas, analogies and insights drawn from your everyday experience

- Keep your mind constantly open and never forget that the trouble with experts is that they always know why things cannot be done

5

five

step three– evaluating and selecting ideas

- Karan Bilimoria – brewing the criteria to achieve the 'big one'
- evaluation allows development, not just selection
- two-phase screening process
- evaluation frameworks for screening ideas
- criteria to use within the frameworks
- business-focused criteria
- person-focused criteria
- prototyping
- Gary Mueller and Internet Securities, Inc. – selecting a venture to suit his needs

Faced with many apparently possible ideas, how will you focus your efforts on developing the most promising, rather than spread yourself thinly across them all?

Your first task is to define 'promising'. Does the market want your idea and, most importantly, will the market pay for it? Is the idea feasible? How will the competition react? And so on.

Don't forget that these underlying questions aren't static – they should contribute to shaping your idea further. After all, Karan Bilimoria originally intended to import an existing Indian beer and elected to have his own Cobra brand brewed only when all the beers already on the market failed to satisfy his key criteria.

But 'promising' goes further than that. In particular, it asks: are you right for the idea and is the idea right for you? Do you have the resources to make it happen – contacts, know-how, money? Will the idea deliver what you want from life? Does it present the level of risk which you are prepared to accept?

Does this sound personal? It should do because you're probably the only person who can fully define what 'promising' means to you, and therefore evaluate and select ideas appropriately.

Does it sound impossible? It shouldn't do. Just look at the processes and techniques which others have successfully employed.

Karan Bilimoria – brewing the criteria to achieve the 'big one'[120]

Cobra beer's founder, Karan Bilimoria, exemplifies the process of establishing clear criteria by which to evaluate and select new business ideas.

Born of a well-connected and highly educated family in India, Karan Bilimoria had always wanted to achieve the 'big one'. Having gained a university business degree from Hyderabad, he read law at Cambridge University before qualifying as a chartered accountant. His extra-curricular exploits at Cambridge University included captaining the polo team and demonstrating his salesmanship by successfully canvassing door-to-door for the post of vice-president of the Students' Union.

His first business venture focused on the import of polo sticks from India, after the Falklands War had halted supplies from Argentina. Despite some success, and despite having considered a number of other import possibilities, including copper wire, leather luxury goods and fabric, his family still teased him for remaining an 'import/export wallah'.

His personal experience contributed to identifying the 'big one' to him. He realised that the Indian curry market was growing in the UK and that the lagers which predominated were a poor match to the Indian cuisine. As Bilimoria put it: 'Real ale and conventional lagers are too gassy for Indian food. They make you feel so bloated.'

his personal experience contributed to identifying the 'big one' to him

The analogy with French restaurants offering French wine, and Chinese restaurants offering Chinese or Asian beer brands such as Tiger or Tsing Tao, gave further credence in Bilimoria's mind to the compellingly simple concept of an Indian-produced beer to accompany Indian food. The idea lay dormant until it was given further impetus during the late 1980s by a chance meeting with a mentor. Bilimoria started to consider importing into the UK the Pals beer which was the main beer served in all the Indian army messes and which Bilimoria knew from his youth because his father had been a general in the Indian army. The option of Pals beer presented a number of obstacles, not least of which was the brand name's echo of a leading UK brand of dog food.

Encouraged by his earlier broad-brush findings, however, Bilimoria undertook further, more detailed research, which highlighted that no beer currently available met his evaluation criteria. These criteria included a strong, smooth taste combining the best qualities of beer and lager, the authenticity of Indian manufacture, plus a nine-month shelf-life to allow the beer to travel through an extended geographical distribution chain. These criteria screened out Pals beer, which in addition to its brand name difficulties did not travel well.

Bilimoria also discovered that the major competitors did not promote themselves heavily in the Indian restaurant sector. Although some data existed on the dynamics of the curry market, no specific research had been undertaken into the ethnic beer market. Confident that he had sufficient data to support his product concept, however, Bilimoria approached Mysore Breweries in Bangalore, the owner of Pals beer, with the request that they brewed his own brand of lager especially for export. Three months were spent in testing and trialling the new product under the expert guidance of the Czech-trained brew master.

Family networks helped Bilimoria identify a source of supply for bottles strong enough for export – bottles for consumption in the Indian home market were recycled and therefore of lesser quality. At 660 ml, the only standard bottles available off the shelf were considerably larger than the UK market norm which Bilimoria had initially specified. Demonstrating an ability worthy of the great Ingvar Kamprad himself to convert problems into opportunities, however, Bilimoria promoted the large bottles as proof of the beer's authentic Indian provenance. ▶

With its strong Indian connotations, Cobra was preferred as the brand name over the alternative of Panther. Bilimoria used his legal training to protect the Cobra brand worldwide. He elected not to patent the brewing recipe, on the grounds that protection was probably unenforceable and that the brand's strength would ultimately lie within its name.

The Cobra brand and product were capable of growth in a number of ways – through attacking mainstream markets outside the Indian restaurant market; through attacking additional global markets; by brewing the beer in other countries, close to market; and by diversifying into other product areas, such as wine, draught beer and lower-strength beer.

Bilimoria actively managed his business risk. When Cobra beer entered a distribution arrangement with Maison Caurette, for example, the level of ongoing debt which resulted was higher than Cobra could withstand if things went wrong. Bilimoria's decision to take out insurance to cover the risk was vindicated some 12 months later when the newly merged Ebury Caurette company went into liquidation. The £60,000 owed to Cobra was fully covered by the insurance.

Bilimoria's left-brain legal and accountancy training was complemented by a right-brain vision of producing the first truly global Indian beer. His whole-brain approach was evident in his assertion that 'every area of your business has to be creative – even raising money'.

His massive personal commitment to the business led him to share a cramped flat with his business partner and his new wife for what must have seemed an eternity. Nor did he shirk from personally delivering Cobra to London restaurants out of the back of 'Albert', his Citroen 2CV. Again, he turned the experience to good effect, forging effective personal relationships with the accounts on which he called.

The success of the 'big one' is demonstrated by Cobra's recent financial performance, with sales for 2004 exceeding £60 million in over 30 countries.

evaluation allows development, not just selection

The specific purpose of this third step of the idea development process – the evaluation and selection of ideas – is to winnow down the multiple ideas, perhaps between five and ten, which you have brought forward from the previous steps into one single leading idea whose implementation you will plan in the fourth step.

The over-arching spirit of Step Three is that the less promising ideas are eliminated early and with the minimum effort possible so that the maximum resource can be directed to the enhancement of the most promising ideas, the best of which goes forward to Step Four. The process is analogous with the medical system of *triage*, which rapidly screens out the cases which do not require specialist intervention from those which do.

The best idea resulting from Step Three will be the one which not only offers the greatest chance of success in the market but also most closely matches your own personal goals, skills, resources and appetite for risk.

The final outcome of the entire idea development process itself will be a robust and viable business idea which can subsequently be expressed in the detailed and structured formality of a business plan. This business plan will codify all the information which you have already gathered and interpreted to date in support of the business idea you have selected.

keeping development options open
Crucially, and in contrast to the final business plan, which provides a fixed plan plus supporting context for a given business idea, both Step Three and Step Four actively encourage and enable ideas to be developed further – reshaped, reconfigured, combined and enhanced.

We saw in the opening entrepreneurial profile how Karan Bilimoria established criteria for Cobra beer which screened out all products currently available on the market, requiring him to reshape his idea so that he commissioned his own brew direct from India, packaged in outsize but highly distinctive bottles. By the same token, we saw earlier how Thomas Edison developed selection criteria for the light bulb filament which would allow him to achieve his grand vision of conquering a mass market. Edison's selection criteria therefore ranked component cost and continuity of supply above pure technical performance. In contrast to his English competitor Swan, these criteria led Edison to reject the technically optimum solution of platinum because its cost was high and continuity of supply could not be guaranteed. Instead, Edison selected carbonised bamboo for the filament because it satisfied the leading criteria of cost-effective implementation and guaranteed supply.

balancing the elements within the business idea

The contrast between Amazon.com's Jeff Bezos and Darryl Mattocks, the founder of the Internet Bookshop, also illustrates the power of the evaluation and planning steps to continue to shape the idea and ensure that all elements of the business idea are in balance.

Bezos' vision for an online business was truly global. He recognised that the two criteria critical to achieving this vision – size of product range and ease of computer-enabled customer selection – would mean that the fixed costs of his visionary business would be very high, while the ongoing variable costs would be very low. As a result, Bezos articulated an early strategic objective for Amazon.com as GBF – Get Big Fast. His financial background gave him the confidence that he could assemble the financial backing required to deliver that strategy.

While Darryl Mattocks may have had a similar grand vision, he perhaps lacked the extreme personal drive and the access to finance enjoyed by Bezos. Because UK venture capitalists saw little potential in the internet and refused to back him, Mattocks depended on a loan of around £50,000 from the Blackwell family, together with the working capital he could generate from his credit card. Mattocks had no option but to scale his Internet Bookshop operations accordingly.

variation on the theme of GBF

A further variation on the themes of GBF and achieving harmony among the business idea elements throughout the idea evaluation step is provided by Body Shop. Anita and Gordon Roddick realised that the criterion of protecting their innovative but relatively easy-to-copy retail concept was best addressed by getting big fast and achieving national coverage. Given their limited financial resources, they selected franchising as a low-cost method of achieving GBF, thereby ensuring that all aspects of their business idea remained in balance.

two-phase screening process

Evaluating business ideas typically follows a two-phase process, with a coarse-screen exercise followed by a more detailed, finer-screened evaluation of those ideas which survive the first phase.

We saw in Chapter 3 how Jeff Bezos generated a list of around 20 product areas which appeared to offer the potential to succeed on the internet, including videos, computer hardware and software. He then force-ranked the product areas according to several different criteria, including that of 'being something that you could only do online, something that couldn't be replicated in the physical world'.[121] Bezos perceived that the sheer size of the product range was critical to internet success:

'First of all you can use computers to sort, search and organise. Second, you can create a super-valuable customer proposition that can only be done online, and that is selection. There are lots of categories where selection is proven to be important: books, in particular, with the book superstores, but also in home construction materials, with Home Depot, and toys with Toys R Us.'[122]

Bezos perceived that the sheer size of the product range was critical to internet success

Bezos used the first evaluation phase to narrow down the potential list of 20 ideas to just two product categories – music and books.

'there are no 800-pound gorillas in bookselling'
Books emerged as the favoured launch product from the second phase because of detailed consideration of two criteria in particular – size of product range and ease of access to supply. In terms of product range, Bezos noted:

'Books are incredibly unusual in one respect, and that is that there are more items in the book category than there are items in any other category by far. There are more than 3 million different titles available and active in print worldwide. Music is the number two category, and there are about 300,000 active music CDs.'[123]

In addition, the book market was highly fragmented from the supplier perspective. With 4,200 US publishers and the market share of the two biggest booksellers limited to 12 per cent, Bezos was reassured that 'there [weren't] any 800-pound gorillas in bookselling'.[124] In contrast, the music industry was controlled by just six major record companies, whose domination of record and CD distribution allowed them to lock out any new business which threatened the traditional record-store format.

It is worth noting that consistent with the recycling principle integral to the entire idea development process, Amazon.com's product range now includes music and videos, ideas which were initially screened out in favour of books.

evaluation frameworks for screening ideas

Although the actual criteria used will necessarily vary from business opportunity to business opportunity and will depend on your personal situation, a number of useful frameworks exist which can help you undertake a two-phase evaluation of business opportunities.

We will look at each of the frameworks in turn before turning to a more detailed discussion of some of the criteria which you may choose to include within the frameworks. The criteria will cover not only business issues but also your personal circumstances, resources and objectives. The overall process is shown diagrammatically in Figure 5.1.

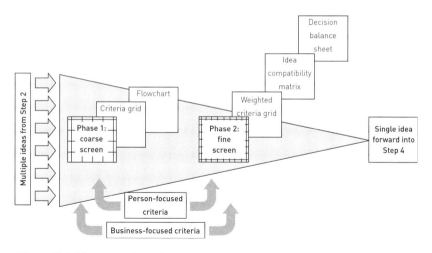

Figure 5.1 The two-phase idea screening process

phase 1: coarse screen

evaluation framework 1: criteria grid The criteria grid method allows you to judge possible business opportunities against a limited number of criteria. You could screen ideas against a specific market or type of opportunity, or against a rough-cut business assessment.

Imagine you are Jeff Bezos and you wish to screen down 20 possible product ideas for online retailing to a more manageable number. The first step is to generate a list of criteria appropriate to the situation – this requires both left-brain and right-brain thinking. You need to be imaginative – if internet security is a potential major concern, then perhaps low unit purchase cost should be a criterion, for example. List the criteria in the grid.

Identify a simple scoring system – perhaps from 0 to 3, where 0 is poor and 3 is excellent. Fill in the chart, taking care to complete one criterion for all alternative ideas before you move to the next criterion. Do not evaluate a single idea against all the criteria at once. This will help you avoid the 'horns and halo' effect where a rating against one criterion may bias your evaluation against other criteria. Again, you will have to apply judgement in the scores you ascribe – decimal point accuracy for the left-brainers is neither possible nor desirable.

Add up the totals to generate a ranking order, as in Figure 5.2.

Product category	Width of product range	Ease of accessing supply	Feasibility of remote selection	Low unit shipping cost	Low unit cost	Totals
Computer hardware	1	1	2	1	0	5
Videos	2	0	3	2	2	9
Music	2	0	3	3	3	11
Computer software	1	1	3	3	1	9
Books	3	3	3	2	3	14
Jewellery	1	3	1	2	0	7

Figure 5.2 Criteria grid for evaluating product categories for online retailing

sorting the wheat from the chaff It is important to remind yourself of the role and purpose of this coarse-screen evaluation grid. It provides the framework to screen out the clearly less promising ideas, but it is not intended to offer fine distinctions between ideas.

The grid does not account for all the relevant criteria – it is limited to the ones you deem most important. It is also unlikely that you will have at your fingertips the precise data to evaluate every idea 100 per cent accurately. The grid is highly valuable in sorting the wheat from the chaff, however, and in encouraging you to think more fully about the strengths and weaknesses of each business idea.

The same type of framework could equally be applied to the headline questions involved in assessing the overall viability of a business idea, as shown in Figure 5.3. We will discuss the actual over-arching criteria in more detail in later sections in this chapter.

Busines idea	Viable market opportunity	Practical feasibility	Ability to protect idea	Financial viability	Level of risk	Degree of fit with personal circumstances	Totals
#1							0
#2							0
#3							0
#4							0
#5							0
#6							0

Figure 5.3 Criteria grid for overall assessment of business ideas

evaluation framework 2: flowchart An alternative method of coarse-screening ideas is to use a simple yes/no flowchart in order automatically to select out ideas which do not satisfy the bare minimum criteria.

Once Karan Bilimoria had decided to source his beer from India, the bare minimum criterion was: does the beer possess a nine-month shelf-life? This single show-stopping criterion led him to screen out all existing products, even before he had applied any taste tests, leaving him no option but to commission the brewing of his own special brand of beer. Three months' worth of Indian-produced prototypes were then evaluated predominantly against their ability to combine the best qualities of beer and lager.

Within the corporate world, planners might quick-screen internal ideas against the scheme in Figures 5.4, for example.

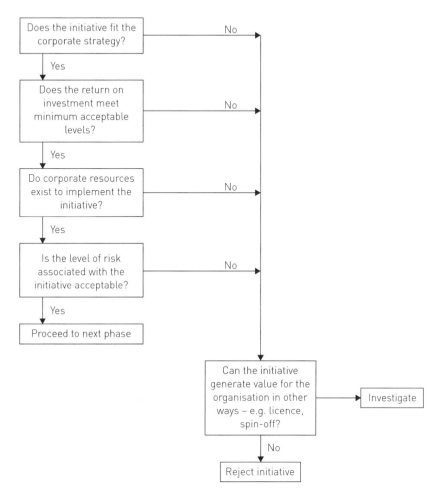

Figure 5.4 Flowchart to screen business ideas against corporate criteria

the instant entrepreneur Leading American entrepreneur Joline Godfrey illustrates perfectly how this type of coarse-screen evaluation may be applied by a major corporation. Having just completed the latest in a number of corporate assignments for Polaroid, Godfrey went on a brief holiday to Mexico

˙and came back with an idea for a business. It was just that simple. Away from the distractions of corporate politics, freed of routines that kept me neatly organized, safe from distracting phones and to-do lists, an idea surfaced . . .

For the next six months I researched, talked with people, travelled, and learned as much as I could about the viability of my idea . . . A full year after that crystalline moment in Zihuatenejo, Mexico, the CEO of Polaroid struck a deal with me: he would fund the development of a prototype and support me for a year if I would agree to spin off the company as a separate entity in which Polaroid would hold a minority position. I agreed before he could change his mind. In an instant, I had become an entrepreneur'.[125]

Godfrey's Mexican idea grew into Odysseum, Inc., which designed and delivered entertaining learning games to Fortune 500 companies. Centrepiece of the company's programme was Photo Odyssey, a film-based learning experience. Though a highly innovative and eventually successful venture, Odysseum, Inc. did not represent a perfect fit with Polaroid's strategic vision and was therefore screened out as an in-house initiative.

making the tough calls Evaluation criteria may also assist you in making tough choices which your emotions might otherwise find impossible. Pauline Pope developed an innovative wheelchair for cerebral palsy sufferers, which recognised that keeping the spine straight as the child grows can help to prevent future deformity.

Christened SAM (Seating and Mobility), her wheelchair design drew on an analogy with motorcycles, whose seating position forces the rider to lean forward on to the petrol tank, keeping the spine straight. Pope teamed up with Sunrise Medical in order to commercialise her design. Subsequent research identified that the product generated considerable interest in the market, but that demand was insufficient to justify the financial investment required by Sunrise Medical.

Although the product was innovative, served a valuable purpose in helping disabled children and offered apparent improvements over existing products, the company's responsibilities to its shareholders would have required it to treat considerations of profit and of business risk as the all-important screening criteria.[126]

phase 2: fine screen

evaluation framework 3: weighted criteria grid As the evaluation process moves from the coarse screens of the first phase to the finer screens of the second phase, you start to evaluate your ideas with more precision. In particular, you can start to weight the criteria according to how important they are, as well as score them. For Edison considering his light bulb filament, price and continuity of supply were more important than technical performance; for Bezos, width of range and a fragmented supplier base were the most important criteria in selecting which product area to pursue.

not all criteria are equal Weighting merely acknowledges that not all criteria are of equal importance in a given situation and to a given individual. For some individuals, for example, the ability to work from home in order to bring up a young family may be the most significant criterion. For others, it is the degree of financial reward. For yet others, it may be that keeping risk below a certain threshold, or ease of implementation, are the key factors.

Your choice of criteria and the weightings which you ascribe to them depend entirely on you. Weighting requires you to exercise judgement in ascribing relative weights to the various criteria. A simple solution is to assign a weighting of 10 to the criterion which you judge to be the most important and adjust the weighting figures given to the other criteria in proportion. In Table 5.1, Idea 1 attracts the same total raw score as Idea 3 but is beaten into second place by Idea 3 once the weightings have been taken into account.

your choice of criteria and the weightings which you ascribe to them depend entirely on you

Table 5.1 Example of weighted evaluation grid

Criteria	Weighting	Idea 1		Idea 2		Idea 3	
		Raw score	Weighted score	Raw score	Weighted score	Raw score	Weighted score
Ability to work from home	10	4	40	1	10	7	70
Low level of risk	8	6	48	2	16	7	56
High financial return	4	2	8	7	28	4	16
Low start-up investment	5	1	5	2	10	1	5
Leverage contacts from previous job	7	9	63	4	28	6	42
Avoid head-on competition with firm A	4	6	24	1	4	3	12
Total scores	–	28	188	17	96	28	201

Note: Raw score of 10 is perfect fit with criterion; raw score of 0 represents no fit with criterion

evaluation framework 4: idea compatibility matrix A further elaboration of the weighting technique is provided by the idea compatibility matrix. This technique matches the attractiveness of the business idea with its compatibility with your resources and goals; in other words, the degree of fit between you and the idea can serve as a screening and evaluation device, as shown in Figure 5.5.

Idea attractivness

		High	Medium	Low
Compatibility with personal circumstances	**High**	Excellent idea – implement	Good idea – implement	Offers drawbacks – may not work
	Medium	Good idea – implement	Offers drawbacks – may not work	Unlikely to work
	Low	Offers drawbacks – may not work	Unlikely to work	Unlikely to work

Figure 5.5 Idea compatibility matrix

Using online book retailing as an example, Jeff Bezos' grand vision would be positioned in the top-left high/high box, whereas Darryl Mattocks' initial grand vision might feature in the bottom-left high/low box, prompting him to reshape his initial idea.

As we shall see later, the key is to be self-aware – there is every merit in recognising that a positive idea in its current configuration may not suit your circumstances or specific abilities.

the benefits of an outsider's objectivity You do not have to be the inventor of an idea to see its potential. Often the reverse is true, where an outsider can perceive the massive potential in a business idea which the inventor or founder themselves perhaps cannot see, sometimes because of their circumstances or specific abilities.

you do not have to be the inventor of an idea to see its potential

We saw in Chapter 3 how Ray Kroc spotted the potential of the single fast-food outlet run by the McDonald brothers. The history of Starbucks exhibits a similar process of an outsider spotting the potential invisible to the founders or incompatible with their ambition. Starbucks Coffee, Tea and Spice was launched in Seattle in 1971 by three men – Jerry Baldwin, Zev Siegel and Gordon Bowker – who shared a passion for fine coffee and tea. Their determination to provide the best-quality coffee beans helped their business to expand to four stores in Seattle within a decade.

Enter Howard Schultz, who in 1981 was a vice-president at Hammarplast, a Swedish maker of stylish kitchen equipment and housewares. Noticing that the Starbucks coffee-bean store had been buying a significant volume of Hammarplast drip coffee-makers, Schultz emulated Ray Kroc and visited the account to find out more. Schultz had the big vision to appreciate immediately the possibilities of the coffee-bean culture and attempted to join the Starbucks operation with a plan to take the concept across the country. The founders did not share Schultz's bigger picture approach, but eventually hired Schultz to head Starbucks' marketing and to oversee the four Seattle stores.

the italian analogy Schultz took the idea further by spotting an analogy with the Italian market. On a visit to Italy he had noticed that coffee bars existed on practically every corner, not only serving excellent espresso but also acting as meeting places or public squares. Numbering around 200,000 throughout the country, they formed a large part of Italy's social framework.

Finding the Starbucks' founding trio unwilling to embrace his reshaped idea on the grounds that 'they had no desire to enter the restaurant business', Schultz struck out on his own. He launched Il Giornale, a string of speciality coffee stores in Seattle modelled on the typical Italian espresso bar. The concept was so successful that Schultz was later able to buy Starbucks for $3.8 million and initiate the programme of store and country roll-outs which has now made Starbucks ubiquitous.[127]

evaluation framework 5: decision balance sheet The decision balance sheet is a useful technique for combining person-focused criteria in an evaluation of specific business ideas. It can also be used for evaluating your whole approach to setting up on your own.

Devised initially by I. L. Janis and subsequently developed in conjunction with L. Mann in the late 1970s, the decision balance sheet helps you structure your decision making by exploring the costs and benefits, the advantages and disadvantages, of different proposed actions.[128] Costs and benefits can be explored not only from your perspective but also from the perspective of others who are significant to you – family, current employers, friends and mentors, perhaps.

Suppose that you want to assess the advantages and disadvantages of setting up on your own. You could construct the table shown in Table 5.2.

Table 5.2 Decision balance sheet for starting your own venture

Reasons to start your own venture	Reasons not to start your own venture
Negative elements about current employment status:	Positive elements about current employment status:
Benefits of starting your own venture:	Disadvantages of starting your own venture:

You should brainstorm ideas for each of the four boxes, taking into account your perspective and that of others significant to you. You should be well aware of the rules of divergent thinking by now and should apply them to this exercise. You can use any or all of the divergent techniques illustrated in previous chapters to generate and explore the ideas – challenge assumptions, seek analogies or use wild ideas to provoke unconventional insights.

When you have had your first attempt at the list, review each cell in the table in the light of your subsequent thinking, ask yourself 'what else?', and then cluster the related 'hits' into 'hotspots'. The finished article might look something like Table 5.3.

Table 5.3 Completed decision balance sheet for starting your own venture

Reasons to start your own venture	Reasons not to start your own venture
Negative elements about current employment status: ● Company won't modify product to address recurrent customer complaints ● Low staff turnover contributes to corporate unwillingness to experiment with new ideas	Positive elements about current employment status: ● Company's profitability is stable, job prospects appear secure ● Company health scheme includes subsidised cover for family ● Generous pension scheme
Benefits of starting your own venture: ● Exploit your insight of how product failure could be overcome by range of value-added products ● Strong personal relationship with major customer experiencing product faults ● Could team up with complementary business skills of partner who has recently been made redundant ● You've always wanted the freedom of being your own boss	Disadvantages of starting your own venture: ● Need for regular guaranteed income to support two teenage children, plus two dependent parents ● No experience of operating within small business sector ● Aggressive price-cutting promotion and legal challenge mounted by current employer against previous colleague who went it alone

Then score each entry using a 10-point scale, where a score of 1 is unimportant, while a score of 10 represents maximum importance. Add up the scores in favour of starting your own venture and compare them with those against. How clear-cut is the outcome? Is the outcome what you had intuitively expected? If not, why not?

A variant on the decision balance sheet described above analyses options in terms of four categories of expected consequences, namely:

● Tangible gains and losses for self

● Tangible gains and losses for significant others

● Self-approval or self-disapproval

● Social approval or disapproval.

Amazon.com – 'minimising regret' The relevance of this technique can be illustrated by Jeff Bezos, whose consideration of whether or not to establish Amazon.com was strongly influenced by what he called 'regret minimisation'.

He described the process during a revealing question and answer session at the Commonwealth Club of California as follows:

'I projected myself to age 80 and I looked back – already, I'm an optimist – and I said, "What I want to have done at that point is to have minimised all the regrets in my life." I knew when I was 80 that I would never, for example, think about why I walked away from my 1994 Wall Street bonus ... At the same time, I knew that I might sincerely regret not having participated in this thing called the Internet that I thought was going to be a revolutionising event."[129]

To apply the technique yourself, list the alternative ideas which you are considering, order them in terms of your initial personal preferences, and then construct a decision balance sheet for each option in the format shown in Table 5.4, following the divergent and convergent thinking processes described above. When you have created a 'trial' balance sheet for all options, review each again in turn to establish whether your later thoughts can spark off any new ideas or insights.

Table 5.4 Decision balance sheet[130]

	Positive anticipations	Negative anticipations
Tangible gains and losses for self:		
Tangible gains and losses for others:		
Self-approval or self-disapproval:		
Social approval or disapproval:		

You should then review all the balance sheets and rank them in order of scored preference. To what extent has the ranking order changed since your intuitive first sort? If so, can you identify why?

The decision balance sheet provides a helpful, structured assessment of alternative ideas from a personal perspective. It also highlights potential problems which you may encounter during implementation – planning how to overcome or at least mitigate these problems is the process which we explore more fully in the following chapter, using techniques such as reverse brainstorming and force-field analysis.

criteria to use within the frameworks

The criteria to use within the various evaluation and selection frameworks can be separated into two broad categories: those which are business-focused and those which focus on you as a person. Both of these broad categories contain a number of headline questions, as shown in Table 5.5. The following sections explore these headline questions. In relation to your personal circumstances and outlook discussed in the later sections, we also offer some simple diagnostic tools to increase your self-awareness.

Table 5.5 Headline criteria for evaluating business ideas

Business-focused criteria

- Existence of viable market opportunity
- Practical feasibility
- Ability to protect the idea
- Financial viability
- Level of risk

Person-focused criteria

- Type and scale of your ambition
- What resources can you access?
- What's your attitude to risk?

As with all the steps within the idea development process, the step of selecting and evaluating business ideas combines right-brain insightful thinking with left-brain analytical thinking. This step is not the purely logical exercise in left-brain thinking suggested by the traditional model of new idea development which 'front-loads' creativity into the initial stage only and throws all subsequent stages over the wall for the left-brained analysts and planners to complete. We described the limitations of this model in Chapter 2. It would be no use undertaking the most complex analytical weighting exercise if the criteria used were inappropriate, for example. In fact, the selection of assessment criteria will benefit from intuitive and imaginative thinking precisely because the criteria will tend to vary from person to person and from opportunity to opportunity.

business-focused criteria
The business-focused headline criteria against which to evaluate and select the various business ideas reflect to a large extent the fundamental questions which any subsequent business plan will require you to answer in more detail. At this stage of the process, however, you are interested in using ball-park figures to guide your decision making. As we discuss below, you should feel comfortable in making the type of simplifying assumption which allows you to see the bigger picture.

the bigger picture

We saw in Chapter 3 the importance of striking the correct balance between under- and over-analysing opportunities, avoiding 'paralysis by analysis' at the same time as ensuring that ideas could withstand at least a basic challenge through the financial numbers.

At this stage in the process, and ahead of the more detailed business plan, it is quite appropriate to adopt a broad-brush approach to the analysis, making simplifying assumptions where you can and avoiding spurious detail. The important element is to sort the wheat from the chaff as effectively and as quickly as you can, so that you maximise the time spent on the most promising ideas.

you don't need accuracy to two decimal points Sometimes, you may have no option but to work with rough-cut numbers. If you are working on your own, you will not enjoy the luxury of accessing the analysis of corporate research departments. You will be dependent on your own time and money and therefore more reliant on information which is already in the public domain.

sometimes, you may have no option but to work with rough-cut numbers

In addition, it may be that your product or service is addressing a market for which no data exists, either because it is too small to gather the attention of the market reporters because it is still in its infancy or because your business idea innovatively straddles a number of different sectors for which no aggregated data yet exist. Karan Bilimoria adopted the bigger picture approach with his Cobra beer, for example, unable to rely on any detailed market research concerning ethnic beers.

Simplifying assumptions may also be in your best interest. If a particular market is detailed to the nth degree, it is likely that others may perceive the same opportunity as you. Equally, a smaller operation can react faster to information which is incomplete, precisely because it is not constrained by a corporate hierarchical system of decision making based on extensive data.

like staff recruitment, only different The increasing level of detail applied to the evaluation and selection of business ideas is similar in nature to the process of recruiting senior staff into companies. The coarse-screening of applicants against key hurdle criteria creates a long list. This long list is then compared in more detail against the criteria of the job specification to create a short list of candidates who will then be assessed using a range of complementary techniques, including interviews, assessment centres and psychometric tests.

It is rare that a company relies on one single technique: it is impossible for the recruitment process to guarantee absolutely a successful appointment, and if the recruitment process takes too long, good candidates are snapped up elsewhere.

business-focused criterion 1: existence of viable market opportunity
The first criterion asks whether a definable market opportunity exists for your proposed product or service.

added-value advantage We saw earlier how the recently published study of three decades of enterprise policy in the Tees Valley had highlighted the risk of 'me-too' products or services driving competitors under on price before themselves suffering an early corporate death, without an added-value proposition to sustain their life.

You therefore need to be sure that you can demonstrate an added-value advantage and that your product or service meets a genuine need for which customers will be prepared to pay. The importance of customers' willingness to pay was poignantly illustrated in an earlier section by the SAM wheelchair, an innovative and socially valuable product which could not generate sufficient demand, however, to justify the financial investment required by Sunrise Medical.

market size Your immersion in the market during the fact-finding phase in step one of the idea development process will now allow you to answer critical questions about the size of the proposed market and its dynamics – is it growing, static or declining? Entering a declining highly competitive market normally represents a quite different challenge and risk to entering a high-growth new market.

competition You need to identify your competition and assess likely competitive reaction – will it allow you to survive? You should never underestimate the magnitude and intensity of competitors' potential responses.

you should never underestimate the magnitude and intensity of competitors' potential responses

The difficulty initially encountered by the cut-price easyCinema in securing first releases from the major vertically integrated film companies almost assumed the status of a 'fatal flaw' in the easyCinema concept. As its website noted with relief:

'easyCinema opened its doors in Milton Keynes a year ago and has been met with high consumer demand while it has struggled to get more and more recent films from distributors. In the past few months, easyCinema has been getting an increasing supply of first run films which tended to be art house or foreign language films. *Shrek 2*, however, represents a mainstream commercial film being shown on first run in easyCinema.'[131]

Mail-order lingerie company Bravissimo had to establish a dummy geographical presence to circumvent a supplier boycott engineered by a local competitor. As Sarah Tremellen, the founder, admitted: 'We decided to start up in Oxford, where my parents live. However, the company was in Oxford on paper only. We set up a P.O. box there and asked them to deliver to Twickenham in Middlesex; we also had a phone service on permanent divert.'[132]

viable route to market You need to be clear that a viable and clear route exists for you to reach the market. In the mid-1980s, Andrew Palmer identified the opportunity for a new food product, namely that of ready-to-eat fresh soup. His research rapidly identified that he would have sell his soup via independent retailers in order to validate the concept before the major UK supermarket chains would consider stocking the product.

In an iteration typical of the evaluation step, Palmer discovered that the independent sector would not risk stocking a new-to-the-world product which only had the four-to-five day shelf-life typical for chilled-food products. The critical success factor thus evolved into the ability to extend the shelf-life of a product made exclusively from natural ingredients. Extensive third-party expertise, including Reading University's Food Technology Department, assisted Palmer in developing a process which allowed a minimum 14-day shelf-life. New Covent Garden Soup Company was now on its way.[133]

You should also consider whether the market is so geographically dispersed that you cannot access it: is buying power concentrated in such a limited number of companies that a superficially attractive market is all but barred to new entrants? Can you reconfigure your business idea to overcome this obstacle or should the idea be eliminated from consideration?

business-focused criterion 2: practical feasibility

A blindingly simple question against which to screen possible ideas simply asks: 'Is this idea deliverable?' We saw in Chapter 3 how the bootleg team at Iridium failed to ask this basic question and overlooked the 'show-stopping' fact that political economics would prevent numerous national governments granting the licences needed by Iridium actually to operate its technically preferred system.

critical success factors A thorough exercise of challenging whether you can translate the seemingly good idea into practice will often highlight the handful of factors which are critical to the success of the venture and will provide some overall indication of the ease with which your business idea could be implemented.

Sometimes the critical success factors are so extreme that they represent a 'fatal flaw' in the business idea. easyCinema's initial inability to secure major first-release films came perilously close to this category, for example. Sometimes you will be able to use your creativity to generate options to overcome them, like Thomas Edison preferring the low cost and guaranteed availability of carbonised bamboo for the lamp filament over the technically superior but commercially risky platinum. At other times, you will say to yourself that a business idea is workable *provided that* this issue is resolved. For both the New Covent Garden Soup Company and for Cobra beer, for example, extended shelf-life represented this critical success factor.

business-focused criterion 3: ability to protect the idea

A further element against which to evaluate business ideas is your ability to protect the idea. Is the idea capable of legal protection, through patents, registered design or copyright?

In order to protect the value in the New Covent Garden Soup Company, for example, Andrew Palmer filed an application to patent the novel cooking process which radically extended the shelf-life of a product made exclusively from natural ingredients. In contrast, Karan Bilimoria protected the Cobra brand name rather than the brewing recipe.

protection other than the law Do other methods exist to protect your idea?

As we saw in Chapter 2, Phil Knight and Bill Bowerman were so successful in importing their running shoes from a distributor in the Far East that the distributor decided to benefit from the 'free' market research by entering the American market direct. The only strategy open to Knight and Bowerman was to manufacture the products themselves in order to protect their brand. Had they started off with own-manufacture, however, their risk and financial investment would clearly have been of a quite different magnitude.

Anita and Gordon Roddick sought to protect the Body Shop idea by perfecting the brand concept and achieving rapid national distribution at low cost through the establishment of a franchise network. In the next chapter, we will see how the Philippines-based Jollibee Foods Corporation also used franchising as a key strategy to restrict McDonald's to second place in the fiercely competitive market for fast food in the Philippines.

can you sustain your business idea? Linked to the idea of protection is the idea of sustainability. No product or service lasts for ever. How will you re-energise the offering, extend the range of products or services, enlarge the customer base, in order to maintain your business idea?

One of the huge strengths of the Cobra brand is its ability to expand, whether into new product areas or new geographical markets, ironically including India. By the same token, Jeff Bezos was clear from an early stage that 'we would focus on expansion into things where we could leverage . . . One is the brand name; two is the set of competencies; and three is our customer base.'[134]

business-focused criterion 4: financial viability

You need to consider whether your business idea offers an opportunity for an independent and financially viable business. To what extent will the likely costs of the business and the likely selling price allow the business to generate a viable profit in the long term? What is the length of time before you achieve break-even? Is the forecast cash-flow viable? How long is it before the cash-flow becomes positive?

Consistent with the bigger picture argument advanced earlier, a back-of-envelope calculation which immediately highlights that the business idea in its current form cannot generate a sustainable cash-flow is more valuable to you than a slavishly developed month-by-month spreadsheet analysis which covers the next decade.

business-focused criterion 5: level of risk We saw in

Chapter 1 that 33 per cent of business start-ups in the UK cease trading within three years. That statistic is a stark reminder that it is impossible completely to eliminate risk. You need to identify the major risks associated with your venture and assess their combined impact and likelihood.

33 per cent of business start-ups in the UK cease trading within three years

risks exist to be managed, not eliminated You should consider plans to manage, reduce or eliminate the major risks highlighted by the analysis. Howard Head, for example, learned from the quality control problems encountered during in-house manufacture of his revolutionary skis that he should eliminate the complex technical risks which the own-manufacture of his outsize aluminium tennis rackets might entail. He achieved this by out-sourcing their production to third-party experts, namely Kunnan Lo in Taiwan.

But residual risks will inevitably remain. As we will see later, your task is to assess what level of risk you will accept.

a step too far with sock shop Under City pressure to expand her UK-based Sock Shop empire, Sophie Mirman launched Sock Shop into the United States. Locating outlets in inner-city stations was a formula which had succeeded in the UK but which did not translate to the US, where high levels of drug-related theft contributed to the launch's failure.

The costs of the high level of debt incurred to finance the expansion were exacerbated by the doubling within one year of interest rates. Sock Shop went into administrative receivership. With the glorious benefit of hindsight, it was a risk which should never have been taken because the company could not afford to lose.

real life keeps intruding In addition, some external eventualities cannot reasonably be foreseen. As we saw in Chapter 1, Trevor Baylis had to abandon his battery-powered shoe concept following the alleged 'Shoe Bomber' episode. Karan Bilimoria had just launched the high-budget 'Curryholic' advertising campaign with Team Saatchi to capitalise on Cobra beer's dominant market position when an article in the *Tandoori* trade magazine which Bilimoria part-owned but over which he exercised no editorial control severely antagonised the Indian curry houses which accounted for the majority of Cobra's turnover. The Cobra business almost went under.

At a less dramatic level during this step of evaluating and selecting ideas, you need to be considering such major risks as the unreliability of customer orders, over-optimistic sales projections, inability to manufacture to appropriate specification and quality levels, and inability to achieve your cost and time estimates. You need to be aware of the realities of starting up – because you may have to chase accounts which other more established players avoid; for example, your risk of bad debts will be correspondingly higher.

innovation and risk The level of risk is also related to the degree of innovation involved. The very highest levels of innovation carry very high risks of failure. Edison demonstrated best practice in innovation management when he promoted electricity to the market as an improvement to gas lighting, for example, rather than as a completely new concept which the market might have rejected outright.

'Me-too' products and services which merely copycat existing market offerings and are devoid of any innovation can be equally risky. The Tees Valley study quoted previously highlighted the significantly high failure rate of new business start-ups in Cleveland during the 1980s. Almost 25 per cent of the start-ups during that period were low entry-cost activities such as motor vehicle repairs, hairdressing and beauty salons, almost exclusively focused on the immediate locality.

Table 5.6 demonstrates the complex relationship between risk of failure, ease of evaluating the opportunity and profit potential. Where on the spectrum would you place your business idea in its current configuration?

Table 5.6 Opportunity conditions associated with new venture innovation[135]

Opportunity conditions	New invention	Highly innovative	Moderately innovative	Slightly innovative	Copycat
Risks	Very high	High	Moderate	Moderate to low	Very high
Evaluation	Very difficult	Difficult	Somewhat difficult	Easy	Easy
Profit potential	Very high	High	High to moderate	Moderate to low	Low to nil

The following sections will help you to explore the extent to which your appetite for risk matches the level of risk which your business idea offers.

person-focused criteria
Being aware of what you actually want to achieve with your business idea, how far you want to go, and being aware of your ability to do so are essential pre-requisites for evaluating business ideas effectively.

As with the business-focused criteria in the previous section, the following person-focused criteria reflect the fundamental issues which any subsequent business plan will require you to answer in more detail. In addition, the criteria reflect two key questions which you should continually be asking yourself, namely: 'Is this venture right for me?' and 'Am I right for this venture?'

person-focused criterion 1: type and scale of your ambition
Jeff Bezos was prepared to sacrifice his home in New York to settle in Seattle, which provided access to a vast pool of computer talent and which was very close to one of the world's largest book wholesalers. In contrast, Darryl Mattocks was highly attached to the university city of Oxford and unwilling to move.

Neither attitude to business start-up was right or wrong. However, it is clear that each attitude exercised a distinctly different influence on the type of business venture which each entrepreneur went on to establish.

honest self-awareness You need to be honest with yourself about the scale of your ambition. Are you like the founders of Starbucks, content to enjoy success within the boundaries of their original retail formula and location, or are you like Howard Schultz, impatient to take on the world?

You need to be honest with yourself about the scale of your ambition

Are you seeking to start up a business so that you can enjoy a more flexible lifestyle, have an outlet for an artistic or sporting talent, or experiment with technologies which interest you? Is it your life ambition to create a business which carries your name and which can be passed on to future generations?

breaking through the glass ceiling Is it the self-fulfilment of being your own boss which drives you?

Chey Garland left school at 16 to work as an office junior. Her secret dreams of becoming managing director were thwarted by the reality that the only women who broke through her employer's glass ceiling were middle-class and well educated. She realised that she would attain her fantasy of becoming managing director of a company only by setting up on her own. Her eponymous company, Garlands Call Centres, generated pre-tax profits in 2004 of £3 million on a turnover of £30 million.[136]

pioneering the concept of 'women returners' Dame Stephanie Shirley founded Freelance Programmers in order to have an intellectually challenging job which fitted in with her plans for a family. One of her many brilliant insights was to realise that she was not alone in wanting to combine a vigorous professional career with bringing up a family.

Xansa (the £2 billion capital company which grew from Freelance Programmers via the FI Group) pioneered the concept of 'women returners' and began as a company of women, for women.

It also began with just £6 of capital.[137]

what are you able to put into the business? Are you like Jill Barker, typical of many start-ups in using a £45,000 redundancy payment to establish Green Baby, or are you like Frederick Smith, risking a multi-million-dollar family trust to establish Federal Express, thereby realising a business idea first articulated in a business school paper?

what will you take out of the business? Are you interested in securing sufficient regular income to survive comfortably? Are you interested in securing quick profit? Or are you committed to achieving significant capital gains from the establishment and sale of a business?

supporting a way of life If your wish is to generate sufficient cash-flow to support a certain way of life, then you do not need to create a business which has an existence fully independent of you. You are in charge 24/7 and if the business were to grow too large, it might prevent you from being personally involved in all aspects of the work or from enjoying your lifestyle.

selling on For those who wish to sell their business in due course, however, an organisation's ability to survive without the hands-on involvement of the founder will inevitably represent a pre-condition for eventual sale. It also means that the founder will have to learn new skills to achieve this transformation, unlike the founder-managers of small enterprises who perform all crucial tasks in their organisation and never have to change their fundamental role.

These new skills will allow the founder to evolve from doing the work, to training others to do it, to establishing outcomes for that work, and finally to managing the context in which the work is undertaken through a more formalised infrastructure and processes.

Can you see yourself evolving in this fashion? Can you make the leap from gifted musician, adept at a number of different instruments in the orchestra, to being part-composer, part-conductor?

personal choices As before, there is no right or wrong answer. It all depends on you, but what you want will inevitably shape the evaluation and selection of business ideas. You need to be aware of what you will be comfortable with and of just how committed you are to the realisation of your product or service idea.

'a proper selfishness' It was Charles Handy who coined the term 'a proper selfishness' to describe the level of commitment required to achieve your potential.[138] Achieving a successful start-up propels 'a proper selfishness' to a new level – success will almost inevitably require an almost improper 24/7 obsession.

Karan Bilimoria worked all hours to bring Cobra beer to fruition, sharing a cramped flat with his business partner and his new wife, delivering the beer personally to the London accounts from 'Albert', his battered Citroen 2CV. Julian Metcalf and Sinclair Beecham, the founders of Pret a Manger, shopped for the food themselves at local markets before making the sandwiches each morning. Their Sunday evening routine regularly involved going to what was then their only store to cook 25 chickens to be ready for the following morning.

Are you ready and able to deliver this level of personal commitment? And are those around you, especially your family, prepared to allow you to do so?

person-focused criterion 2: what resources can you access? Reviewing your checklist of resources is an important element in the process. Finance inevitably features high on the list, but is by no means the only resource which you should consider. Contacts, knowledge and know-how are also extremely important.

finance With the typical business start-up, venture capital is not the most likely source of funding. The ability of Jeff Bezos or Frederick Smith to structure multi-million-dollar deals is unusual. Your own savings, redundancy payments, a remortgage on your house, loans from friends and family, bank loans, credit from suppliers, government-funded start-up loans or research grants, with possible additional funding from business angels, are all much more likely options to begin with.

The underlying question to answer here is the extent to which you are able to access the level of finance required by the proposed business idea in its current configuration. Can you reduce your financing needs by gaining extended credit from suppliers, for example, or by gaining the free use of resources, like Richard Branson, who secured the premises for his first Oxford Street record shop rent-free? Or can the need for finance be reduced by a different configuration of the business model, like the franchise model which gained the cash-strapped Body Shop the means to achieve rapid national distribution?

contacts The significance of contacts as a resource should not be underestimated. Contacts can open doors to customers, suppliers and sources of finance. They can offer temporary facilities; they can provide endorsement to third parties for you; they can contribute insight and ideas for further development; and they can use their own networks to put you in contact with additional specialist expertise. Karan Bilimoria used his extensive network in India, for example, to source a beer bottle which would survive distribution to the UK.

Sometimes a customer's loyalty to an organisation's employee exceeds loyalty to the organisation. If you currently working for a firm, how strong are your ties with customers – if you strike out on your own, will customers risk coming with you rather than stick with the security blanket of the established organisation? And if the customers do come with you, how will your previous organisation react commercially?

An established network of contacts is also an important selling argument to providers of finance. Strong contacts allow you to overcome the objection that you are new to the business – you may be a 'start-up virgin' but your strong contacts will form an important part of the 'the 50,000 chunks of experience' evoked by Nobel prize-winner Herbert Simon, of the Department of Psychology at Carnegie-Mellon University, as prerequisites for successful entrepreneurs. Ask yourself: how strong is your network? How assiduously have you maintained it? How committed to you personally as well as commercially are its members?

knowledge and know-how Alongside who you know is what you know – how good is your industry knowledge and experience? When you are acting on your own behalf, will you be able to exercise the same authority and impact which you might previously have gained from working for an established brand name? Where you have gaps in your knowledge, how quickly can you fill them, either by accessing the knowledge directly, by identifying an individual or organisation with the relevant knowledge, or by involving a specialist broker such as Knowledge Transfer Partnership?[139]

In the early days of the business, you as founder will be performing most if not all the tasks associated with running a business, from selling to invoicing to keeping the books. Have you got the skills at the basic level, together with the commitment to do this?

person-focused criterion 3: what's your attitude to risk?

We saw earlier in this chapter how you should identify the major risks from a business perspective. It is equally important that you gauge your own attitude to risk. An effective starting point is to consider what you might be risking by setting up your own venture.

what are you putting at risk? Establishing any venture creates enormous strain on you, those around you and your resources. The risk that the venture might fail exacerbates the strain by placing four different elements of your life at risk: your finances, your career, your family and friends and your emotional well-being.

financial risk For most new start-ups, the individual will have to commit a significant proportion of their savings and other resources, up to and including their house. The long-term comfort of a regular monthly salary will almost inevitably feel like a thing of the past. Should the venture fail, all your resources are likely to be lost.

Are you prepared to risk personal bankruptcy in order to start your own business? Could you withstand the pressures evoked by Anne Notley, co-founder of the Iron Bed Company, when she wrote: 'You have to have nerves of steel and be prepared to take risks. You have to be able to put it all on the line knowing you could lose everything.'[140]

career risk Although the pre-start-up phase of a new business venture can sometimes be undertaken within the organisational comfort of paid employment, the moment comes when you have to sacrifice salary, benefits and apparent security to dedicate yourself full-time to your new venture. Should the venture fail, is there any way back to your former employer? Will you be stigmatised in the eyes of other potential employers by apparent failure?

family and social risk When a journalist asked whether she was able to see or speak often to her busy husband, Veronica Berlusconi, wife of the Italian prime minister, had her tongue firmly in her cheek when she replied: 'Yes, I not only speak to him on the telephone, sometimes I even see him on the television.'[141]

The time commitment and 'proper selfishness' described earlier in connection with starting a business are no different to being the Italian prime minister, except that you probably appear on television slightly less frequently – starting a business can actually deprive your family of a whole slice of their life.

It may be that the money is simply not available to recruit outside talent of the appropriate calibre to help you run the operation. Alternatively, potential recruits may feel your venture is too risky an investment of their career. In these cases, there is a real risk that you become locked in to the business, working hours which never seem to end, and that you remain constantly at the mercy of sickness or burn-out.

If your business crowds out your family, what chances do your friends stand? If the business succeeds, will you consider that the sacrifice has been worthwhile? And suppose the business fails, what then?

emotional well-being The psychological impact of a financial disaster can be dramatic and long-lasting. Have you got the emotional resilience required to bounce back if your venture fails?

That is not to say that it cannot be done – Sophie Mirman bounced back from Sock Shop by founding Trotters, offering couture for kids, for example – but the difficulties of accomplishing this type of comeback are not to be under-estimated.[142] Are you prepared to risk having to put your emotional resilience to the most extreme test?

These types of risk incurred by entrepreneurial start-up can be compared against 'conventional' careers within organisations, as Table 5.7 demonstrates.

risk comfort zone You need to consider all the elements described above in defining the borders of your risk comfort zone. Clarity over your attitude to risk will allow you to eliminate ideas which in their current configuration fall outside this comfort zone.

Table 5.7 A comparison between the potential of entrepreneurial and conventional careers for satisfying economic, social and personal development needs[143]

	Entrepreneurial career	Conventional career
Economic needs	Can offer the possibility of high financial rewards in the long-term.	Financial rewards typically lower, but secure and predictable.
	Income may be low in early stages and risks are high.	Risks are relatively low.
Social needs	Entrepreneur creates organisational change.	Established organisation usually provides good stage for making social relationships.
	A great deal of freedom to create and control network of social relationships.	Manager may have only limited scope to control potential of social relationships formed.
	Social status of the entrepreneur usually high.	Social status of manager variable.
Personal development needs	Entrepreneur in control of own destiny.	Good potential to pursue personal development.
	Possibility of creating an 'entire new world'.	The direction of personal development may need to be compromised to overall organisational objectives and values.
	Venture may be powerful vehicle for personal development and expression of personal values. However, this is dependent on success of venture.	Career options limited and subject to internal competition.

It may be that the risk analysis will trigger you to reconfigure your business idea – licensing an innovative idea rather than implementing it yourself will reduce your personal risks, albeit by trading off the level of your return. The analysis also provides a framework for evaluating those ideas which remain within the frame.

Figure 5.6 highlights that not every entrepreneur shares the same attitude to risk and return. In the model, profit seeking is associated with a strong desire to maximise profits; activity seeking refers to other activities associated with entrepreneurship, such as independence or intrinsic interest in the work undertaken by the enterprise.

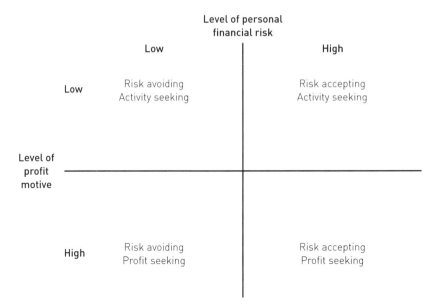

Figure 5.6 Identifying your risk comfort zone[144]

not every entrepreneur shares the same attitude to risk and return

In the case of Federal Express founder Frederick Smith, his active service during the Vietnam War contributed significantly to shaping his attitude to perceiving and accepting risk: 'I think probably my experience in the service [made me realize that] the currency of exchange in FedEx was just money, it wasn't people's arms and legs or lives . . . I was willing to take a chance, because losing wasn't the worst thing in the world that could happen to you.'[145]

What you need to do is to establish where within the grid your personal preferences place you. You then need to consider the extent to which the individual business ideas with their varying levels of risk match your risk comfort zone. If an idea does not match, you should consider either rejecting the idea or reconfiguring it so that it does match. Where an idea does match, you can evaluate the degree of the match as either strong, medium or weak, and carry the score forward into later stages of the evaluation.

prototyping

Although prototyping has a role to play throughout the idea development process, its role is particularly pronounced during the third step of evaluating and selecting ideas.

We saw earlier how Iridium's failure to undertake extensive technical prototyping deprived it of significant feedback before the big-bang launch in 1997, especially in terms of product performance inside buildings or on the streets of cities with tall buildings. Conversely, the positive impact of prototypes was demonstrated in the previous chapter by Darryl Lenz, who unwittingly prototyped a combined suitcase and child seat which prospective customers immediately wanted to buy.

getting stuck on Post-it® notes

The story of the Post-it note also illustrates the power of prototypes. Arthur Fry and his colleagues produced more than enough Post-it note prototypes to supply all of 3M's offices. The process of discovery which hit 3M employees when they first used the new-to-the-world concept was vividly described by Jack Wilkins, marketing director at the time: 'Once people started using them, it was like handing them marijuana. Once you start using it, you can't stop.'[146]

This addictive power was thrown into relief by the product's commercial launch, which initially relied on a brochure which omitted any samples. By itself, the brochure failed to generate any interest whatsoever.

a prototype is worth a million words

If a picture is worth a thousand words, a prototype is worth a million. While prototyping was once the province of large engineering projects, modern technology allied with imagination make the benefits of prototyping available to every venture.

A prototype does not have to be fully functional – it can be just a solid model to demonstrate shape, supplemented where necessary by working prototypes of key functional elements of the product to validate feasibility or demonstrate operation. The closer to implementation you are, the closer the prototype should be to the form of the first production unit. Estimates suggest that around 80 per cent of manufacturing costs are decided during the early design stages of a product, so the earlier you can eliminate failures the better. Much better to have screened out non-runners using rough non-functional models at a very early stage of the evaluation process than to have a close-to-reality prototype which suddenly reveals a 'fatal flaw'.

a prototype does not have to be fully functional – it can be just a solid model to demonstrate shape

There is nothing new about prototypes. Sir Christopher Wren built a large-scale model of the innovative St Paul's Cathedral which he had designed to replace the medieval cathedral lost in the Great Fire of London of 1666. The scale model allowed him to convince the various project stakeholders, from King Charles II to the City financiers, none of whom could interpret two-dimensional drawings, to approve his grand design.

Effective prototyping delivers a number of benefits, from the perspective both of designing the product or service and of selling it.

design benefits of prototyping
Prototypes form an integral part of the innovation process from the designer's viewpoint. Prototyping contributes to how the various elements of the product or service actually work. We have shown in previous chapters how extensive the prototype process can be: James Dyson created 5,127 versions of his Dual Cyclone vacuum cleaner; Thomas Edison prototyped over 1,600 materials to identify the correct lamp filament; and Howard Head saw more than 40 different ski designs literally destruction-tested before he found the winning formula. Focused prototyping allows critical problems to be resolved one by one.

The very act of prototyping will encourage further discoveries, precisely because prototyping requires you to challenge and explore boundaries. As Thomas Edison once remarked: 'The real measure of success is the number of experiments that can be crowded into 24 hours.'

sales benefits of prototyping
Individual language, culture and personal preconception can often prevent a shared understanding of what is being proposed. These communication problems are exacerbated when the subject under discussion is highly innovative and lacks a pre-existing frame of reference.

As we saw in the discussion on user observation in Chapter 3, qualitative market research on existing products can be misleading, let alone market research on products and services which are new to the market. Crucially for this phase of the idea development process, therefore, visual or physical prototypes allow customer feedback to be generated and communicated effectively.

see it, touch it, feel it, taste it You cannot beat customers actually being able to see, touch, feel and taste your product or service. New Covent Garden Soup Company created the idea of 'Soup of the Month', introducing a new and unusual flavour such as Spinach and Nutmeg on to retailers' shelves every month to evaluate customer reaction. Close monitoring of this real-time test market allowed informed decisions to be made on whether the prototype should be included in the standard product range.

ganging up on glitches Prototyping is standard practice in the software industry, where key users are granted access to new software ahead of full launch in order to facilitate product improvement and eliminate glitches.

you cannot beat customers actually being able to see, touch, feel and taste your product or service

Intuit routinely canvasses for customers to beta test forthcoming releases, acting on the maxim that the best way to refine your product is to share it early and often with potential end-users. This highly person-centred approach to prototyping was emphasised by *Inc.com* magazine's report of Intuit's 'Follow-Me-Home' testing method: 'Intuit representatives observe new users when they first use the product. "You watch their eyebrows, where they hesitate, where they have a quizzical look," says Cook [Scott Cook, founder of Intuit]. "Every glitch, every momentary hesitation is our fault." The testing helps the company figure out which areas to work on each time it updates its products."[147]

the slippery slope of commitment By suggesting improvements to prototypes, potential customers are starting to descend the slippery slope of commitment to the product or service which should result in orders for you. Exposure of the product or service prototype to potential customers also helps shift your focus from 'Can it be made?' to 'Will it add value to the customer when used?'.

There is no excuse not to use prototypes. Take the arts industry as an example. Before committing to full creative production, musicians routinely prepare demo tapes, while authors develop plot outlines and sample chapters. Film studios regularly make a mockery of artistic integrity by previewing films with different versions of the ending to judge from real-life feedback which of the endings plays best with the audience.

prototyping for services

Prototypes are as relevant to services as they are to products. In the late 1990s when the internet was still in its infancy, the Prudential bank was considering the launch of a telephone- and internet-based banking venture. The bank considered that while using a name such as pru.com would allow the bank to capitalise on the brand's equity, the stretch between the image of Prudential and the new brand was too big. The brand name of Egg made its way on to the shortlist by virtue of breaking all known rules of the stuffy banking world, as well as being simple and easy to remember.

But would it work? The agency team mocked up the brand as it would look after the launch, with a complete suite of Egg credit cards, chequebooks and advertising. Significantly, prospective customers were shown the mock-ups but were not explicitly asked whether they liked the name. Prototypes allowed the agency team to concentrate on noting actual customer reactions to the concept and brand name in practice rather than having to solicit feedback to the service proposition and the brand name either in isolation or in the abstract. The rest is history.[148]

quick and dirty

By the same token, Bill Gross of Idealab! prototyped his Dell Computers-inspired notion of selling cars directly to end-customers online, not by following the convention of creating a complex temporary website but by posting an extremely simple website intended merely to validate the idea.

Gross hired a chief executive with the brief to sell just one car – this car would be bought from a dealer and sold on as a loss-making one-off, the cost being justified by the value of vindicating the concept. To Gross's surprise, the site received over 1,000 hits on its first day, resulting in the sale of four cars. That quick-and-dirty prototyping exercise led to the foundation of CarsDirect.com.

It is significant that a large measure of the success of Internet Securities, Inc., showcased in the case study at the end of the chapter, stems from the company's decision to move rapidly into the financial information sector with an off-the-shelf IT solution rather than invest cost and time in the development of a higher-specification bespoke package.

expectation management

It is important to avoid undoing the good you can achieve with prospective customers by forgetting to manage their expectations. If you are not clear with your prospects about the purpose and scope of the prototype, misunderstandings will arise. Either they will criticise the fit and finish of a rough-cut prototype which was created only to demonstrate practical usability, or they will assume that the conversion of the prototypes into a finished product is a 'just job'.

Only if you manage expectations appropriately can you be sure to receive the full benefits from prototyping.

prototypes and divergent thinking

The creation of prototypes is not restricted to left-brain thinking – far from it. Divergent thinking is as important at the prototyping stage as at any other step in the idea development process. Where can you obtain cheap, if not free, components to use in a mock-up? Where could you easily simulate the product in use?

Tom Kelley reports how an IDEO design team wanted to test whether its new design of goggles for snowboarders would remain fog-free in freezing conditions. Baking in the heat of the Californian summer, they were unable to secure the funds from the clients to fly down to New Zealand, where it was winter. Instead, the team brainstormed out the idea of trialling the goggles in the industrial-sized freezer of a local family-run ice-cream factory. Meanwhile, IDEO legend also has it that part of a key prototype for the first Apple mouse was a $2 butter dish bought from a discount store.[149]

Best-practice divergent thinking might also lead you to apply the technique of reversals to prototyping – perhaps you should turn yourself into a prototype customer.

California-based Interval Research Corporation did just this. The company equipped its 20-something-year-old whizz-kid computer designers with gloves, weights for their arms and legs, plus spectacles with clouded glass so that they could experience at first hand what it would be like for the elderly to operate the physical controls of the next generation of televisions and other electronic equipment.[150]

All in all, the power of prototypes should never be underestimated. Gary Mueller of Internet Securities, Inc. summed it up eloquently when he described the reaction of an early prospect: 'The client was like a kid in a candy shop. It was one of those moments when you know you're really on to something.'

Gary Mueller and Internet Securities, Inc. – selecting a venture to suit his needs[151]

Gary Mueller's launch of Internet Securities, Inc.
exemplifies good practice for the idea development process in general. In particular, it demonstrates best practice for coarse-screening multiple ideas ahead of a more detailed evaluation of those with the most all-round promise.

Gary Mueller graduated with top honours in biology in 1988 from Harvard College and won a Fulbright Scholarship to travel to Germany and Eastern Europe. His presence in Berlin in 1989 when the wall came down brought home to him the significance of the opportunities involved in regenerating Eastern Europe. He turned down admissions to a number of top medical schools, including Harvard and Yale, to work on a number of privatisation projects in Eastern Europe and the former Soviet Union with the John F. Kennedy School of Government at Harvard.

His family's background was in entrepreneurship – his grandfather had established a manufacturing business, his father had set up a packing plant and his mother had founded a store. His uncle had either run or set up seven different businesses. Studying an MBA at Harvard Business School was a logical next step for Mueller.

As a summer job after his first year at business school, Mueller joined a group undertaking privatisation work in Poland. Given that no database service existed which had information on publicly traded companies in Poland, newspapers and word of mouth were often the main sources of information. As Mueller himself expressed it: 'There is a paucity of detailed news in these [emerging] countries. When you get news, it's often "headline" news that's not very detailed. If you're investing in these markets, you need the meat.'[152] He did not take the business idea of providing that 'meat' any further at that point, however.

While on his business course, Mueller considered a number of other business ideas, including setting up a food packaging company in Russia, which he discounted on the grounds of excessive risk, and establishing a bottled water company in Poland, which he rejected as too capital-intensive.

To allow himself to manage the wealth of apparent opportunities offered by the emerging markets of Eastern Europe, Mueller developed six criteria against which to coarse-screen ideas, shown on Table 5.8.

Table 5.8 Coarse-screen criteria

Coarse-screen criteria	Rationale
Low start-up costs	Could finance start-up from friends and family and limit downside risk
Low variable costs once business established	Control the rate of cash-burn
Low capital intensity	Minimise investment required
Rapid break-even	Recognise political instability inherent in emerging markets and gain rapid feedback on market acceptability of idea
Proven business rather than completely new idea	Reduce risk by mimicking what worked in developed countries – successful start-ups in Eastern Europe included English-language publications, restaurant franchises and copy centres
High market potential	Satisfy personal and business ambition

During his time at Harvard Business School, a colleague on the course put Mueller in touch with his father, Ludwig Gelobter. Having emigrated from Poland to the United States in his youth, Gelobter had been in the first wave of entrepreneurs returning to Poland. He was enjoying considerable success with a number of start-up ventures, including the establishment of *What, Where, When?*, Warsaw's equivalent to London's printed events-listing magazine, *Time Out. What, Where, When?* addressed the unmet need which Gelobter had identified among western visitors to Warsaw for even the most basic information about what was going on. ▶

Mueller and Gelobter struck up an immediate rapport. As a result of further productive meetings, Mueller spent time in Warsaw researching how he could contribute to the further development of Gelobter's publishing ventures. One of the options Mueller proposed was that he should split his time between working for Gelobter and pursuing his own business development interests.

Mueller made a number of useful contacts in Poland, including the cousin of a former Polish colleague who had worked at the Warsaw Stock Exchange and now wrote a daily column about the stock market for the leading financial daily. In parallel with his consideration of the publishing venture, Mueller's interest in the financial information business was reawakened by the financial strategy course at Harvard Business School which focused on two online companies – Technical Data Corporation and BRC. Mueller decided to re-evaluate the idea of some type of online service for Eastern Europe which he had previously shelved. The outcome of this re-evaluation took the form of a business school project.

In the early 1990s, the internet was still in its infancy. Regarding the internet as a 'toy for techies', many established organisations adopted a 'wait-and-see' attitude to the internet, rather than risk cannibalising their existing business generated through conventional channels.

In order to obtain a broad-brush assessment of the technological feasibility of the idea, Mueller contacted his brother George, a research engineer at Carnegie Mellon University with extensive experience of advanced systems integration and programming. George Mueller, together with his colleague Jae Chang, reassured Gary of the project's technical feasibility: internet technology and access were becoming cheaper and simpler, hardware costs were falling some 40 per cent per annum and the required database program could be adapted from off-the-shelf programs, rather than commissioned as bespoke (and expensive) software. The opportunity to assume first-mover advantage undoubtedly existed.

Gary Mueller again brought his wider network into play, gaining invaluable access to experts in the online financial information industry, among others, to help refine his business idea. Turning his back on the six-figure salaries, generous starting bonuses and apparently risk-free futures accepted by his business school peers from the leading consultancy and investment companies, Gary Mueller set to work in evaluating his idea of an online business. Recognising the explosive growth in Eastern European stock markets, together with the significant growth in inward foreign investment for which timely and accurate information was crucial, Mueller proposed to meet the currently unfilled market need for an online database service which provided in-depth financial information.

The target market comprised domestic and international brokers, traders, investors and analysts. The information would include fundamental financial data, together with news, press releases and analyst reports. Information would include data 'exclusive' to the service and would be available in both the host language and in English. User access was by internet or direct dial-up.

The critical nature of the information made the market highly insensitive to price.

In terms of competitive strategy, Mueller sought to avoid head-to-head competition with Reuters and Telerate, which both operated in Eastern Europe and which focused on real-time stock prices and carried only very limited news stories.

Mueller's service would not list such real-time information. While his concept mimicked a number of similarities with the service provided by Bloomberg, Mueller considered that Bloomberg's strategic focus was on the developed markets and that by moving quickly into Poland as a test market, Mueller would be able to enter Eastern Europe 'under the radar' and thereby secure first-mover advantage.

Mueller was also blessed with colleagues in the form of his brother and Jae Chang who were prepared to work for free in the expectation of the so-called 'sweat equity' which they would earn in the medium term. Mueller was clear that within three to five years they would sell the operation to a major online business or strategic partner.

The low investment costs required to start up, together with the partners' collective willingness to forgo salaries while the business became established, meant that Mueller would be able to set up his business idea with around $130,000 raised from his entrepreneurial uncle, his parents, himself and his brother.

Mueller used practical demonstrations wherever possible to promote the service. As he said of a very early presentation to one of London's ▶

leading investment banks: 'The client was like a kid in a candy shop. It was one of those moments when you know you're really on to something.'[153]

Gary Mueller founded Internet Securities, Inc. (ISI) in 1994 and launched ISI Emerging Markets into Poland in 1995. Expansion into other Eastern European countries soon followed. In 1999, Euromoney Institutional Investor plc purchased 80 per cent of ISI for $43 million.

Internet Securities, Inc. now delivers online hard-to-get information from more than 8,500 information providers on more than 55 emerging markets, with 22 regional offices in addition to worldwide and European headquarters in New York and London respectively. Professional recognition includes a 'must-have' ranking from *Information World Review*, a first place ranking by the *Wall Street Journal Europe* among business websites and 'Best of the Web' rating from *Forbes* magazine for four years running.

key points

- The best idea to take forward from this step will not only offer the greatest chance of success in the market but will also most closely match your personal goals, skills, resources and appetite for risk

- Be honest with yourself in assessing what you want and are able to put into the business idea and what you wish to take from it

- There are few right or wrong answers, only what is best for you

- Remember that this step of the process allows you to continue reshaping, reconfiguring or combining your emerging business ideas

- Follow a two-phase process, with a coarse-screen exercise followed by a more detailed, finer-screened evaluation of those ideas which survive

- Quick-and-dirty analysis which rapidly highlights a potential show-stopper is worth its weight in gold

- Prototypes are worth a million words

- This key step in the idea development process needs intuition and imagination just as much as logic and analysis

planning for implementation

- Frederick Smith – overcoming the obstacles to Fedex
- the importance of planning for implementation
- increasing the likelihood of successful implementation
- the blocks to implementation
- techniques to identify blocks to implementation
- guiding principles for overcoming blocks to implementation
- practical examples of overcoming blocks to implementation
- milestone planning
- Jollibee Foods Corporation – planning to beat a giant

Planning for implementation merely involves creating the list of positive actions required to bring your idea to market. True or false?

And if things are going to go wrong during implementation, the best time to sort them out is as they occur. True or false?

False on both counts. The most effective planning involves the creative identification of all those elements which could potentially block you from implementing your idea. For the fledgling Federal Express, the key block was the regulation of the air freight industry. For you, it could be competition, finance, the stifling power of convention or the inability to protect your idea.

Planning then resolves those blocks. It might overturn them, mitigate their impact, circumvent them or even transform them into an advantage. It might make you flex and develop your business idea further to take account of an immutable obstacle.

But effective planning will stop you from having to cross your fingers and just hope that it will be alright on the night.

Because if you do, it won't.

Frederick Smith – overcoming the obstacles to Fedex[153]

Frederick Smith exemplifies the ability to overcome, circumvent and turn to one's advantage potential obstacles to implementation.

Frederick Smith was born into a family steeped in transport – his grandfather had been a steamboat captain on the Mississippi river and his enterprising father had made significant money from such initiatives as establishing the earliest Dixie Greyhound bus lines. Having lost his father at an early age, Smith was brought up by his mother, whose significant influence included the development of his love of reading broadly and deeply which he always retained. As Smith later remarked: 'There are a lot of good lessons in history, and other peoples' experiences in the past, that could be exactly the solution to the problem you're looking for.'[154]

At the age of 15, he started his first business, Ardent Record Company, recording songs in a small garage with two friends. Around this time, he also learnt to fly. Later he studied political science and economics at Yale University, where in 1965 he wrote a paper on the logistical challenges facing firms in the newly emerging information technology sector. Given that companies could not afford to maintain large inventories of expensive spare parts for computers and other data-processing machines, Smith argued that an opportunity existed for an overnight door-to-door delivery system to enable the leading computer companies to offer reliable after-sales service. Legend has it that the paper received only a modest grade. He let the idea lie for the time being.

After serving one 'hitch' in ground combat in Vietnam for which he was highly decorated, Smith flew 230 air reconnaissance missions as a US marine. His four-and-a-half years' service in the Vietnam War taught him many lessons about human nature and leadership; about the relative importance of business affairs compared with the carnage of war; and about the wasteful inefficiencies of an air and ground logistics system which was not integrated.

On his return from Vietnam in 1969, he joined his step-father's aviation sales and repair business, Arkansas Aviation, which was struggling financially. During the successful turnaround of this company, Smith experienced at first hand the difficulties of obtaining spare parts rapidly. Most of the air freight in the US was shipped through passenger aircraft, and conventional industry thinking held that freight was the poor sister of passenger traffic. The overall transportation system, such as it was, constituted a fragmented patchwork quilt of airlines combined with haulage companies which operated local networks.

This first-hand experience, coupled with the insights gained from his tours of duty during the Vietnam War, crystallised his university business idea. 'What the hell', he said to himself, 'let's try to put it together.'[155]

As primary customer targets, Smith chose high-technology companies needing to ship high-value, time-sensitive items quickly and reliably. He commissioned two market research organisations, operating independently, to undertake feasibility studies on his proposal for an overnight package delivery system. Both agencies confirmed the idea's potential, highlighting massive market size and growth against a finding that 90 per cent of commercial airlines did not operate after 10 p.m.

Smith's big vision was based on an analogy which he had perceived with the banking sector. The banks operated a hub and spoke system, by which cheques were sent to one central point before being distributed back out to individual banks. Smith's integrated delivery system would collect time-sensitive parcels from within a 25-mile radius of key cities (the spokes), fly them to a central location (the hub) and then sort the parcels before flying them back out to the spokes. Rather than participate in a traditional and fragmented and locally focused transport sector, Smith intended to create an entirely new industry. ▶

Smith's big vision was based on an analogy with the banking sector

Smith incorporated Federal Express in 1971, intending to establish operations at Little Rock, Arkansas, because of its central location. The barriers he faced were considerable. The business concept did not lend itself to a gradual roll-out. A significantly high minimum level of infrastructure would have to be in place for the concept to be attractive to customers. Although Smith was able to put up $4 million of his own money, $80 million was still required. The financial community was reluctant to provide funding to establish such a large undertaking. Integrated express delivery services had been operated before – by the Indian and French Post Offices, for example, and by American Airlines shortly after World War Two – but no venture to date had succeeded.

An additional major block was that the air freight industry was heavily regulated. Furthermore, the authorities at Little Rock, his preferred central location, were reluctant to incur expenditure on upgrading the facilities for the benefit of a fledgling enterprise which in their eyes was likely to fail.

Smith attacked the various barriers with courage and conviction. He cited the independent market research agencies' reports to eventually secure funding from corporate investors. He used his passion and influencing skills to generate short-term capital from General Dynamics, which was apparently convinced as much by Smith's enthusiasm for his business model as by financial motive. Smith's enthusiasm extended to tracking down General Dynamics' hospitalised financial officer in order to close a deal by a particular deadline. Smith sailed extremely close to the wind in securing bank loans on his family trust, of which his sisters were also trustees. The sisters considered that a due process of consultation had not been followed.

Smith chose to buy small corporate jets at highly competitive rates from Pan Am, partly because prices had collapsed in the wake of the oil crisis-induced recession and partly because he intended to operate Federal Express under the provision for air-taxi services so as to circumvent mainstream airline regulations. Even to achieve this, Smith had to persuade Washington to increase the maximum weight limit because the corporate jets which he was buying exceeded the current limit.

In 1973, Smith located his premises in Memphis, Tennessee, where the more entrepreneurial authorities were keen to support him, realising that the overnight delivery operation could create jobs, put the airport to profitable use at night and establish the city as a trans-shipment centre.

Guided by the principle of asset parsimony, Smith rented old hangar space at extremely favourable terms.

He conducted the first beta test in March 1973, with planes flying in from 12 cities in the East and Midwest. Six parcels were carried. Undeterred, the company extended the test the following month to a fuller network of 25 cities. The more positive results from that test represented the birth of the air express industry.

To keep things simple and to avoid re-inventing the wheel, Smith recruited a number of staff from competitor UPS to enable him to copy elements of the UPS organisational system. He continually combined his inspirational and business skills in recruiting other employees who were entrepreneurial, possessed deep experience in their specialist field while often lacking corporate experience. Most importantly, aspiring recruits had to demonstrate that they were willing to make sacrifices for the company.

Smith possessed the interpersonal skills to sell the dream of what the company could become and to inspire supreme loyalty – when pressure from the shareholders and a lawsuit from his sisters in relation to the family trust brought him close to resignation, Federal Express senior managers threatened to resign en masse if Smith went ahead with his resignation.

Smith was never a man to be daunted by criticism: 'Folks are entitled to [criticise]. It's a free country, increasingly a free world, so let them take their best shot. If they're right, they may tell you something you didn't know before.'[156] His determination and self-belief were tested to the full in 1974, however, when Federal Express was on the verge of bankruptcy. As he laconically phrased it two years later: 'Everything was going wrong, except the fundamentals of the business were proving every single day that the idea was right.'[157]

The early success of the venture required flexibility, particularly in terms of securing larger aircraft. Starting in 1975, Smith lobbied government authorities to overturn restrictive regulations which not only prevented Federal Express from transporting payloads in excess of 7,500 pounds, but which also dictated pricing structures. It took until 1977 for the regulations to be overturned, an event which triggered Federal Express to purchase seven Boeing 727s, each with a load capacity of 40,000 pounds.

Close observation of customers made Smith aware that information about a shipment was just as valuable as the contents of that

▶

shipment or its physical delivery. COSMOS®, a centralised computer tracking system, was duly launched in 1979.

Smith used analogical thinking to great effect when he realised that the handheld barcode scanners used in grocery stores represented the best-in-class business process which he should incorporate. The Federal Express SuperTracker® was introduced in 1986.

Initially, customers made no-charge telephone calls to establish progress of their delivery. Launched in 1994 to allow customers to access their own shipment details directly, Federal Express's internet site (www.fedex.com) is generally acknowledged to be an internet classic, exploiting interactive functionality to improve the quality and accuracy offered to customers while reducing the supplier's own cost.

Smith structured the company on three interlinked principles – people, service and profits. Enlightened human resource policies inspired staff to go the extra mile. The recent Tom Hanks film, *Cast Away*, glorified this purple-blooded staff commitment to such an extent that critics agonised whether *Cast Away* was a commercial within a story or a story within a commercial. In turn, the superior service levels lock in premium-paying customers, who then contribute to the final element of the trinity, profits.

Subsequent developments extended Federal Express's geographical, technological and service reach. The founder's unerring conviction was a consistent thread within the development. As Smith said: 'Very rarely have I ever seen any business or major undertaking that goes in a straight line. There's zigs and zags, victories and defeat, and you have to be propelled by that conviction that what you're doing is right and what you're doing is important.'[158]

'very rarely have I ever seen any business or major undertaking that goes in a straight line'

Federal Express became the first US company to attain an annual revenue of $1 billion in ten years without merger or acquisition. It reported profits for 2003 of around $830 million on revenues of $22.5 billion. Vindication indeed of Frederick Smith's first secret of being a successful entrepreneur: 'Have a compelling business idea, one that is differentiated and sustainable.'[159]

the importance of planning for implementation

The specific purpose of this fourth step of the idea development process – planning for implementation – is to increase the likelihood of turning your idea into a successful entrepreneurial venture by identifying, and then resolving, potential blocks to implementation.

The blocks which you face will take many forms, from competitive reaction to lack of technical know-how, from lack of finance to inability to protect your idea. Resolving the blocks, or acknowledging that you must recycle your idea further back into the idea development process, will save considerable heartbreak later on in the implementation process proper.

We saw in earlier chapters how Mike Gooley's first mining foray and the Iridium project were both jeopardised by early failure to consider the political blocks to implementation. In contrast, the Federal Express case study demonstrated the step-change benefits which Frederick Smith secured by overturning the onerous regulations which characterised the airline business.

ideas are useless unless implemented
Implementation matters so much because ideas on their own have little value. Unless actually implemented into products or services which generate new value, ideas are literally of no use. It is successful implementation which separates the entrepreneur from the inventor, however creative.

successful implementation separates the entrepreneur from the inventor, however creative

The British track record of failure to transform invention into successful innovations which profit the inventor includes many notable names. This track record stretches back into history. John Kay, inventor of the flying shuttle in 1733, for example, had his house wrecked by textile industry workers who considered that his convention-breaking machine threatened their livelihoods. With the government unwilling to uphold his patent, and in constant fear of the mob, Kay fled to France where he died in obscure poverty.

More recent inventors to whom contemporary public acknowledgement and financial reward were largely denied include Sir Frank Whittle, inventor of the jet engine, and Sir Christopher Cockerell, inventor of the Hovercraft.

corporate dilettantes The obstacles to implementation which exist within organisations, let alone in the external world, represent particular challenges to the would-be innovator.

In a particularly stern *Harvard Business Review* article entitled 'Creativity is not enough', Theodore Levitt condemns as irresponsible the compulsive idea generators whose distaste for the mundane realities of organisational life make them incapable of executing real projects.[160] Levitt views these throw-it-over-the-wall-my-task-is-now-finished creative specialists as ineffectual dilettantes with literally nothing to show. For Levitt, such so-called creatives are not worthy of the name – they are just talkers, not true creative artists whose work can actually be measured. After all, innovation is creativity which has been made to work.

increasing the likelihood of successful implementation

Thorough planning increases the likelihood of successful implementation. It is much better to have foreseen the problems and issues at the planning stage, and to have considered creatively how to overcome them or mitigate their effects, than to encounter stumbling blocks for the first time during implementation itself.

In the Internet Securities, Inc. case study in the previous chapter, we saw how Gary Mueller identified that a potential block to successful implementation of the company was its relative ease of imitation by competitors. He also recognised that the strengths of his business idea included his ease of access to the specialist communities in the Warsaw stock exchange and in financial journalism.

His elegant solution to the potential implementation block was to capitalise on his access to financial specialists by maximising the sources of financial information 'exclusive' to Internet Securities, Inc. The introduction of 'exclusive' material created barriers to entry, making imitation of his business model much more difficult.

satisfying the critical success factors The fourth and final step of the idea development process explores, resolves and balances implementation issues which may have been raised at broad-brush level during the previous steps. It is during this fourth step that you can determine whether the business idea's critical success factors can truly be satisfied.

This step still requires whole-brain creativity in finding solutions to the blocks to implementation which you are likely to foresee in every functional area. As in previous steps, you need to combine the divergent skills to generate options with the convergent skills to close in on practical solutions. This step offers yet more opportunities, therefore, for the underlying business idea to be developed further.

At the conclusion of this fourth and final step, you will be ready to codify all the elements of your business idea into a formal business plan.

the blocks to implementation The blocks to implementation will obviously vary from situation to situation, but will typically include at least some, if not all, of the types of potential blocks shown in Figure 6.1. We discuss in turn each of the types of block which you are likely to encounter, recognising that each business opportunity will provide its specific mix and profile of obstacles.

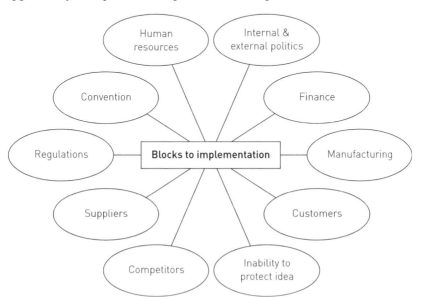

Figure 6.1 Blocks to implementation

convention The section on boundary-hopping in Chapter 3 illustrated just how strong conventional thinking within a sector can be. The natural inclination of conventional thinking to reject or eliminate non-conformism and outsiders is immense, whether motivated by values and beliefs, self-interest, lack of imagination or lack of faith in the innovator. Conventional thinking can apply equally to competitors, suppliers, financial backers, regulatory authorities and, crucially of course, customers.

We saw earlier how lack of big-company clout initially held back James Dyson, when his development grant application for his Dual Cyclone was rejected by the Secretary of State for Wales. The rejection assumed that if the product really did represent a superior offering, then one of the big conventional manufacturers would already be producing it.

The conventional Swedish furniture market literally closed ranks in an attempt to exclude Ingvar Kamprad. By forcing Kamprad to site his stores out of town, stocked with products made from outside Sweden, the competitors contributed to their own demise by steering Kamprad towards his low-cost business model targeted at the emerging market of young house-owners seeking affordable new furniture.

the natural inclination of conventional thinking to reject or eliminate non-conformism and outsiders is immense

if you want a bank loan, wear a suit and carry a folder The refusal by Anita Roddick's bank manager to grant her a £4,000 loan when she turned up with the children and wearing jeans contrasts with the subsequent successful application by her husband, Gordon. Legend has it that he satisfied convention by 'wearing a suit and carrying a gobbledegook-filled business plan in a plastic folder'.[161]

women don't work and software doesn't sell Dame Stephanie Shirley challenged a number of conventions in the 1960s when she founded the FI Group, which developed into the £1 billion-turnover business technology company, Xansa plc.

Contemporary attitudes held that 'no one expected much from women in work because all expectations then were about home and family responsibilities'.[162] Not only did she found and run her own business, she also exclusively recruited women, recognising that there was a huge pool of untapped human resources in the form of women with IT skills who had left their jobs to raise children. In addition, Dame Stephanie challenged the convention that 'there weren't any software developers in the commercial world because software was considered relatively unimportant and given away free with hardware'.[163]

people power Monsanto, producer of genetically modified food, experienced the full power of convention when it sought to introduce its products into the European market. It failed to win the public debate on the benefits of genetically modified food and its potential to reduce world famine and disease.

Once the products were launched, Monsanto compounded the communication failure by appearing not to offer a clearly labelled choice to consumers between organic and genetically modified food. Monsanto eventually withdrew from the European market.

is it just me who's mad or is it the others? A particularly poignant illustration of conventional group-think is offered by the story of Charles Merrill. At the acceleration point of the great bull market in 1928, Merrill started to obsess that the American stock market was bound to collapse. Conventional thinking among his peers that the stock-buying spree would continue was so powerful that Merrill was advised to seek professional help.

A psychiatrist duly attended Merrill, but was able to reassure him that his mental faculties were in perfect order. The very next morning, both psychiatrist and patient started to sell their stocks. Merrill's exit from the stock market at least a year before it crashed provided him with the means subsequently to establish his firm, Merrill Lynch.

perfecting the known rather than addressing the unknown In the 1870s, Alexander Bell and Elisha Gray were both working independently on an urgent problem with the telegraph network, namely how to send more than one message over the wire at any given time. Experiments by both led both to realise that speech could also be transmitted over the wire, provided a transmitter were available to convert speech into electronic signals.

It is certainly the case that Bell filed his patent application literally hours before the patent caveat of Elisha Gray. On the basis of its earlier filing time and on the subtle distinctions between a caveat and an actual patent application, the US Patent Office awarded Alexander Bell, not Elisha Gray, the patent for the telephone.

It is vigorously argued in some circles, however, that Gray could have won the race comfortably, had he not been discouraged by businessmen who believed that the telephone would never be profitable and had he not as a result put his design to one side.[164] Not so Bell, who defied conventional thinking in order to break new ground with the telephone rather than persist with perfecting the existing technology of the telegraph.

the glorious benefit of hindsight The previous examples all illustrate that the natural tendency of convention to crush innovation should never be underestimated. After all, the Hall of Shame for conventional thinkers boasts many famous exhibits, some of which are catalogued in Table 6.1. Even though doubts exist about the provenance of a few of the exhibits, the light projected on to the exhibits by the glorious benefit of hindsight ensures a good display.

Table 6.1 The glorious benefit of hindsight

'Chicken Noodle News'.	Competitors' description of Cable News Network (CNN) when it launched
'Who the hell wants to hear actors talk?'	Harry M. Warner, president of Warner Brothers Pictures, 1927
'There is no reason anyone would want a computer in their home.'	Ken Olson, president, chairman and founder of Digital Equipment Corp., 1977
'Heavier-than-air flying machines are impossible.'	Lord Kelvin, president, Royal Society, 1895
'[Television] won't hold any market it captures after the first six months. People will soon get tired of staring at a plywood box every night.'	Darryl F. Zanuck, head of 20th Century Fox, 1946
'The horse is here to stay. The automobile is only a fad, a novelty.'	President of the Michigan Savings Bank, offering market advice to Horace Rackham, Henry Ford's lawyer
'I think I may say without contradiction that when the Paris Exhibition closes, electric light will close with it and no more will be heard of it.'	Erasmus Wilson, Oxford Professor, 1899

regulations Sometimes blocks to implementation come in the form of regulations. We saw earlier how regulatory blocks represented major potential stumbling blocks for Iridium and Federal Express. Iridium failed to identify that national governments were unlikely to grant operating licences which deprived them of regular income. In contrast, Federal Express was well aware of the regulatory blocks. As a result, the company lobbied central government extremely hard. Federal Express succeeded initially in getting the weight thresholds for air taxi services increased and subsequently in achieving the complete deregulation of the entire air freight industry.

internal and external politics
The world of politics has not changed much since 1513, when Machiavelli claimed:

'There is nothing more difficult to take in hand, more perilous to conduct or more uncertain in its success than to take the lead in the introduction of a new order of things. Innovation makes enemies of all those who prospered under the old regime and only lukewarm support is forthcoming from all those who would prosper under the new.'

It is most likely that you will be seeking to give life to your idea in just such circumstances. Your idea will probably be competing in an environment where its fit to corporate strategy is all-important, where corporate strategy may change, the not-invented-here syndrome holds sway, the culture is risk-averse, financial hurdle rates are extremely aggressive, your initial sponsor has just left and so on.

The great and the good are not immune from the impact of this phenomenon. Howard Schultz had to quit his job at Starbucks in order to realise his own idea for coffee bars because the idea did not fit the strategy adopted by the founding trio of Starbucks. Only when Schultz bought the company did Starbucks adopt the coffee-bar formula for which it is now famous.

H. Ross Perot, founder of global giant Electronic Data Systems (EDS), was a salesman for IBM when he suggested that the company should create a service organisation which would design, install and operate electronic data-processing systems on a fixed-contract basis. Unable to convince IBM senior management of the proposal's fit with corporate strategy, Perot left and established EDS with $1,000 of savings.

customers
Generally attributed to Ralph Waldo Emerson, the adage that 'if you build a better mousetrap, then the world will beat a path to your door' is unfortunately incorrect. As earnest marketers have pointed out, the adage does not take account of market awareness, customers'

actual needs (do they have a mouse problem?), customers' perceived needs (people who have mice but are not aware of their existence), the definition of 'better' (style-conscious customers may consider that a better mousetrap offers designer hues rather than enhanced technical effectiveness) or the effort of beating the path (is customer perception of product value strong enough to outweigh the effort of obtaining the product?). Lack of acceptance by customers of apparently superior products will often represent a major potential stumbling block.

overlooking the basics Sometimes the block lies in customers' inability to make use of the innovation.

lack of acceptance by customers of apparently superior products will often represent a major potential stumbling block

Boo.com created a technically brilliant internet concept for selling fashion goods online, including zoom and 360° rotation facilities, a mannequin which you could dress in the clothes which you were considering, and so on. The ultimate success of the venture was doomed, however, by customers' lack of access to computer facilities of sufficient power to take advantage of the complex functionality. Early estimates indicated that less than 25 per cent of those who tried to access the website actually succeeded. Macintosh users could not access the site at all, which hardly fitted the brand positioning of 'geek chic'.

the fear of the radically new At other times, the block lies in customers' fear of embracing the radically new. This realisation led Edison to position the new technology of electrical lighting as an added-value version of existing gas lighting. Similarly, Sony recognised that a major implementation block to launching the Sony Walkman was its new-to-the-world nature, which might intimidate customers. Its creative response was to employ actors to use the Walkman in the main park in Tokyo, thereby 'normalising' the product's use.

Discount broker Charles Schwab recognised that security concerns on behalf of customers represented a major block to implementation. The provision of instantaneous computer confirmation eliminated that obstacle. By the same token, Schwab identified that customers perceived standard office hours as a potential limitation, one which he overcame by designing 24-hour/7-days-per-week operation into the business model.

enduring loyalty to the old In contrast, senior managers behind the unsuccessful launch in 1985 of New Coke failed to identify correctly customers' loyalty to the old brand and their reluctance to embrace the new. The decision by Coca-Cola simultaneously to withdraw the old brand was apparently based on the encouraging results from market research which had inadvertently suggested to participants that the new brand might be in addition to, rather than a replacement for, the tried and tested formula.

Three months after the launch of New Coke, the old brand was restored under the title 'Coca-Cola Classic'. The corporate climb-down over what was portrayed as a national symbol achieved the type of saturation news coverage normally reserved for disasters or diplomatic crises.[165]

finance It is almost inevitable that finance will represent one of the major blocks to implementation. While the 'big-money model' of business start-up has a certain glamour, the reality of starting your own business is often more to do with supplementing savings by borrowing money from friends, family, banks and credit cards than it is to do with seeking funds from angel investors or venture capitalists.

As we will see in the case study at the end of this chapter, for example, the £310-million-turnover Jollibee Foods Corporation had its origins in just two ice-cream parlours, established by Tony Tan Caktiong with a loan from his father.

It is equally a question of reducing or eliminating expenditure wherever possible, like Internet Securities, Inc. opting for off-the-shelf software, Jeff Bezos making desktops out of cheap doors or Michael Dell using standard componentry for his customised Dell computers to minimise the level of inventory and overall cost.

human resources Recruiting and retaining appropriate staff can be a major block for a business start-up because money may be tight or non-existent, you want to avoid as much financial commitment as possible, and staff may not wish to work for you, perceiving the venture as too risky, perhaps.

We saw in the Federal Express case study how Frederick Smith sought staff who demonstrated specific entrepreneurial qualities and how 'selling the dream' to those employees was an important part of the recruitment process.

For Dame Stephanie Shirley, the founder of Xansa plc, an early block was the male domination of the IT sector. So male-oriented was the sector that she was forced to sign her early business development letters as 'Steve' in order to get through the customers' doors for a first meeting. She turned the problem into a competitive advantage by tapping into the pool of highly motivated, although not particularly well-paid, women returners.

converting blocks into opportunities Dame Stephanie Shirley's strategy echoes that of Ingvar Kamprad, who turned the lack of funds to employ trained business professionals into an advantage. Kamprad recruited bright but non-qualified staff whose very open-mindedness assisted IKEA in breaking convention across so many other areas of its operation. They also cost less than their business-brainwashed peers.

manufacturing Throughout this text, we have seen examples of how manufacturing has represented a potential block to implementation.

eliminating conventional costs Sometimes this has been because of cost. For Swatch, an initial block was the inability to achieve the desired retail price point when producing a watch using conventional technology and processes.

By challenging the assumptions of conventional watch manufacture, Swatch designers reduced the number of working components from 150 to 51, replaced high-cost materials such as leather and metal with lower cost alternatives, such as plastic, and developed cheaper assembly techniques. Total manufacturing costs ended up 30 per cent less than those of competing products sourced from such areas as Hong Kong.[166]

necessity as a mother of invention For Anita Roddick, the manufacturing blocks stemmed from lack of resources. Painting her first Body Shop dark green to cover the damp patches, Roddick and her small local manufacturer produced the 25 launch products from readily available ingredients. They sold the products in urine-sample bottles. Without enough bottles, she decided to offer refills in customers' own containers.

It is worth noting in passing that similar finance-driven blocks to implementation applied to marketing. Two nearby funeral directors threatened to sue her if she used the Body Shop name. She saw them off by phoning the story anonymously to the *Brighton Evening Argus*, which gave it centre-spread and taught her that you never need pay for advertising.[167]

thinking outside the conventional supply chain We saw in Chapter 2 how Ingvar Kamprad overcame the manufacturing blocks imposed by the Swedish retail furniture cartel by forging good relations with low-cost Polish manufacturers and by identifying spare manufacturing capacity held by such non-traditional production sources as ski manufacturers and shirt makers.

a problem outsourced is a problem eliminated Sometimes manufacturing has represented a block to implementation because of lack of know-how. Recognising the intense difficulties encountered while manufacturing the Head skis in-house, for example, Howard Head avoided repetition of the block by outsourcing the technically complex production of his outsize aluminium tennis rackets to Kunnan Lo in Taiwan.

experts always know why things cannot be done The 'experts' in the field regarded Andrew Palmer's requirement for a process to extend the shelf-life of his fresh soup as an insurmountable obstacle. Palmer's persistent challenge to conventional wisdom, his refusal to accept defeat, together with the support of Reading University's Food Technology Department, finally eliminated the block by developing a feasible, and patentable, manufacturing process which would underpin the success of the New Covent Garden Soup Company.

suppliers Suppliers should not be overlooked as a potential block. Perhaps they will not advance credit to a start-up company. Perhaps they do not have the technical ability consistently to achieve your specification – quality considerations contributed to Karan Bilimoria's decision to transfer the brewing of Cobra, 'the beer from Bangalore', to Bedford after about six years, for example.

At other times, suppliers may have been warned off from supplying you, which was the problem faced by Ingvar Kamprad or by Sarah Tremellen of Bravissimo, as we saw in the previous chapter. And at other times, suppliers may consider that it is not in their interests to deal with you, a problem faced by easyCinema in its early days.

competitors Competitive reaction is clearly one of the likeliest blocks to implementation. IKEA's experience demonstrated the full gamut of competitive reaction, ranging from exclusion from trade fairs to legal challenge, and organisation of a boycott among potential suppliers.

competitive reaction is clearly one of the likeliest blocks to implementation

We saw earlier how Internet Securities, Inc. identified competitive reaction as a major implementation block, leading the company to avoid head-on competition with the American players already present in Poland and to fly in 'under the radar'.

Hoover paid James Dyson the most sincere form of competitive flattery by seeking to imitate his Dual Cyclone vacuum cleaner.

As the concluding case study will demonstrate, Tony Tan Caktiong had to overcome the psychological block of McDonald's' forthcoming entry into the Philippines' fast-food market when he pre-emptively launched his Filipino version. Caktiong's triumph was to be the only entrepreneur who has ever managed to keep McDonald's in the number-two slot.

inability to protect your idea Linked to competition is the idea of protecting your idea. James Dyson beat off Hoover by taking the company to court for patent infringement, while Andrew Palmer patented his process for extending the shelf-life of his fresh soup.

But suppose you lack the funds to patent-protect your idea or suppose the idea will not sustain protection, making you vulnerable to rapid imitation by others? Clearly these were the type of issues identified by the Roddicks when they sought rapid and national coverage through franchising for the Body Shop concept, or by Internet Securities, Inc. when it developed the range of sources 'exclusive' to it, or by Karan Bilimoria, when he developed the brand values of Cobra beer rather than protect the brewing formula.

techniques to identify blocks to implementation

A number of techniques exist to help you identify the blocks to implementation which are specific to your particular idea. These include reverse brainstorming, force-field analysis and commitment charting, which focuses particularly on the interpersonal blocks to implementation. We discuss each technique in turn.

technique 1: reverse brainstorming
As its name suggests, reverse brainstorming follows the same process as conventional brainstorming, except that it concentrates on obstacles and blocks.

Perverse though it may sound, it is important that the exercise is carried out in a highly positive fashion which does not evaluate the problems identified. The very act of articulating the problems may make the exercise appear highly critical and negative – it should not be. The exercise should be viewed as the opportunity for a highly creative and legitimate exploration of what could go wrong, hence its affectionate nickname of 'bitching with attitude'.

confronting the fear of failure It is important to remember that the more exhaustive the exercise, the more robust will be the platform for generating solutions and increasing the likelihood of the venture's success. By proactively identifying problems and generating solutions, you can start to overcome the debilitating effect created by fear of failure which inevitably afflicts many start-up businesses.

by proactively identifying problems and generating solutions, you can start to overcome the debilitating effect created by fear of failure

Given the positive intention of reverse brainstorming, it is important that it is not confused with 'blame-storming', the term neatly coined by *Wired* magazine to describe the exercise of harnessing group creativity to identify multiple scapegoats for failure.

reverse brainstorming: step one The first step is to carry out a brainstorming exercise on exactly the same basis as conventional brainstorming, but focusing on elements which can block implementation or simply go wrong.

Apply the same rules for divergent thinking as with conventional brainstorming: go for quantity; piggy-back ideas wherever you can, using 'wild ideas' as the spur to more practicable, yet still unexpected, ideas; and suspend all critical judgement. The temptation to become judgemental of the individual ideas during a robust period of what could be construed as sustained criticism is very tempting but must be avoided.

At this stage, it is not important that you differentiate cause from effect, an exercise which will be undertaken during the next convergent phase. It is important to surface every type and scale of problem imaginable – from the type of problem that wakes you up in a sweat at night, to the nagging doubt at the back of your mind which just will not go away, to other entrepreneurs in other sectors whose experience made you think 'There, but for the grace of God, go I', to the type of problem you had not considered until now.

A mind-map of the issues facing Ingvar Kamprad's attempt to enter the Swedish furniture market might have included the elements shown in Figure 6.2 below, for example.

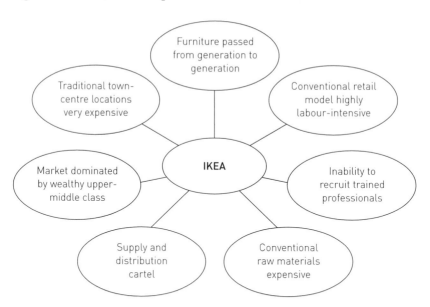

Figure 6.2 Mind-map of blocks to implementation for IKEA

reverse brainstorming: step two The second step moves you back into convergent thinking. You should cluster related themes together; disentangle causes from their effects; enhance and develop the strong ideas, combining ideas where appropriate; and eliminate the 'wild ideas' and 'intermediate impossibles' where they have led up a blind alley.

At all times, remember to apply affirmative evaluation – train yourself to identify the good aspects in every idea, however apparently outlandish, before you criticise it.

fishbone analysis Developed by Professor Kaoru Ishikawa, so-called fishbone analysis is an effective way of exploring the relationship between cause and effect.

On your writing surface, draw a long arrow horizontally across the page to represent the backbone of the fish. At the right-hand side, write down the potential block to implementation – this is the head of the fish. Next, you should draw fishbones at roughly 45° from the backbone to identify the likely major causes of the potential block. Once you have done this, draw further small bones off each of the major causes to mark further breakdowns of each cause. Highlight any causes that appear more than once because they may have a particular significance. Circle anything that seems to be a 'key' cause, so that you can concentrate on it subsequently.

By way of example, imagine that you were Andrew Palmer, seeking to identify and explore the blocks which would prevent you from manufacturing to the required volume and quality levels. Your fishbone diagram might then include some of the elements shown in Figure 6.3.

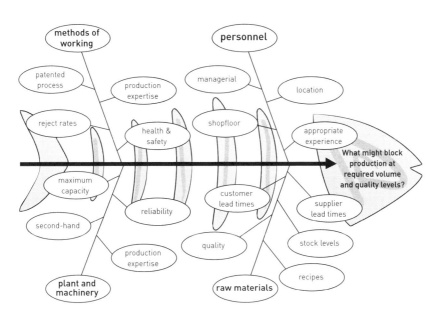

Figure 6.3 Fishbone analysis of potential manufacturing blocks for New Covent Garden Soup Company

reverse brainstorming: step three The final step of the reverse brainstorming technique requires you to provide a rough-cut priority ranking of implementation blocks to address. This is best achieved by using a simple grid which evaluates blocks to implementation according to the scale of the impact and the likelihood of their occurrence. Such grids are frequently used as a risk management tool. A suggested scoring mechanism is shown in Table 6.2.

Table 6.2 Matrix for prioritising blocks to implementation

Block to implementation	Impact	Likelihood	Combined score
Block A	4	5	20
Block B	2	3	6
Block C	3	2	6
Block D	3	4	12

Scoring machanism:
Impact:
minor	1
significant	2
important	3
very important	4
catastrophic	5

Likelihood:
extremely unlikely	1
unlikely	2
feasible	3
probable	4
expected	5

reduce likelihood of occurrence There are at least two iterations to this process – the first iteration identifies the blocks and their impact assuming that you take no action. Your task is to prioritise the blocks according to their combined score – in Table 6.2, Block A would attract your attention first. As a result of the first iteration, you then investigate ways of reducing the likelihood that the blocks will occur. Karan Bilimoria discovered that there was a strong likelihood that political issues would block him from making direct contact with the entire network of Indian restaurants which represented his core market. To avoid this block occurring, he founded a trade magazine, *Tandoori*, whose distribution to the entire network allowed him to establish direct contact with his core customers.

the first iteration identifies the blocks and their impact assuming that you take no action

reduce impact of 'residual risk' The second iteration takes account of the likelihood that the blocks will occur, after you have taken whatever action is open to you. The focus of managing this so-called 'residual risk' then transfers to reducing the impact of the block in question.

Considering it inevitable that competitors would seek to emulate his Internet Securities, Inc. business model – scoring 5 for likelihood in our earlier grid – Gary Mueller maximised the range of material exclusive to him. Aware that competitors would seek to imitate his Cobra beer, and that patent protection of the precise brewing formula would not stop this competitive reaction, Karan Bilimoria invested heavily in building the brand to reduce the impact of competitive reaction.

technique 2: force-field analysis
This technique acknowledges that implementation of innovative ideas typically faces both positive ('driving') and negative ('restraining') forces. It provides a framework for identifying the various forces which are likely to be at play, evaluating their relative impact, and generating ideas for overcoming the negative forces while capitalising on the positive forces.

It is rare that an innovation faces forces which, overall, are initially balanced in its favour – far from it. The technique is helpful, therefore, in establishing how to achieve a better balance between driving and restraining forces. A defined and growing market need which is not currently satisfied by products or services on the market would constitute a major positive force, while regulatory restrictions or the inability to secure raw material supplies would clearly represent negative forces.

step one: brainstorm the forces The first step involves brainstorming the various forces at play around your business idea, observing all the usual rules for divergent thinking. Think of all the positive forces as well as the negative forces – avoid taking anything for granted and make sure that you capture all your ideas.

step two: cluster the forces into themes Move into a convergent phase of thinking, finding clusters of themes, combining ideas where you can. At the end of this step, a helpful approach is to divide your writing surface with a vertical rule and list the driving forces on the left and the restraining forces on the right.

step three: evaluate the forces The next task is to evaluate the relative impact of each force. Suppose that Gary Mueller had created an early version of a force-field analysis for Internet Securities, Inc., then his analysis might have included the elements shown in Figure 6.4. As the simple hypothetical model shows, the best approach is to reflect the relative weight of the force in the relative length of the arrow. This allows the major driving or restraining forces to be immediately evident.

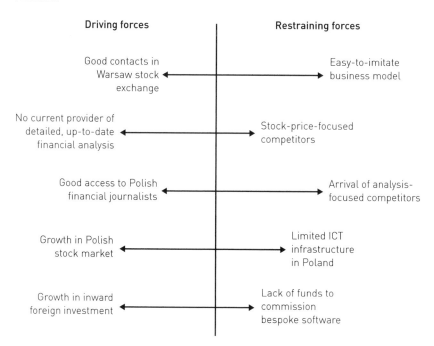

Figure 6.4 Force-field analysis for Internet Securities, Inc.'s launch into Poland

technique 3: commitment chart

The commitment chart develops further the idea of positive and negative forces which affect implementation, particularly as they apply to specific stakeholders. It is a particularly useful tool, therefore, for considering the likely impact of innovations within organisations, as well as for independent start-ups.

The first stage in the technique involves mapping your perception of where key stakeholders stand in relation to the innovation. Are they for it, against it or merely indifferent? Once the map is completed, the task is to identify how to capitalise on the existing support of key stakeholders, how to win over or at least neutralise the antagonists and how to win over or at least not antagonise those who are indifferent.

A commitment chart for Frederick Smith's proposed Federal Express project might have included the elements shown in the Figure 6.5.

Stakeholder	For	Indifferent	Against
Family trust-holders			✗
Little Rock airport authorities			✗
Memphis airport authorities	✓		
General Dynamics	✓		
Investment banking community		O	
Air freight industry			✗
Federal Express employees	✓		
Government aviation authorities		O	

Figure 6.5 Commitment chart for Federal Express launch

guiding principles for overcoming blocks to implementation

A number of guiding principles inform this final stage of planning for implementation. They include asset parsimony, keeping things simple, the need continually to influence and sell, exercising vigilance and flexibility, and applying the process and techniques outlined in the first three steps of the idea development process.

easyJet combined a number of these principles. In its exercise of asset parsimony the company minimised staff numbers, eliminated business processes and offered a no-frills service on two leased Boeing 737s. It kept things simple by outsourcing a range of back-up services such as maintenance, passenger handling and aircraft handling. The high profile of Stelios Haji-Ioannou meant that the brand was continually being promoted (flooding the inaugural flight of its competitor go! with orange-uniformed easyJet employees, for example). Multi-skilling the staff ensured operational flexibility.

We will discuss in turn each of the guiding principles in more detail.

asset parsimony Earlier chapters showed how Phil Knight commissioned the Nike logo for $35 from a design student; Richard Branson started Virgin Records in rent-free accommodation in Oxford Street; and Karan Bilimoria delivered Cobra beer from the back of his battered Citroen 2CV.

The 'big-money model' of business start-up has a certain glamour. The reality, however, more often involves hard personal effort and the ability to supplement savings by borrowing money from friends, family, banks and credit cards than it does angel investors or venture capitalists.

the 'small-money model' Research undertaken by Amar Bhide highlighted how over 80 per cent of companies on the 1989 *Inc.* '500' list of the fastest growing private companies in the United States were financed according to the 'small-money model' of bootstrap financing.[168] This finding is consistent with a 1991 American study which identified that for 74 per cent of the start-up sample, personal savings had represented the primary source of finance; 77 per cent of the sample had been launched with $50,000 or less, 46 per cent were launched with $10,000 or less.[169]

The 'small-money model' provides you with the benefit of retaining control of the business start-up.

parsimony forces ingenuity Parsimony also encourages, if not demands, ingenuity. It is comparable in its effect to targeting zero stock in a just-in-time production system – problems previously hidden behind stock buffers are revealed and demand immediate solution.

Howard Head, for example, claimed that had he raised all the funds which he required at the outset, he would have failed by spending the funds too early on the wrong version of the metal ski. Ingvar Kamprad echoed this sentiment, claiming that 'expensive solutions . . . are often signs of mediocrity. We have no interest in a solution until we know what it costs'.[170] IKEA's company culture sustains the importance of asset parsimony. Corporate mythology recounts how Kamprad drove around a city at night in order to find an appropriately economical hotel and how he prevented a senior executive from flying first-class to an important meeting. Equally, the company's website explicitly promotes the IKEA value of 'finding simple solutions, scrimping and saving in every direction. Except on ideas'.[171]

'expensive solutions are often signs of mediocrity'

focus resources where they matter The frugality of Amazon.com offers a stark contrast to the apparently more indulgent strategy of Boo.com, which was intended by its founders to be technically awesome and ultra hip in all its operations in order to appeal to the affluent young.

Amazon.com concentrated all available funds on development of its website and business model and allowed little or nothing for the niceties of office life, such as desks. It tended to be the Amazon.com staff themselves who made the desks from doors. Jeff Bezos tells the self-deprecating story of how he almost blew the appointment of a senior financial director whom he had been trying to recruit for months by ringing him to check how high the 'desk' should be made.[172]

In contrast, the founders of Boo.com were highly image-conscious, regarding themselves as the vanguard of the second-generation internet entrepreneurs. They invested heavily in luxurious offices in major cities such as London, New York, Stockholm, Paris, Amsterdam and Munich. They were reported to have spent $250,000 on flat-screen monitors for the staff. When added to the investment in purchasing and integrating 'best-of-breed' electronic transaction software, the infrastructure costs significantly outweighed sales revenue, burning cash in early 2000 at a rate of over $1 million per week.

five golden rules It is worth bearing in mind the five golden rules for asset parsimony attributed to Ian MacMillan, director of Wharton's Snider Entrepreneurial Center:[173]

- Do not buy new what you can buy second-hand
- Do not buy second-hand what you can rent
- Do not rent what you can borrow
- Do not borrow what can be begged
- Do not beg what can be salvaged.

generate early cash-flow Lack of funds will also force you to concentrate on bringing sales revenue as early as possible into the business. Gary Mueller, for example, introduced an up-front monthly subscription with unlimited use for Internet Securities, Inc. in Poland rather than a retrospective payment by usage, in order to generate regular up-front cash-flow.

Property developers also exemplify this process – they do not wait until the two-dimensional architects' drawings of forthcoming developments are converted into bricks and mortar before they start their sales campaigns. Instead, they create online virtual tours of the project as early as possible to stimulate interest and then create a show-house immediately that they arrive on site in order to pre-sell the properties and generate cash-flow.

keep things simple

Legend has it that Albert Einstein was once asked why he also used hand soap for shaving in preference to shaving foam. He is supposed to have replied: 'Two soaps? That is too complicated!' Apocryphal as the story may be, it does illustrate a value acknowledged as central to Einstein's creativity – namely, the importance of simplification.

In terms of business start-up, the need to keep things simple is entirely consistent with asset parsimony. Jeff Bezos launched Amazon.com with a highly functional website, where basic functionality and rapid loading preceded style and editorial content. Getting started simply, economically and quickly was what mattered – refinements could be introduced over time.

> the need to keep things simple is entirely consistent with asset parsimony

The task facing Boo.com was a challenge of a different order. The technical solution required from the outset to overcome customers' inability to actually feel the clothes on offer and to physically try them on was so complex that it stretched managers' ability beyond breaking point. When Boo.com went into liquidation after just six months of active trading, it had spent over $128 million.

limit your areas of uniqueness

Keeping things simple allows you to avoid unnecessary risk and exposure. Rock-climbers, for example, are urged to maintain three points of contact with the rock face at all times – while one hand may be reaching for a new and previously undiscovered hand-hold, the other hand plus both feet should be firmly locked to the rock to avoid additional risk. A business start-up is similar, in that it is often in your interests to exploit a few areas of uniqueness and use standard, easily available elements for the other operational elements which make up your business idea.

Internet Securities, Inc., for example, launched its financial information service by tailoring an off-the-shelf software package rather than investing in a bespoke system. Similarly, Michael Dell launched his highly innovative direct-to-consumer Dell Computer operation using entirely standard components. Likewise, Karan Bilimoria accepted beer bottles whose size was standard to India but outsize for the UK market because it avoided the need to commission an additional bespoke element in the Cobra beer concept.

the need continually to influence and sell No matter

how compelling the advantages of your new business idea appear to be, these advantages mean nothing if appropriate people other than yourself cannot be persuaded of their value. This means you must continually influence, and sell to, all those on whom you depend for money, labour, support, endorsement or sales.

This applies as much to the pre-implementation planning stage as it does to the implementation stage and thereafter. Remember Gary Mueller, continually using his influencing skills to enlarge his network of contacts, using them for insights into e-commerce or the Warsaw stock exchange.

Whether you are seeking to influence a hard-pressed boss, to whom your idea if presented in the raw may well just represent further work, or whether you are seeking the support of an outside backer who is regularly barraged with such requests, you can follow the simple four-step influencing process outlined in *Re-inventing Influence – how to get things done in a world without authority* (see Table 6.3).[174]

The task ahead is often complicated for the individual entrepreneur by a perceived lack of credibility among stakeholders. As we have seen earlier, James Dyson and Anita Roddick both suffered in one way or another from this adverse perception.

You should remember that every interaction represents a chance to talk up your business idea. It is all part of the selling effort. It also provides the opportunity for feedback from other people's points of view which yet again may provoke further improvement in your business idea.

Table 6.3 Four-step influencing process

Step One: know yourself	Be clear about who you are – your beliefs, values and assumptions – and what you want to achieve
Step Two: identify your target	Pick out and analyse which targets are essential for achieving your goals and how to gather multiple clues in order correctly to evaluate and effectively manage these targets
Step Three: diagnose the system	Identify how organisations work in reality; access the 'hidden system' of culture and networks which determines what types of influencing behaviour are acceptable more strongly than the 'proper' channels of authority
Step Four: decide on strategy and tactics	Identify the appropriate strategy of influence – soft or strong – then select multiple tactical weapons of influence appropriate to the specific target. Tactics include pressure, upwards appeals, exchange, coalitions, ingratiation, rational persuasion, inspirational appeals and consultation

the 'elevator pitch' It is worth preparing a brief 'elevator pitch' about the idea, a sales pitch which would convince someone to back your idea during the course of a typical ride in a lift.

it is worth preparing a brief 'elevator pitch' about the idea

Investment giant JP Morgan is reported to have trained the young Boo.com entrepreneurs to deliver their pitch to potential investors in just four minutes flat.[175]

vigilance and flexibility As we have argued throughout the text, our model of the various phases within the idea development process is rooted in research, but necessarily over-simplifies the process as it actually works in practice.

On the ground, the idea development process can never be an absolutely clear-cut set of discrete steps which follow each other in rigid linear fashion. The reality is much more fuzzy, with steps overlapping, reoccurring 'out of sequence', with information and ideas constantly recycling between the various steps.

real life doesn't stop just because you're planning Events in the external world regularly intrude and impact on the best-laid plans. The co-founders of online betting exchange Betfair, for example, were in the midst of finalising their finance arrangements when a rival company, Flutter, appeared out of nowhere to beat them to the launch. Edward

Wray and Andrew Black considered giving up, but demonstrating the typical persistence of true entrepreneurs, continued to launch successfully in 2000. Having merged with Flutter in 2002, Betfair won the Queen's Award for Enterprise in 2003.

In addition, internal politics, the law of unintended consequences, changes in corporate strategy, all mean that the idea development process can never be micro-managed so that it runs like clockwork. This fluidity places two particular entrepreneurial attributes at a premium – vigilance in detecting the unforeseen as early as possible and flexibility in reacting to it.

The Minnesota Innovation Research Program team created an apt metaphor when they described the innovation process as similar to navigating an uncharted river – while unable to control exactly where the river goes and how it behaves, the successful entrepreneur does possess the skills to steer towards a favourable destination.

learning from experience The enterprise-award-winning company Travel Counsellors illustrates effectively the power of reacting flexibly to new information and experience. Among a number of business start-ups, entrepreneur David Speakman had founded a conventional travel agency which had achieved a steady turnover of £500,000. The failure of another of his businesses, a restaurant, led him to define the key criteria for his ideal business. These criteria included no fixed labour costs, commission-only sales, large volume and low overheads. In the light of his analysis of the business failure, and inspired by the American trend-spotter Faith Popcorn, who predicted that more people would shop and work from home in the future, Speakman completely reconfigured his travel agency in 1994. He armed his travel agents with laptops and mobile phones, enabling them to visit mostly baby-boomers in their own homes and provide an extremely high level of tailored service.

Turnover of Travel Counsellors plc in 2003 had soared close to £100 million.[176]

focused reapplication of the idea development process
A final guiding principle is that once the apparent blocks to implementation have been identified, you should treat the process of resolving the blocks using exactly the same process and techniques as you used in the first three steps of the idea development process itself.

This means that you should challenge the blocks, explore and possibly redefine them. You should generate ideas for resolving the redefined blocks and then evaluate and select the best solutions to pursue. In other words, you are following the process model for idea development, but at a more detailed level, often focused on problems or issues within individual business functions.

The strength of the model for idea development is that it can successfully be used at a number of different levels – its flexibility in use is similar to business modelling techniques such as portfolio analysis, which can be applied at the level of holding company/subsidiaries, subsidiary/strategic business units, strategic business unit/product ranges, and right down to the level of product range/individual stock-keeping unit.

The reapplication of the idea development process, together with the additional techniques specific to this fourth step, means that planning for implementation should follow the series of iterative divergent and convergent phases illustrated in the Figure 6.6.

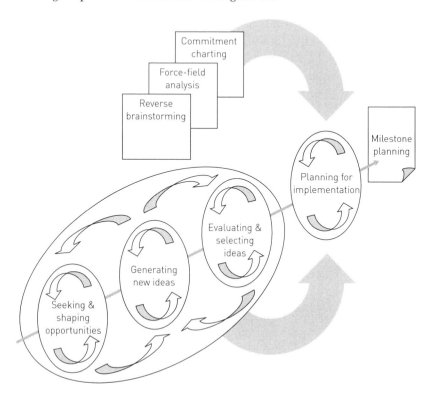

Figure 6.6 Step Four – planning for implementation

practical examples of overcoming blocks to implementation

By way of example, the following section illustrates how the model of idea development and its techniques could be applied to the major functional area of finance. It shows how the idea development model encourages you to redefine the problem of finance, facilitates the generation of ideas, and allows those ideas to be evaluated. The section also demonstrates how the other guiding principles can inform the process.

We restrict discussion to the *process* of addressing and resolving financial blocks – it clearly lies outside the scope of this text to explore the finance area from a left-brained perspective focused on detailed content.

step 1: redefining the financial block to implementation

As we saw earlier, the 'big-money model' of business start-up is more spoken about than applied in practice. In terms of the problem-solving model, therefore, it is all the more important that you avoid any immediate rush to solve the apparent problem of raising a particular amount of money. It is much better first of all to challenge the problem definition using the techniques which were discussed at Step One: seeking and shaping opportunities.

> the 'big-money model' of business start-up is more spoken about than applied in practice

Use the '5 Whys' technique to explore why you consider you need a specific amount. Use the technique again to challenge why particular costs have to be incurred, bearing in mind the five rules of asset parsimony. Jeff Bezos stripped out all ancillary costs, including desks; in contrast, Boo.com was so convinced of the need to present an holistic image of a leading-edge internet enterprise that significant sums were spent on state-of-the-art offices located in some of the world's most expensive cities. Like easyJet, what tasks can you outsource in order to avoid investment in either physical or human capital?

Examine how you have phrased your financial problem – what assumptions does it reveal? Instead of *raising* money, suppose you earned it through sale, or were offered it as a gift? Instead of raising *money*, suppose you raised expertise, a long-term sales contract or an influential endorsement? Matt Stevenson, founder of Reef One which manufactures a high-tech approach to the traditional fish bowl called the 'Biorb', so impressed a wholesaler to whom he demonstrated an early prototype made in his parents' attic that the wholesaler bought Stevenson's entire output for the first nine months in order to secure exclusivity of distribution.[177]

Explore the boundaries of the problem – look at other start-ups in the sector: core users of finance, as it were; look at other sectors for lead users who may have redefined the problem in different ways which may inspire you.

Perhaps you choose to redefine the financial problem as how to start your business without raising any external funds.

step 2: generating ideas to resolve the financial block to implementation It is then time to consider using the tools and techniques from Step 2: generating ideas.

Having used a checklist to identify the main functional areas where you could reduce cost, you could choose to focus on staff costs. Had IKEA applied the SCAMPER technique to staff costs, the results could have included those in Table 6.4.

Table 6.4 Application of SCAMPER technique to IKEA staff costs

Substitute	Instead of trained business professionals, recruit open-minded non-graduates; substitute customers for retail assistants – provide customers with own tape measures, self-service warehouse, high quality of product display and catalogue information
Combine	Train personnel on information desks to serve the dual function of salespeople and of accounts clerks; warehouse staff could also assist customers
Adapt	Incorporate good ideas from individual stores into standard corporate design
Magnify (or minify)	Magnify staff responsibility and 'corporate ownership' by rewarding enterprising behaviour; magnify effective selling time (as opposed to providing information); minify customer service levels; minify business expenses
Put to other uses	Rotate staff between functions in order to increase internal efficiency, provide management development and reduce staff turnover because of perceived job enrichment
Eliminate	Eliminate managers' ability to 'hide behind the hierarchy' and so flush out under-performance
Rearrange (or reverse)	Ensure managers work in front line to retain contact with reality of retail

You could use rule reversal to ask yourself 'What could I not pay for?' and then explore the boundaries of that particular question. This might lead you to review what expenses would not be incurred because you delete them from your shopping list.

if you don't need it, don't buy it Remember that if you don't need something, don't get it. Remember too that the internet is an excellent vehicle to present a window on the world which can be quite at variance with reality.

Launched in 1998 with just $50,000 in seed capital, Cold Fusion Sports, Inc. wasted little money on its ramshackle store and offices in a San Francisco neighbourhood pocked by dance clubs and auto-parts dealers. Jumbles of old boots and packing boxes cluttered up rooms divided by sheets of corrugated metal and used doors.

Instead, the company focused exclusively on its 'virtual store' of discounted snowboards and associated gear and, especially in its early years, on creating a community of interest by publishing weather reports and travel information, customer comments and photographs. With 90 per cent of its business executed through the internet, the company targeted sales of over $5 million within three years.[178]

securing win-win Rule reversal might lead you to consider what you could get for free, on extended credit or on particularly advantageous terms.

Founded by ex-academic Jimmy Doherty, the Essex Pig Company benefits from the waste fruit pulp and unwanted orange pips supplied free of charge by local maker of Tiptree preserves, Wilkin & Sons Limited. Both sides gain: 'Jimmy's Farm' reduces the costs of feeding its free-range rare breed pigs; Wilkin & Sons delivers on its recycling programme.[179]

still waiting for that order The start-up days of Amazon.com reveal a striking example of boundary examination. To keep costs down, Jeff Bezos needed to buy single copies of titles from wholesalers rather than the ten-book minimum orders which industry convention required. Noticing that the wholesalers stipulated a minimum *order* quantity rather than a minimum *delivered* quantity, Bezos hit upon the idea of bulking up his orders for single copies of required titles with nine copies of an obscure book on lichens which none of the wholesalers carried.[180] Bezos thereby maximised his flexibility by minimising his stock levels.

the start-up days of Amazon.com reveal a striking example of boundary examination

Flexibility was the aim of Michael Dell's strategy of providing tailor-made personal computers from standard componentry – the levels of both finished goods stock and of parts were held at the absolute minimum.

charge rather than be charged Pushing the question of 'What could I not pay for?' still further might lead you to consider that not paying for something could extend beyond 'something for nothing' to actually being paid for that something.

Suppose you are a small film company working on low budgets – how to avoid paying for film extras in addition to the main cast? The production company for *Following Yago*, a comedy film shot in August 2004, solved the problem by advertising for investors who would each contribute a minimum of £200 for the additional entitlement to appear as an extra.

how about bionics? You might use bionics to consider where in nature might the problem of limited resources for a fledgling entity have been solved. This might lead you to consider the analogy of the cuckoo, which might in turn prompt you to share resources with another, complementary, start-up, for example. How can you make yourself the dominant partner in the relationship? Can you find an organisation to whom your value exceeds its value to you? Could you establish your venture within a business incubator unit, taking advantage of a range of services specifically designed to help early-stage businesses?

force-fitting for resource ideas You may wish to generate further ideas about where you could access all the resources which you seek to acquire for minimum outlay. These resources may include office or warehouse space, professional endorsement, technical expertise, customer knowledge and so on.

You could use the force-fitting technique, for example, to inform your search for these resources. You could list all your resource requirements against your network of contacts and consider every cell in the matrix. The exercise may reveal useful leads which your assumptions had previously led you to overlook. Perhaps you have assumed that a particular customer is good only for sales, but actually may provide start-up advice or introductions to other non-competing customers. Perhaps a supplier will provide sales leads for you on the grounds that their business ultimately benefits.

Karan Bilimoria took this approach to extremes when he persuaded the Indian supplier of his beer, Mysore Breweries, to provide him with a letter of credit in addition to shipping the first consignment of beer, so that the brewery in effect bought the beer from themselves.

step 3: evaluating and selecting ideas to resolve the financial block to implementation

Assuming that you have generated a number of options for resolving the redefined financial problem, you can then turn to techniques for evaluating and selecting the best options. You could undertake a rough-cut screening against criteria such as ease of implementation or degree of business control which is lost.

Fine screening could involve a criteria grid which prioritises the various options against the financial benefit involved moderated by the likelihood of its achievement.

milestone planning

Now that you have identified the blocks to implementation and have created and selected solutions to overcome them, the final task within the fourth step of the idea development process is the identification of key events and activities, definition of their timing and inter-dependencies, and articulation of the assumptions which underlie your business case and which will be tested against reality at each milestone.

A number of techniques and tools of varying complexity exist to achieve this. They include Research Planning Diagram, Program Evaluation Review Technique (PERT), Critical Path Analysis, GANNT chart and so on.

Milestone planning is one of the more effective techniques and was brought into particular prominence by a seminal *Harvard Business Review* article by Zenas Block and Ian MacMillan.[181] This technique recognises that the actual implementation process for your new business idea will progress via a number of major events, known as milestones, which must happen in the course of turning your business idea into a viable business in practice.

Milestone planning helps you move at the lowest possible cost and level of risk from one milestone to the next rather than follow slavishly a fixed plan based on erroneous assumptions. The milestones will tend to be generic for any business start-up. However, the precise description of each milestone will be specific to your particular situation. In addition, the precise questions which you should ask yourself at each milestone to test your underlying assumptions will be particular to you. In many instances, the milestones will represent achievement of the solutions to the implementation blocks. Without a process to extend the shelf-life of his fresh soups, for example, Andrew Palmer would have been denied a viable business model for the New Covent Garden Soup Company.

milestones as reality checks

The principle is that during actual implementation you achieve each milestone before you move on to the next one. This means that every milestone offers the opportunity to decide whether and how to proceed to the next milestone.

every milestone offers the opportunity to decide whether and how to proceed to the next milestone

It may be that a particular milestone confirms that the established strategy and direction are correct. Alternatively, it may highlight that corrections are required, suggest new and unexpected opportunities, or indicate that the project be slowed down, accelerated or even aborted. In the case of Swatch discussed earlier, production prototyping identified that the number and quality of materials would need to be radically adjusted in order for the target retail price point to be achieved.

By identifying the must-achieve events, milestone planning is practical and goal-oriented. Consistent with the guiding principle of maintaining flexibility articulated earlier, it also provides the framework for making running changes to your business idea in the light of continuous feedback from the environment. This ability to take corrective action, and to compare your planning assumptions against reality, creates a growing body of ever-harder information and helps you manage the implementation risk.

step 1: identify milestones

The first step is to identify the key events which will stand as milestones – it is important to focus on the outcome of specific activities, not the activities per se. The milestones are those events or actions which must definitely occur in order that your objectives are achieved. You should also identify what learning will be taken from each event.

step 2: identify linkages among events

The simplest way to achieve this is to ask yourself what other events must be accomplished before each event, and what events could or should be postponed until each event is completed.

step 3: document the key assumptions that underlie the milestones

Being clear about your planning assumptions and the precisely defined outcome represented by each milestone will allow you to verify the assumptions, or not, as each milestone is achieved. Modifying your assumptions in the light of experience may then lead you to reconfigure the business idea or to modify subsequent milestones.

Ensure that the milestones test all your assumptions. If that is not the case, create a milestone to do so, being clear how you will gather the hard information which will replace the assumption.

step 4: re-plan in the light of information

As each milestone is reached, and hard information becomes available to replace assumption, re-plan the future milestones in the light of this information. Review your list of predetermined questions for each milestone to decide whether to go, no-go or change direction.

A typical milestone planning approach is shown in Table 6.5.

Table 6.5 Typical milestone approach

	Milestone description	Key questions
1	Formulation of basic idea for the new venture	● Have you established to your satisfaction that a market opportunity and need exist for the new venture? ● Have the concept testing and rapid prototyping exercises validated your business idea? (Completion of the four steps of the idea development process should represent achievement of this milestone)
2	Completion of finished prototype	● What assumptions did you initially make about processes, labour, equipment, suppliers and raw materials? ● What have you learned from the prototyping process and what impact does this learning have on subsequent milestones, on your financial requirements and on launch timings? ● Has the prototyping process revealed new opportunities, either for new products, new uses or new customers?
3	Raising outside funding	● Are financial stakeholders attracted by your business idea? ● Do you need to modify your business idea in the light of feedback?
4	Executing pilot operation	● Have initial manufacturing operations challenged any of the assumptions underpinning your business idea in relation to materials, processes, personnel, reject rates and so on? ● Does feedback indicate that you should modify cost estimates or production methods?
5	Market testing	● Why are customers buying the product? ● Why are target customers not buying the product? ● Does the product perform in use as you intended? ● Should you modify marketing strategy and objectives?
6	Full production start-up	● Can you manufacture and deliver in terms of production rates, costs and quality according to the assumptions which you revised at pilot operation stage?
7	Sale to first major account	● How does your product compare with those of competitors in the broad market rather than just on a test basis? ● Do you need to modify your sales strategy? ● Do you need to revise your assumptions on customer service levels?
8	Reaction by competition	● Have competitors reacted in the fashion you anticipated? ● What measures are required to counter unforeseen competitive reaction?

9	Redesign or redirection of strategy	In the light of actual operations, are any changes to strategy required?
		Have additional opportunities for follow-up products been revealed?
10	First major price change	Major price revision may be triggered by changes in competition, production costs or manufacturing processes – does your business remain viable if any adverse price change is permanent?
		How can costs be restructured to restore viability?

Using the wide range of tools and techniques available to plan for implementation is a key final step in the idea development process. Often it will represent the difference between success and failure. And as we will see in the following case study, it can sometimes create success from apparent impossibility.

After all, who would want to take on McDonald's in a national fast-food market, particularly when they had no money, limited business skills and no expertise in fast food? Only someone who possessed one element which McDonald's could never have and which could be deployed to overcome every single block to implementation. And that someone was Tony Tan Caktiong of Jollibee Foods Corporation.

Jollibee Foods Corporation – planning to beat a giant[182]

some fast-food entrepreneurs might consider that taking on McDonald's represented an insurmountable obstacle. After all, no company had ever taken on McDonald's in a national fast-food market and won.

But Tony Tan Caktiong overcame this and a number of other major potential blocks when he battled his way to a 65 per cent share of the fiercely competitive Philippines market with Jollibee Foods. The success of his Philippines-based globally recognised fast-food company won him the award in 2004 of Ernst & Young World Entrepreneur of the Year.

Caktiong was born in the Fujian province of China, where his father was a cook in a temple. When Caktiong was 11 years old, his father ▶

accepted an invitation to move the family to Davao in the southern islands of the Philippines in order to set up a Chinese restaurant.

After graduating from the University of Sto. Tomas in 1975 with a degree in chemical engineering, Caktiong responded to an advertisement posted by an ice-cream parlour looking for franchisees. Borrowing the initial capital from his father, Caktiong set up two ice-cream parlours in the Philippines' capital of Manila. Following cultural convention, his siblings came to Manila to help. While Caktiong and his wife managed one of the stores, his brother and sister handled the other.

Caktiong's hands-on style and close rapport with the customers made him realise that a market existed for more than just the ice-cream which his two stores currently sold. The ice-cream parlours started serving hot sandwiches and other meals, whose sales soon outstripped ice-cream.

Inspired by the global popularity of such fast-food companies as McDonald's, which had yet to enter the Philippines, Caktiong acted on the feedback from his two stores. The company changed its name in 1978 from the Magnolia Ice Cream House to Jolly Bee, and despite the fact that 'no bank dared to touch them', established seven outlets to explore fully the possibilities of the hamburger concept. The name was shortened to Jollibee several months later, with the happy bee symbolising industriousness and the creation of pleasurable food.

Caktiong's strategy to pre-empt the entry of McDonald's into the Philippines was bold. Other American fast-food giants such as Burger King were already in the market and McDonald's was understood to be preparing entry plans. Caktiong observed that the foreign fast-food outlets did not localise their products to cater for Filipino tastes. Caktiong knew little about fast-food operations. His tangible resources were extremely limited compared with the gigantic financial muscle and operational expertise of the American multinationals. In addition, the business skills available from within his family were limited and Chinese-Filipino tradition dictated that management positions were retained within the clan.

Caktiong realised, however, that he possessed one key factor which the multinational companies could never obtain: '[our] indisputable edge is our knowledge of our fellow Filipinos and their taste.'

In 1979, he undertook a two-week tour of the United States together with his brother. They immersed themselves in the fast-food market in order to identify best operational practice. Right from the start, they were willing to copy best-in-class business processes so that they could concentrate their efforts in the Philippines on their specific areas of uniqueness. Subsequently, Caktiong regularly reviewed best management practice from western economies, particularly in relation to human resources, and incorporated it into Jollibee's operations.

Caktiong also challenged cultural traditions by recruiting outside the family: 'Early on, we organised the structure by hiring professionals. We realised that in terms of marketing, finance, human resources, we did not have the skill.' The company also outsourced its IT activity.

Frugality became an explicit company value. Profits were reinvested into the business. To this day, Caktiong and his family prefer to fly economy class rather than business class.

Caktiong registered the Jollibee trademark in the Philippines and overseas. He also adopted franchising to increase the reach and speed of his geographical coverage, while limiting his financial exposure.

The exercise of benchmarking best practice contributed significantly to Jollibee's robust business process. The creation of an holistic brand which appealed not only to the Filipino palate but also to Filipino culture was the next challenge. Caktiong completely redefined the conventional concept of fast food to suit the local market. Recognising that the Filipinos enjoyed eating out in groups and ordering different dishes, Jollibee offered a much wider menu than conventional fast-food restaurants.

Caktiong's sister created special recipes to appeal to local tastes. A significant additional advantage of using local ingredients such as noodles and chicken was the avoidance of the import bills faced by the traditional fast-food competitors as they brought in potato and beef products. The nature of Jollibee's recipes was a closely guarded secret within the company – the few individuals who needed to know were bound by stringent confidentiality agreements.

By focusing on aromatic herbs and spices, the menu appealed explicitly to the emotions and values of his home market. As Caktiong explained: 'There is a ritual involved in the way we Filipinos eat. Whether we lift ▶

the lid of the pot on the fire or slowly unwrap a hamburger sandwich, we first introduce ourselves to a meal by taking a big whiff of its aroma. This awakens our senses and our appetites. To the Asian, sniffing is part of our culture, so it's definitely not bad manners.' This cultural aptness was captured in the advertising strap-line of 'Langhap-sarap', which translates into 'You can smell how delicious it tastes'.

Focused on the eponymous bee, Jollibee's advertising was deeply rooted in the traditional Filipino values of family and love for children. The bee achieved the iconic status within the Philippines of Ronald McDonald in other global markets. Jollibee also pioneered the consistent use by staff of a traditional Filipino greeting, 'Magandang Umaga Po', to signify the company's pride in 'our heritage as a 100 per cent Filipino-owned corporation'.

'We also believe in social investing,' claimed Caktiong, and in 'being supportive of our host communities and actively contributing to nation-building.' Numerous high-profile social initiatives engaged the commitment of the wider stakeholder communities on which Jollibee depended. These initiatives included poverty housing projects, educational programmes for children and the employment of a significant number of hearing-impaired workers.

When McDonald's entered the Philippines' market in 1981, the received wisdom was that Jollibee would be crushed. Far from it. Caktiong positioned the move by McDonald's as an opportunity for his management team to learn at first hand from the operations of a global multinational. Jollibee adjusted its own operations accordingly. Caktiong also adopted a so-called 2:1 strategy, opening two Jollibee stores for every one opened by the new market entrant.

Market research undertaken in 1995 revealed that Jollibee achieved almost 100 per cent brand recognition, prompting Miguel Jose Navarrete, the company's chief financial officer, to remark that Jollibee's reach in the Philippines was equalled only by the government and by the Catholic Church.

The company's financial success created a virtuous circle. Its central position in Filipino culture was epitomised by the 'Jollibee indicator'. Based on the company's sales, this was accepted as an unofficial measure of the health of the wider Filipino economy.

The robust business model and formidable brand identity combined to make Jollibee a powerful franchise proposition. Of its 450 Jollibee stores, around 50 per cent were franchised. The business process model was documented down to the last detail in order that brand identity and operating practice could be consistent across the entire Jollibee network. New stores were assembled from pre-constructed elements in order to ensure consistent image and to control cost. Extensive training and development were offered throughout the system to employees, franchisees and suppliers.

Ever vigilant for growth possibilities, Jollibee entrenched its position during the temporary market withdrawal during 1989–90 by its American competitors, including McDonald's, prompted by the failed military coup. Its flexibility of operation was highlighted during the Philippines' recession of 1997, when Jollibee introduced so-called Value Meals, which cost customers less than a snack from a street-side hawker's stall. Jollibee maintained its margins by negotiating cost reductions from suppliers and by bringing bread bakery in-house.

Jollibee grew within the Philippines not only through organic growth but also through the acquisition of such complementary brands as Greenwich (pizza and pasta), Chowking (Chinese quick service segment), and Delifrance (French-style speciality cafés).

Recognising that the global fast-food players had been hampered by not adapting their product to local tastes, Jollibee gave priority in its own foreign expansion to countries where it could easily achieve local customisation. Rather than go head to head with McDonald's in its first overseas forays, Jollibee selected smaller countries such as Brunei, Guam and Vietnam to pilot its operations. A significant number of Filipino nationals worked in these countries, providing a ready customer base for the Jollibee concept. Current priorities for Jollibee's overseas expansion include Indonesia and China.

As president and 65 per cent owner of a globally recognised operation now achieving annual sales in excess of £310 million, Tony Tan Caktiong provides proof positive that nimble entrepreneurs really can slay the giants.

key points

- Time invested now in identifying – and resolving – what could go wrong is time well spent

- Make sure that you take nothing for granted in considering where the blocks to implementation will come from

- Apply structured techniques to identify the blocks which are specific to your idea

- Follow the guiding principles for overcoming blocks to implementation in order to increase the likelihood of success

- Even at this fourth step, be prepared to adjust or recycle your business idea in the light of emerging information and insight

- This planning step needs imagination and intuition equally as much as logic and analysis

- Persevere – remember ideas on their own have no value until successfully put into practice

- Good luck!

appendices

appendix 1: possible solutions to ambiguous picture

Smokey the Bear

Longhorn steer or whale's tail

Alfred Hitchcock and Alfred's brother

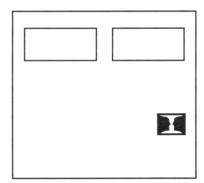

The key hole

Seal or sombrero or coathanger

Two cars parked back to back, bumper to bumper

Appendix 2: References

1 *Business Journal*, Milwaukee, 20 April 1998

2 *Sources*: Dyson, J. *Against All Odds* (London: Orion, 1997); Dyson company website: www.dyson.co.uk; Cook, P. *Best Practice Creativity* (London: Gower, 1998)

3 'Fly higher with an angel,' *Sunday Times*, 12 January 2003

4 Burns, P. *Entrepreneurship and Small Business* (Basingstoke: Palgrave, 2001)

5 Drucker, P. *Innovation and Entrepreneurship* (Oxford: Butterworth-Heinemann, revised edition, 1994)

6 Basadur, Min. *The Power of Innovation* (London: Pearson Education, 1995)

7 Timmons, J. and Olin, F. *New Venture Creation – Entrepreneurship for the 21st Century* (New York: McGraw-Hill, 2004)

8 Davis, W. *The Innovators* (London: Ebury Press, 1987)

9 Baylis, T. *Clock This, My Life as an Inventor* (London: Headline, 1999)

10 Timmons, J. and Olin, F. *New Venture Creation – Entrepreneurship for the 21st Century* (New York: McGraw-Hill, 2004)

11 Commissioned by the Chancellor of the Exchequer, Lambert Review of Business–University Collaboration, December 2003

12 Personal interview with Trevor Baylis, 'Wind-up genius,' *Earthmatters*, summer 2002

13 Van de Ven, A. *et al.*, *The Innovation Journey* (New York: Oxford University Press, 1999)

14 Godfrey, J. *Our Wildest Dreams* (New York: HarperBusiness, 1992)

15 Timmons, J. and Olin, F. *New Venture Creation – Entrepreneurship for the 21st Century* (New York: McGraw-Hill, 2004)

16 Posted at www.sbs.gov.uk/content/analytical/statistics/survival-jan-2004.pdf

17 'Google search – and destroy,' *Sunday Times*, 4 April 2004

18 'High Stakes,' *The Engineer*, 24 October 2003

19 Cited in LeBoeuf, M. *How to Develop and Profit from your Creative Powers* (London: Piatkus, 1990)

20 Baylis, T. *Clock This, My Life as an Inventor* (London: Headline, 1999)

21 'Fly higher with an angel,' *Sunday Times*, 12 January 2003

22 Henry, J. *Creativity and Perception in Management* (Milton Keynes: Open University, 2001)

23 *Sources*: Marks, A. 'The Sinclair C5 – Why Did it Fail?' *Management Decision*, Vol 28, No 4, 1990; *The Engineer*, 24 October 2003; *Sinclair User*, March 1985

24 *Sources*: Hartley, R. *Management Mistakes and Successes* (New York: John Wiley and Sons, 1991); Hamel, G. 'Killer strategies that make shareholders rich,' *Fortune*, 23 June 1997; Collins, J. and Porras, J. 'Building your company's vision,' *Harvard Business Review*, September–October 1996; www.nike.com/nikebiz

25 von Oech, R. *A Whack on the Side of the Head* (New York: Warner Books, 1998)

26 Drucker, P. *Innovation and Entrepreneurship* (Oxford: Butterworth-Heinemann, revised edition, 1994)

27 Lewis, D. *Mind Skills: Giving your child a brighter future* (London: Souvenir Press, 1987)

28 Zimmerer, T. and Scarborough, N. *Essentials of Entrepreneurship and Small Business Management* (New Jersey: Pearson Education, 2002)

29 Henry, J. *Creative Management* (London: Sage Publications, 2nd edition, 2001)

30 Shallcross, D. and Gawienowski, A. 'Top experts address issues on creativity gap in higher education,' *Journal of Creative Behaviour* 23, No 2, 1989, p 75

31 Kanter, R. *The Change Masters* (London: Unwin, 1983)

32 Marton, F. *et al.* 'A Nobel's eye view of scientific intuition: discussions with Nobel prize-winners in physics, chemistry and medicine (1970–1986),' *International Journal of Science Education*, 1994, 16, pp 457–73

33 Zuckerman, E. 'William Gates III,' *People Weekly*, 20 August 1990

34 Van de Ven, A. *et al.*, *The Innovation Journey* (New York: Oxford University Press, 1999)

35 Posted at www.angelfire.com/wi/2brains/test.html (Left-brain/right-brain questionnaire) and at www.angelfire.com/wi/2brains/key.html (Key)

36 'My Wife and My Mother-in-Law' by W. E. Hill, published in *Puck* magazine, 1915, believed to be based on an anonymous German postcard from 1888

37 Reprinted with permission from Basadur, M. *The Power of Innovation* (London: Pearson Education, 1995)

38 Osborn, A. *Applied Imagination* (New York: Charles Scribner's Sons, 3rd revised edition, 1963)

39 *Sources:* Kamprad, I. *Testament of a Furniture Dealer*, internal IKEA document, 20 December 1976; *Financial Times*, 4 March 2003; www.ikea.co.uk; 'Ingvar Kamprad – IKEA Founder,' posted at http://entrepreneurs.about.com; 'The gospel according to Ikea,' *Guardian*, 26 June 2000; Larson, A. *Competitive Implications of Environmental Regulation: A case study on IKEA* (Washington: The Management Institute for Environment & Business, June 1996)

40 *Sources*: Kotha, S. 'Competing on the Internet: The case of Amazon.com,' *European Management Journal*, Vol 16, No 2, 1998, pp 212–22; 'A fable concerning ambition,' *The Economist*, 19 June 1997; Clark, T. 'Newsmakers: Jeff Bezos, Turning to a Global Page,' *CNET News.com*, 8 April 1998; www.amazon.com; 'A bookstore by any other name,' speech by Jeff Bezos to the Commonwealth Club of California, 27 July 1998, posted at www.commonwealthclub.org

41 Kotha, S. 'Competing on the Internet: The case of Amazon.com,' *European Management Journal*, Vol 16, No 2, 1998, pp 212–22

42 Steiner, R. *My First Break – How Entrepreneurs Get Started* (London: News International, 1998)

43 Nutt, P. 'Types of Organizational Decision Processes,' *Administrative Science Quarterly*, Vol 29, 1984, pp 414–50

44 Osborn, A. *Applied Imagination* (New York: Charles Scribner's Sons, 3rd revised edition, 1963)

45 Greene, F., Mole, K. and Storey, D. 'Does more mean worse? Three decades of enterprise policy in the Tees Valley,' *Urban Studies*, Vol 41, No 7, June 2004

46 Getzels, J. and Csikszentmihalyi, M. *The Creative Vision: A Longitudinal Study of Problem-Finding in Art* (New York: Wiley-Interscience, 1976)

47 Albrecht, K. *Brain Power – Learn to improve your thinking skills* (New Jersey: Prentice-Hall, 1980)

48 Reprinted with permission from Albrecht, K. *Brain Power – Learn to improve your thinking skills* (New Jersey: Prentice-Hall, 1980)

252

49 'Bertelsmann's Bismarck,' *The Economist*, 7 November 1998

50 von Stamm, B. *Managing Innovation, Design & Creativity* (Chichester: John Wiley and Sons, 2003)

51 Kelley, T. *The Art of Innovation – Lessons in Creativity from IDEO, America's Leading Design Firm* (London: HarperCollins Business, 2002)

52 Chun, J. 'Theory of Creativity,' *Entrepreneur*, October 1997, p 130

53 Obituary of Norman Heatley, *The Guardian*, 8 January 2004

54 Wujec, T. *Five Star Mind* (New York: Broadway Books, 1995)

55 Burns, P. *Entrepreneurship and Small Business* (Basingstoke: Palgrave, 2001)

56 Drucker, P. *Innovation and Entrepreneurship* (Oxford: Butterworth-Heinemann, revised edition, 1994)

57 Time's 100 Most Important People of the Century, posted at www.time.com/time/time100/builder/profile/Kroc.html

58 'Gateshead revisited at cutting edge of shopping,' *The Times*, 26 February 2004

59 Reprinted with permission from Kaplan, J. *Patterns of Entrepreneurship* (New Jersey: John Wiley & Sons, 2003)

60 Leonard, D. and Rayport, J. 'Spark innovation through empathetic design,' in *Harvard Business Review on Breakthrough Thinking* (Boston: Harvard Business School Press, 1999)

61 Epstein, R. 'How to get a great idea,' *Reader's Digest*, December 1992, p 104

62 'The Band-Aid Brand Story,' posted at www.bandaid.com/brand_story.shtml

63 Design Museum website: (www.designmuseum.org/designerex/craig-johnston.htm)

64 'Queen's Awards for Enterprise,' *The Times*, 21 April 2004

65 'Rugby's great underachievers no more,' *The Guardian*, 5 October 2003

66 Kelley, T. *The Art of Innovation – Lessons in Creativity from IDEO, America's Leading Design Firm* (London: HarperCollins Business, 2002)

67 Crate and Barrel history, posted at www.crateandbarrel.com/aboutus/history.asp

68 Brown, M. and Rickards, T. 'How to create creativity,' *Management Today*, August 1982, pp 38–41

69 Gettler, L. 'Stephen Millar: The Vinter's Tale,' *Management Today*, March 2003, posted at www.aim.com.au/resources; Bartlett, C. and Ghoshal, S. 'Going global: lessons from late movers,' *Harvard Business Review*, March–April 2000

70 Kim, C. and Mauborgne, R. 'Creating new market space,' in *Harvard Business Review on Innovation* (Boston: Harvard Business School Press, 2001)

71 Ibid.

72 'Father of an industry,' *Design News*, 6 March 2000

73 Best Friends Pet Resorts and Salons' website (www.bestfriendspetcare.com)

74 Kim, C. and Mauborgne, R. 'Creating new market space,' in *Harvard Business Review on Innovation* (Boston: Harvard Business School Press, 2001)

75 Steiner, R. *My First Break – How Entrepreneurs Get Started* (London: News International, 1998)

76 'Creating technology in pursuit of dreams,' *The Times*, 27 March 2004

77 *Sources*: Bennahum, D. 'The United Nations of Iridium,' *Wired,* Issue 6.10, October 1998; Leibovich, M. 'A dream come back to earth; missteps, shortfalls,

glitches have Iridium scaling back expectations for its satellite phone service,' *The Washington Post*, 24 May 1999; Kelley, T. *The Art of Innovation* (London: HarperCollins Business, 2002); Flower, J. 'Iridium,' *Wired*, Issue 1.05, November 1993

78 Bennahum, D. 'The United Nations of Iridium,' *Wired*, Issue 6.10, October 1998

79 Leibovich, M. 'A dream come back to earth; missteps, shortfalls, glitches have Iridium scaling back expectations for its satellite phone service,' *The Washington Post*, 24 May 1999

80 *Sources*: Landrum, G. N. *Profiles of Genius: Thirteen Creative Men Who Changed the World* (New York: Prometheus Books, 1993); Kennedy, R. 'I'm giving up the thing world – Howard Head,' *Sports Illustrated*, 29 September 1980; Peters, T. and Waterman Jr, R. *In Search of Excellence* (New York: Harper & Row, 1982); 'Howard Head, Ski Inventor' posted at Lemelson Centre for the Study of Invention and Innovation website, www.si.edu/lemelson/centerpieces/iap/inventors_hea.html

81 Kennedy, R. 'I'm giving up the thing world – Howard Head', *Sports Illustrated*, 29 September 1980

82 *Sports Illustrated*, 1974

83 From Howard Head's keynote address at Entrepreneur's Night of UCLA Graduate School of Business, 1984, quoted in Timmons, J. and Olin, F. *New Venture Creation – Entrepreneurship for the 21st Century* (New York: McGraw-Hill, 2004)

84 www.newcoventgardenfood.com

85 Poincaré, H. *Mathematical Creation*, 1908

86 Osborn, A. *Applied Imagination* (New York: Charles Scribner's Sons, 3rd revised edition, 1963)

87 Davis, G., Roweton, W., Train, A., Warren, T. and Houtman, S. *Laboratory Studies of Creative Thinking Techniques: The Checklist and Morphological Synthesis Methods*, Technical Report No 94, Wisconsin Research and Development Center for Cognitive Learning, University of Wisconsin, 1969

88 Eberle, R. *Scamper: Games for Imagination Development* (Buffalo, New York: D.O.K. Press, 1972)

89 Kim, C. and Mauborgne, R. 'Creating new market space,' in *Harvard Business Review on Innovation* (Boston: Harvard Business School Press, 2001)

90 Entry for Thomas Edison on Lemelson Center website, www.si.edu/lemelson/edison/000_story_02.asp

91 Kelley, T. *The Art of Innovation – Lessons in Creativity from IDEO, America's Leading Design Firm* (London: HarperCollins Business, 2002)

92 www.llb.co.uk

93 Law, A. *Open Minds* (London: Orion Business, 1998)

94 'How parenthood delivered a brainchild,' *Financial Times*, 7 January 2004

95 Ansoff, I. *Corporate Strategy* (London: Penguin, 1968)

96 Greene, F., Mole, K. and Storey, D. 'Does more mean worse? Three decades of enterprise policy in the Tees Valley,' *Urban Studies*, Vol 41, No 7, June 2004

97 'Careers for women on tap,' *The Independent*, 6 May 2004

98 Ibid.

99 'Mr Rooter's Woman of the Year,' *Plumbing and Mechanical Magazine*, August 2002

100 Rickards, T. *Creativity and Problem-solving at Work* (Aldershot: Gower Publishing, 1997)

101 Information from Swatch company website, www.swatch-shop.co.uk/accesscollection.htm

102 Osborn, A. *Applied Imagination* (New York: Charles Scribner's Sons, 3rd revised edition, 1963)

103 Kelley, T. *The Art of Innovation – Lessons in Creativity from IDEO, America's Leading Design Firm* (London: HarperCollins Business, 2002)

104 Ibid.

105 Buzan, A. *Use Your Head* (London: Ariel Books, 1974)

106 Sutton, R. *Weird Ideas That Work – 11½ ways to promote, manage and sustain innovation* (London: Allen Lane, The Penguin Press, 2002)

107 www.si.edu/lemelson/centerpieces/iap/inventors_edi.html

108 'At last, an (almost) indestructible book children can really get their teeth into,' *The Times*, 29 May 2004

109 Pentland, B. *Process Grammars: a generative approach to process redesign*, draft paper posted at http://ccs.mit.edu/papers/CCSWP178/ccswp178.html

110 Rogers, B. *Seize the Future for Your Business – using imagination to power growth* (London: International Thomson Business Press, 1998)

111 www.designmuseum.org/designerex/craig-johnston.htm

112 Hargadon, A. and Sutton, R. 'Building an Innovation Factory,' in *Harvard Business Review on Innovation* (Boston: Harvard Business School Press, 2001)

113 Kelley, T. *The Art of Innovation – Lessons in Creativity from IDEO, America's Leading Design Firm* (London: HarperCollins Business, 2002)

114 Chun, J. 'Theory of Creativity,' *Entrepreneur*, October 1997

115 Smit, T. *eden* (London: Corgi, 2002)

116 De Bono, E. *Lateral Thinking* (London: Penguin Books, 1990)

117 Steiner, R. *My First Break – How Entrepreneurs Get Started* (London: News International, 1998)

118 Grossman, S. 'Releasing problem-solving energies,' *Training and Development Journal* 38, pp 94–8, 1984

119 *Sources*: Lemelson Center website, including www.si.edu/lemelson/centerpieces/iap/inventors_edi.html; Baldwin, N. *Edison: Inventing the Century* (Chicago: University of Chicago Press, 2001); Clark, R. *Edison – The man who made the future* (London: Macdonalds and Jane's Publishers Ltd, 1977)

120 *Sources*: Steiner, R. *My First Break – How Entrepreneurs Get Started* (London: News International, 1998); 'Will India fall for the charm of King Cobra?' *The Observer*, 18 January 2004; www.startups.co.uk; BBC News Online:http://news.bbc.co.uk/1/hi/in_depth/business/2003/small_business; Cobra Beer website: www.cobrabeer.com; Article 13: www.article13.com

121 Jeff Bezos' speech to the Commonwealth Club of California, 27 July 1998, posted at www.commonwealthclub.org

122 Ibid.

123 Ibid.

124 Kotha, S. 'Competing on the Internet: The Case of Amazon.com,' *European Management Journal*, Vol 16, No 2, 1998, pp 212–22

125 Godfrey, J. *Our Wildest Dreams* (New York: HarperBusiness, 1992)

126 Trott, P. *Innovation Management and New Product Development* (Harlow: Pearson Education Limited, 2002)

127 National Commission on Entrepreneurship, posted at www.zeromillion.com/entrepreneurship/stories/howard-schultz.html

128 Janis, I. L. and Mann, L. *Decision Making* (New York: The Free Press, 1977)

129 Jeff Bezos' response to questions at the Commonwealth Club of California, 27 July 1998, posted at www.commonwealthclub.org

130 Janis, I. L. and Mann, L. *Decision Making* (New York: The Free Press, 1977)

131 www.easyCinema.com

132 www.startups.co.uk

133 FoodForum: www.foodforum.org.uk; New Covent Garden Soup Company website: www.newcoventgardenfood.com

134 'Turning to a global page,' *CNET News.com*, 8 April 1998

135 Adapted from Burch, J. G. *Entrepreneurship*, (New York: Wiley, 1986) p 72

136 'Self-made woman finds her true calling,' *Sunday Times*, 27 June 2004

137 Dame Stephanie Shirley, keynote speech to mi2g event at Lloyd's of London, 30 January 2002: 'An entrepreneur's story – growing a digitally networked organisation with values'

138 Handy, C. *The Hungry Spirit: Beyond capitalism – a quest for purpose in the modern world* (London: Arrow Books, 1998)

139 www.ktponline.org.uk

140 'My first break: Anne Notley and Simon Notley,' *Sunday Times*, 28 January 2001

141 'Hell hath no fury like a first lady scorned,' *Sunday Times,* 27 June 2004

142 www.trotters.co.uk

143 Wickham, P. *Strategic Entrepreneurship: A decision-making approach to new venture creation and management* (Harlow: Pearson Education Limited, 2001)

144 Monroy, T. and Folger, R. 'A typology of entrepreneurial styles: beyond economic rationality,' *Journal of Private Enterprise* IX, No 2 ,1993, pp 64–79

145 Interview with Academy of Achievement, 23 May 1998, posted at www.achievement.org

146 Henry, J. and Walker, D. (Eds) *Managing Innovation* (London: Sage, 1999)

147 *Inc.com* magazine, January 1995: www.inc.com

148 Taylor, D. *The Brand Gym* (Chichester: John Wiley & Sons, 2003)

149 Kelley, T. *The Art of Innovation – Lessons in Creativity from IDEO, America's Leading Design Firm* (London: HarperCollins Business, 2002)

150 Leonard, D. and Rayport, J. 'Spark innovation through empathetic design,' in *Harvard Business Review on Breakthrough Thinking* (Boston: Harvard Business School Press, 1999)

151 *Sources*: Internet Securities, Inc. website: www.securities.com; *Boston Business Journal*, 29 November 1996; Harvard Business School online: www.alumni.hbs.edu/bulletin/1998/april/mueller.html; Timmons, J. and Olin, F. *New Venture Creation – Entrepreneurship for the 21st Century* (New York: McGraw-Hill, 2004)

152 *Boston Business Journal*, 2 December 1996, posted at http://boston.bizjournals.com/boston/stories/1996/12/02/story6.html

153 'Internet Securities, Gary G. Mueller (MBA , 94)' posted at HBS Bulletin online: www.alumni.hbs.edu/bulletin/1998/april/mueller.html/1998/april/mueller.html

154 *Sources*: Academy of Achievement, interview with Frederick W. Smith on 23 May 1998 at Jackson Hole, Wyoming, posted at www.achievement.org; *The Story of Fedex – a chronicle of achievements*, posted at www.sri.com; 'Fred Smith's FedEx isn't looking back at 30 years,' Karin Miller, 26 November 2001, posted at www.oakridger.com; www.fedex.com; Reichert, B. 'A review of 'overnight success: Federal Express and its renegade creator,' *Journal of Business Leadership*, 2000–2001, posted at www.anbf.org

155 Academy of Achievement, op. cit.

156 Ibid.

157 Ibid.

158 Ibid.

159 Ibid.

160 Posted at www.fedex.com

161 Levitt, T. 'Creativity is not enough,' *Harvard Business Review*, May/June 1963

162 World Vision Award for Development Initiative 1991, posted at www.worldaware.org.uk

163 'An entrepreneur's story – growing a digitally networked organisation with values,' keynote speech by Dame Stephanie Shirley to mi2g event at Lloyds of London, 30 January 2002

164 Fielding, R. 'Technology pioneer still fighting,' *Computing*, 1 November 2002

165 Flatow, I. *They all laughed . . .* (New York: HarperCollins, 1992)

166 Hartley, R. *Management Mistakes and Successes* (New York: John Wiley & Sons, Inc., 2003)

167 Kim, W. and Mauborgne, R. 'Knowing a winning business idea when you see one,' in *Harvard Business Review on Innovation* (Boston: Harvard Business School Press, 2001)

168 World Vision Award for Development Initiative 1991, posted at www.worldaware.org.uk

169 Bhide, A. 'Bootstrap finance: the art of start-ups,' *Harvard Business Review*, November–December 1992

170 Roberts, E. *Entrepreneurs in High Technology: Lessons from MIT and Beyond* (New York: Oxford University Press, 1991)

171 IKEA's value statement, *Testament of a Furniture Dealer*

172 www.ikea.com

173 'A bookstore by any other name,' speech by Jeff Bezos to the Commonwealth Club of California, 27 July 1998, posted at www.commonwealthclub.org

174 Quoted in McGrath, R. 'The parsimonious path to profit,' in Birley, S. and Muzyka, D. (Eds) *Mastering Entrepreneurship* (London: Pearson Education, 2000)

175 Bragg, M. *Reinventing Influence: how to get things done in a world without authority* (London: Pearson Professional Limited, 1996)

176 Miller, K. L. 'Hitting The Wall At Boo,' *Newsweek*, 17 July 2000

177 www.travelcounsellors.com

178 Bridge, R. 'Fish bowl guru makes waves with novel tank,' *Sunday Times*, 30 May 2004; www.startups.co.uk

179 Ingebretse, M. 'Swim with the Big Fish,' posted at www.wellsfargo.com; www.the-house.com

180 *Tiptree News*, Summer 2004, posted at www.tiptree.com

181 'A bookstore by any other name,' speech by Jeff Bezos to the Commonwealth Club of California, 27 July 1998, posted at www.commonwealthclub.org

1812 Block, Z. and MacMillan, I. 'Milestones for successful venture planning,' *Harvard Business Review*, September–October 1985

183 *Sources*: 'Jollibee beats rival McDonald's at its own game,' *Business World*, 28 June 2004; Quimpo-Espino, M. 'This Jolly man deserves his 'langhap sarap' success, *Philippine Daily Inquirer*, 26 June 2004; www.jollibee.com.ph; Ramirez, J. 'The secret of Tony Tan Caktiong's success: 'be happy!', *The Philippine Star*, 24 June 2004; speech by Tony Tan Caktiong to Asian franchisers, reported in *BizNews Asia*, 27 January 2003; Bartlett, C. and Ghoshal, S. 'Going global: lessons from late movers,' *Harvard Business Review*, March–April 2000

index